Druidry
A Practical & Inspirational Guide

Druidry
A Practical & Inspirational Guide

by Philip Shallcrass (Greywolf)

Pretanic Press

Pretanic Press (BDO),
PO Box 1217,
Devizes,
Wiltshire SN10 4XA,
UK
pretanicpress.com

1st edition, Piatkus Books, 2000.
2nd, revised and expanded edition, Pretanic Press, 2023.

Dedicated to: Eleanor Jane Shallcrass (née Kilpatrick), 1954-2000

Hardback ISBN: 978-1-915604-00-2
Paperback ISBN: 978-1-915604-01-9
E-book ISBN: 978-1-915604-02-6

CONTENTS

Illustrations ... v

Preface to the 2ⁿᵈ Edition ... 1

including Dogmas & Catmas; A Note on Dates; A Note on Gender; A Pronunciation Guide; Acknowledgements

Introduction: **Why Druidry, Why Now?** ... 9

Part One:
The Circle Is Unbroken

Chapter 1: **Rekindling the Sacred Fires** ... 13

including The Sources of Modern Druidry; Druidry as Native Spirituality; The Paths of Bard, Ovate & Druid; Core Concepts; Ethics

Chapter 2: **Beginnings** ... 31

including Honouring Our Ancestors; The Altar; Druids Today; The Reformed Druids of North America (RDNA); The Order of Bards, Ovates and Druids (OBOD); The British Druid Order (BDO); A Druid Fellowship (ADF); The Ancient Druid Order (ADO); The Gorsedd of Bards of the Isle of Britain; The Ancient Order of Druids(AOD); Druids, Antiquarians & Artists; Bardic Schools & Druid Survivals; Classical Druids; Druid Roots & Celtic Identity

Chapter 3: **The Sacred Circle** ... 65

including The Aura: Circle of the Self; Sensing the Aura; Casting the Circle; Weaving the Web; The Cardinal Directions; Making Your Own Map; Working with the Circle; The Wheel of the Year; Walking the Circle

Part Two:
Inspiration & Creativity: The Path of the Bard

Chapter 4: **Flowing Spirit, Feminine Spirit** ... 85

including Sensing Awen; Chanting Awen; Seeking Awen; Poetry & the Cell of Song; Creative Dreaming

Chapter 5: **Ancestral Voices** ... 97

including Many Blessings; Tales of the Gods; Cycles of the Sun; *The Mabinogion*; The Story of Taliesin; Arthur, Merlin & the Matter of Britain;

Gawain & the Greene Knight; Ireland: The Mythological Cycle; The Ulster
Cycle; The Fenian Cycle; The Historical Cycle; A World of Legend

Part Three:
Healing & Awareness: The Path of the Ovate

Chapter 6: **Seership & Divination** ... 123
including Signs & Omens; Second Sight; The Language of Birds; Ogham: the
Secret Language; Ogham Divination

Chapter 7: **Healing** ... 137
including Journeys of the Soul; The Ancestor Tree; Herbs & Healer Gods;
Healing & the Faery Folk; The Place of Healing; A Time to Live, a Time to
Die

Part Four:
Ritual & Change: The Path of the Druid

Chapter 8: **Ritual** ... 149
including The Gorsedd Rite; Opening the Circle; Calling the Quarters;
Handfasting; Blessing for Children; Bardic Initiation; Honouring the Departed;
Sharing Bread & Mead; Closing the Circle; Greeting the Day

Chapter 9: **Change** ... 167
including Boundaries Between the Worlds; Power Animals & Animal Powers;
In the Paw-prints of the Wolf; Shape-Shifting; Eagle Dancing; On the Edge
Between the Worlds; Hale & Farewell

Resources ... 182
including Druid Groups; Pagan, Ecological & Conservation Groups; Select
Bibliography & Discography

Index ... 191

Illustrations

Title page & pages 29 & 194: Antlered shaman/druid/god with horned serpent, detail from the 1st century BCE Gundestrup Cauldron. Wikimedia Commons.

Page vi: Cauldron, block print by the author from *The Druid Tarot*, © 2022.

Page 8: 'Wild Sweeney,' pencil, ink and oil pastel drawing by Greywolf, 2013.

Page 16: Life-sized female figure carved from alder, Iron Age circa 600 BCE, photographed shortly after its excavation in 1880. Public domain.

Page 30: 2022 © collage by the author from 2013 © photo of Joe Shallcrass by Elaine Gregory and 1704 engraving after a drawing by William Stukeley.

Page 35: Dragon Hill rite of passage. Photo © by Elaine Gregory, 2006.

Page 38: Ritualists after an animal spirit ceremony in a reconstructed Iron Age roundhouse, May Day, © 2016. Photographer unknown.

Page 43: 20th anniversary gathering of the Gorsedd of Bards of Caer Abiri in 2013. Photo © by Elaine Gregory.

Page 46: Contemporary sketch of the stonemason, poet, Druid revivalist and literary forger, Edward Williams, a.k.a. Iolo Morganwg. Wikimedia Commons.

Page 47: 1908 photo from Winston Churchill's initiation into the Ancient Order of Druids. Public domain.

Page 49: Detail from 1802 self-portrait by William Blake. Public domain.

Page 50: Harper from the *Worms Bible*, Germany, 12th century, Harley MS 2804, f. 3v. Public domain.

Page 54: Block print of the 1st century BCE Iron Age bronze 'Druid' figurine from Neuvy-en-Sullias, France, from *The Druid Tarot* © 2022 by the author.

Page 55: © 1998 pencil drawing by the author of 1st century BCE bronze figurines of a bard and naked dancers from Neuvy-en-Sullias, France.

Page 61: (top) Blocked forecourt of the West Kennet Long Barrow, Wiltshire, with Silbury Hill in the background at right of frame. Photo by the author, © 2014; (bottom) the Gorsedd of Bards of Cor Gawr greeting the Midsummer sunrise, Stonehenge, 1999. Photo © by Rob Adams.

Page 70: Diagram showing the four cardinal directions and elements marked by the 'aces' from *The Druid Tarot*, © 2022 by the author.

Page 75: Wheel of the Year diagram by the author, © 2022.

Pages 83, 177 & 179: Ink painted silhouettes by Fee Sanderson, © 2018.

Page 84: BDO Awen Tree symbol by the author, © 2018.

Page 128: Woodcut of a Magpie by Thomas Bewick from his *A History of British Birds*, 1797. Public domain.

Page 129: Ogham alphabet diagram by the author, © 2022.

Page 133: Fionn's Roof-Tree diagram from folio 170r of the 14th century Irish *Book of Ballymote*, enhanced by the author. Wikimedia Commons.

Page 148: Dr. William Price in Druid costume, circa 1870. Public domain.

Page 173: Greywolf and Wolf cloak. Photo by Elaine Gregory, © 2016.

My own true cauldron of devotion,
deity-drawn from the mysterious abyss of the elements;
a fitting find that ennobles every belly or womb,
pouring forth a fearful stream of speech from the mouth.

From the author's translation of
'The Cauldron of Poesy' (see pages 28-30).

Preface to the 2nd Edition

The first edition of this book proved more influential than I ever imagined when the organisers of the London 2012 Paralympic Games asked permission to use parts of the ritual given in chapter 8 in their closing ceremony, which was called 'The Festival of the Flame' and themed around the four classical elements of Earth, Water, Fire and Air. So, on the night of September 9th 2012, Rory Mackenzie, a former army medic who had lost a leg to a roadside bomb in Iraq, ascended on a platform high above a packed Olympic Stadium and spoke calls to the four quarters that Emma Restall Orr (Bobcat) and I had composed fifteen years earlier for a multi-faith ceremony held in Volunteer Park in Seattle. Our invocations appeared amid wild steam-punk pyrotechnics and were broadcast live to around 8 million people in the UK and millions more worldwide at the start of a show that featured Coldplay, Rihanna and Jay-Z. Modern Pagan Druidry as manifested by the British Druid Order (BDO) and in this book had gone truly global. Subsequent feedback showed that our words resonated not only with the festival organisers, but with folk around the world, especially, of course, with fellow Druids and Pagans.

Early in 1998, a year before the first edition was written, Ellie, my wife of fifteen years, was diagnosed with Acute Myeloid Leukaemia. Writing began while she was in remission following an initial bone marrow transplant. After a relapse in the autumn of 1999, work on the book was completed between hospital visits and while our two children, then aged five and seven, were in school. Under the circumstances, I was surprised and pleased to deliver the manuscript to the publishers on time.

On New Year's Eve, 1999-2000, while the rest of the world held massive street parties, worried about aircraft falling from the sky and toasters rebelling because of the Y2K bug that was going to make all our computers crash at the turn of midnight, or gathered on mountain tops waiting for aliens to beam them up to waiting mother ships, I was in an isolation room in the Intensive Care Unit of a London teaching hospital, working with Ellie using techniques learned through a quarter of a century of the study and practice of Druidry as she slid in and out of consciousness. A few hours earlier, her medical team had told me she had between 12 and 48 hours to live. I had to translate that news to our children as best I could. After midnight, while most patients slept and nursing visits were few, I walked the borderlands between life and death with Ellie, even crossing over into the otherworld, seeking aid from guides and higher powers in her cause, weaving healing magic with and for her. Just before dawn I knew we'd done enough and that she would, once again, confound the doctors and live beyond their expectations.

As the Sun rose on the year 2000, I walked through eerily silent, deserted London streets bedecked with wind-blown, multi-coloured streamers trailing from lampposts, balloons and paper hats floating along pavements piled here and there with crates of empty champagne bottles. Surreal scarcely begins to cover it. Later that morning, I was told that Ellie's blood cell counts had increased dramatically overnight for no reason her medical team could discern.

Ellie lived for a further five months, long enough to see the first edition published, with its dedication to her. She put her time to good use, preparing herself and our children for her passing before finally succumbing to a further round of treatment rather than to the illness itself in May, 2000. The last event we attended together as a family was the May Day weekend Jack-in-the-Green Festival in Hastings, with its powerful symbolism of death and rebirth. Ellie died a few days later in our local hospital. As she exhaled her final breath, a sparkling cluster of golden motes of light gathered above her chest, coalescing into a beautiful butterfly which flew out through the closed window into the grey and rainswept afternoon outside. Her spirit had literally flown and I was privileged to see it depart, freeing her from the physical body that had become a crumbling cage.

Being alone in that hospital room with Ellie, I was able to make ceremony for her departing spirit. Having a guitar with me, as part of the rite I sang a song called 'The Islands of the Blest,' from an 8th century Irish tale called 'The Voyage of Bran,' part of which features in chapter 4 of this book (pages 98-9). This and other songs in our tradition were, I believe, intended to be sung in just such circumstances, helping guide departing souls to the wonderful refuge of the Earthly Paradise that lies across the western ocean, beyond the setting Sun. Thus, as it is throughout life, Druidry is there beyond its physical ending, offering the peace and solace that come with understanding.

Finding myself a single parent to two small children and faced with the mass of paperwork that must be tackled following a death, though the advance helped cover ongoing expenses, I had neither the time nor the inclination to do publicity for the book. As a result, it sold fewer copies than the publishers hoped and much of the print run was pulped. This gave the book rarity value, so that copies have occasionally changed hands online for over £1000. I have often thought of bringing out a new edition, and am grateful to all those who have prompted, pushed and prodded me to finally get around to it.

Reading through the original text, I was pleased to find how well it held up. The theories and opinions expressed are ones I still stand by, which is just as well since they form the basic framework around which the British Druid Order's distance learning courses are built (see the Resources section). In this new edition, parts of the original text are retained but I have taken the opportunity to rewrite and expand it extensively, more than doubling the book in length. The word limit set by the original publisher meant that many topics could not be explored in the kind of depth they warranted. On the contrary, the manuscript had to be trimmed repeatedly to bring it down to the required length, leaving me painfully aware of what was lost in the process. Now, with no word limit, what was reluctantly contracted has been expanded, not just restoring what was cut but adding much more. In 1999, I had intended to include footnotes. My editor argued against them on the basis that they slow down reading. In retrospect, I agree, so where references to sources are necessary, they are included in brackets (...) in the body of the text.

Since the first edition was published, it's been particularly gratifying to hear from folk whose first encounter with Druidry was through my little book and who have actively pursued it as a way of life ever since. That is, after all, why it was written. Almost equally gratifying is that even old hands with decades of experience in Druidry and Paganism have told me that, although intended as an introductory book, it opened up new ways of looking at the tradition for them.

My own journey in the tradition began in 1974 with a vision of Druidry as a unique, powerful, indigenous British and European spirituality. This vision has been central to my life ever since, saving my life and sanity, inspiring my songs and poetry, fuelling my creativity, enhancing my writing, taking me to other continents and other worlds, introducing me to the old gods of our lands, placing me in the midst of magic, informing my relationships with my ancestors and the spirits of the natural world and bringing me to meet many of the most talented, wonderful, magical people I've ever encountered. The sense of wonder, magic and power it engenders in me fuels my desire to share it with others. Furthermore, I believe that the vision of Druidry presented in these pages not only has the power to enhance individual lives, but can contribute significantly towards making our world a better, more equitable, more tolerant, more peaceful and greener place in which to live, for ourselves and future generations. With this in mind, it is a genuine pleasure to make this new edition available.

Before we set out on the quest proper, however, there are a few things we need to clarify, beginning with...

Dogmas & Catmas

There are no dogmas in Druidry, only catmas. Dogmas are rigidly held beliefs, often received from others, that tend to stifle freedom of thought and expression. Catmas, a concept invented by Robert Anton Wilson, co-author of the *Illuminatus* trilogy (Dell Publishing, 1975), are fluidly held beliefs, held only so long as they have value or until they are superseded by our growth in experience and understanding. Catmas offer the freedom to behave as if beliefs are true, allowing us to thoroughly test their worth. For example, one of my catmas is that spirits of nature are as real as the computer on which I'm writing these words, if not infinitely more so. Many years ago I believed differently. My opinion may change again. My present catma, however, enables me to interact with nature spirits well and with respect. You may believe such spirits to be poetic metaphors, psychological projections or simple hallucinations. That's fine. All I ask is that you allow yourself the catmatic freedom to try out for yourself the belief systems that underlie this book and see if they work for you. So, before we begin, let your dogmas off their leashes and allow them to run free. They may race around in chaotic confusion for a while but give them time and you may find that, one by one, they shape-shift into self-reliant, cool catmas.

A Note on Dates

The dating in this book replaces the Christian system of BC and AD, Before Christ and *Anno Domini* ('Year of Our Lord'), with the culturally broader BCE and CE, Before the Common Era and in the Common Era. This system has been adopted by students of comparative religion, history, prehistory and non-European cultures as being more inclusive of the many belief systems that make up the rich diversity of human experience.

A Note on Gender

I don't use the word Druidess. A Druid is a Druid, whatever their gender. Gender itself is not, and never has been, a simple binary of male and female. Some folk are non-gendered, bi-gendered or trans-gendered. The construction of language over several millennia has, however, tended to differentiate between male and female so that it is difficult to avoid using gender-specific terms, particularly when looking at how our ancestors viewed the world. To avoid frequent repetition of terms such as 'she or he' or neologisms such as 's/he' I alternate more or less randomly between 'he' and 'she' in the text. Similarly, I sometimes use the plural 'gods' to mean deities of all genders or none while using 'god' and 'goddess' for individual deities as appropriate.

A Pronunciation Guide

Modern Druids draw some of our inspiration from texts preserved in manuscripts produced in medieval Wales and Ireland. English speakers often find some Welsh and Irish words and names difficult to pronounce. Both languages have letters, or pairs of letters, that are pronounced differently from English. It therefore seems appropriate to offer a few pointers before we begin. Don't worry about memorising them because where 'difficult' names appear we will give their pronunciation in square brackets [...] after their first appearance. Our pronunciation guides use common English letters and sometimes represent syllables by short English words. We chose this method rather than phonetic symbols because most people have no idea what phonetic symbols represent. Our guides take no account of regional variations in dialect between, say, North and South Wales or Ulster and Connaught. Instead, we approximate the most commonly used pronunciations.

In spoken Welsh, the strongest emphasis is usually on the penultimate syllable. We indicate this by capitalising that syllable. So our pronunciation guide for Yr Wyddfa, the Welsh name of Mount Snowdon, would look like this: [ur WITH-va].

English speakers often have difficulty with the Welsh double 'l.' There is no exact equivalent in spoken English, but it can be mastered with a little practice. 'Ll' is pronounced something like 'thl' with the 'th' as in 'thin' but preceded by a slight 'ch' sound, as in Scottish 'loch.' We therefore render 'll' as 'chthl' in our pronunciation guides.

Double 'd' in Welsh, 'dd,' is always pronounced like the hard 'th' in 'the' or 'there.' Single 'd' is similar to English but can be harder, almost like the 't' in 'baton.'

Double 'f' in Welsh, 'ff,' is pronounced as 'f' in 'fine' or 'folly.' Single 'f' is pronounced as 'v' in 'van.'

In Welsh, the letter 'y' is usually pronounced like the 'e' in 'winter,' but at the end of words as the 'e' in 'we.'

'W' at the beginning of words is pronounced as in English 'want,' 'wet,' etc.. In the middle or at the end of words, it is usually pronounced more like the 'oo' in 'boot' or 'shoot.'

'C' in Welsh is always pronounced hard as in 'cat.'

'G' is always hard as in 'get.'

English speakers generally find Irish Gaelic more difficult than Welsh due to the number of letters that are either not pronounced at all or pronounced very differently from how they would be in English. An example is the alternative Gaelic name of the Irish capital, Dublin, which is written Baile Átha Cliath. An English speaker might expect this to be pronounced 'bailey ather cleeath.' Locally, however, it is pronounced 'blear clear,' regionally 'bally a clear' or 'barley aha clear.' With such variation in pronunciation, and the rules by which sounds mutate being so complicated and, in the case of Old Irish, so uncertain, rather than attempt to tabulate them here, we will simply give our best approximation of how each name is pronounced in square brackets [...] the first time it occurs.

Acknowledgements

Many people, both seen and unseen, human and non-human, have contributed to the inspiration and support that have made this book, and my life, possible. In more or less chronological order, I offer profound thanks to my mother, Doris, a radical, astute, fiercely independent-minded woman who taught me to read and write from the age of two and supported me through much subsequent strangeness; Jack 'King' Kirby, whose renditions of *The Mighty Thor* and All-Father Odin for Marvel comics in the 1960s were my introduction to Paganism; Steve Ditko, whose *Doctor Strange* comics of the same era awakened me to the possibilities of ritual magic; Leslie Davie and George Blacker, who patiently tried to teach me Art and English Language respectively; Jenni and Claire, who introduced me to the joys of love and the sorrows of parting; Robin Williamson, Mike Heron, Rose Simpson and Christina 'Licorice' McKechnie for The Incredible String Band, the perfect musical accompaniment to spiritual seeking; Ravi Shankar and the Third Ear Band, ditto; the Ancient One; Toni Rampling, who opened up worlds of wonder, beauty and magic while we danced together on the edge; Richard 'Scarf' Gregory, soul brother; Tim, for first guitar lessons and more; starry-eyed John W. of the gleaming golden aura; Janet, Flossie and the Bexhill babes, shining like the summer Sun; David Bowie; Robert Graves, for showing me I was a Druid; Mircea Eliade, for further clues to sanity; Ceridwen, patroness of bards; Gary, Pam and the Grove of the Badger; Gwyn ap Nudd, winter king; Gwydion, antlered lord of forests; Arianrhod of the starry skies; MDB, Andy, Reg, Carl, Martin, Josh and the Simons for musical mayhem; Bill Carter and The Screaming Blue Messiahs, ditto; Robyn Hitchcock; Annie Lennox; Ellie, for everything; Dickon, Joe and Maie, who have brought so much to my life; Philip and Stephanie Carr-Gomm, good friends for many years; Ronald Hutton, without whose friendship life would be poorer and this book less historically sound (remaining inaccuracies being entirely my own); Ana; Bobcat, whose companionship on many strange adventures taught me more than words can say; Georgien Wybenga and Fire-keeper Walter, during whose ceremony the Wolf Who Walks with Fire came to me; the wild Wolf people of the world; Raven, Steve, Hette, Debbie, Graham, Robert; the Thunder Eagles of Yr Wyddfa; Andy, Kevan, Brother Brochfael; Woden, wisest of wights; Leon and Allen, Ani, Amy, Gail; the Quileute nation and the Makah, who welcomed me into their sacred circle when I had lost my way; Elaine and Garth, whose warmth and generosity have added so much to so many lives, not least my own; Bodger, Barry and Ann, Fee; Adam, Ady, Amanda, Andrew, Arian, Ben, Flick, Paul and the BDO Circle of Elders; 'the Norways,' Kyrre, Morten, LeNa, Wil, Bobby and Anita for sacred sounds and chaga spirit; The World Drum family; Kate Rusby; Frank Olding for Taliesin translations and tutoring; Brendan Myers for philosophical insights and permission to quote; and all other co-conspirators in the cosmic mystery who have shared their lives, wisdom, love and laughter with me. To those not named who should be, I ask your forgiveness and thank you for all that you are and all that you have been to me.

To you all I say, hale* and blessed be!

Greywolf /|\

Wiltshire, *Gwyl Forwyn* 2023

*The 1st edition had 'hail' not 'hale.' English 'hail' comes from Old English *haegl*, meaning 'frozen rain.' English 'hale,' which sounds identical, comes from Old Norse *heill*, meaning 'health, prosperity, good luck.' Despite which, 'hail' came to be the common spelling used for the salutation. Reverting to 'hale' makes it clear that we're wishing each other well-being, not frosty storms. 'Blessed be' is a common saying in modern Witchcraft, or Wicca. Having been initiated as a High Priest of Alexandrian Wicca in the 1970s, I began using the phrase in Druid contexts, attracting some criticism from fellow Druids. I continue to use it because it is clear, elegant and concise.

Introduction:
Why Druidry, Why Now?

Hale and welcome! You are about to enter a world in which people and animals talk to each other and take on each other's shapes, where you can learn to speak and read the language of trees, a world of visions, spirit guides, journeys into other worlds, ancestral teachers, past lives and gods who are at once ancient and ever young: such is the world of the Druid, but what is a Druid?

We know from classical Greek and Roman writers that Druids were central to an educated elite that existed in north-western Europe since at least the late Iron Age. They were teachers, philosophers, counsellors, law-givers, priests and magicians. More than a thousand years later, Druids were still active in some of those roles in medieval Ireland, and perhaps also in Scotland and Wales. But what relevance does this ancient tradition have for us today? That many do still find it relevant is shown by the fact that the last decade of the previous century and the early decades of this one have seen an explosion of interest in Druidry as a spiritual path. As evidence of this, in 1990 there were no 'how-to' books covering modern Druid beliefs and practices, by 2000 four introductory books were in print and in 2022, as I work on this new edition of my own contribution, a brief web-search reveals more than a dozen introductions and many more books offering in-depth coverage of particular 'flavours' of Druidry or focusing on specific aspects of the tradition. Demand for talks and workshops on modern Druidry has likewise expanded. Thirty years ago, it was hard to find any Druid-run or Druid-related events. Now there are several to choose from each weekend. Why, then, has a spiritual system rooted in the prehistoric past found renewed relevance in our digital age? What is there in the teachings and practices of our ancestors that continues to speak to us across the centuries?

A large part of the answer lies in connection, or rather in a web of connections encompassing past, present and future, birth, life and death, the physical world and other worlds beyond. These connections are accessible to us today because of the rediscovery and recreation of Druidry as a Pagan spiritual path that has taken place over the last sixty years or so. We'll look at that process in this book, and at how it led to the modern spiritual Druidry that has become its dominant form.

The deep connection with the natural world offered by this spiritual Druidry is a strong part of its appeal at a time when global warming and climate change are at the forefront of many minds, especially those of the young who will have longest to live with their potentially disastrous consequences. Many Druids, young and old, therefore support active campaigning groups like Extinction Rebellion (XR). In the UK, Druid ceremonies placing natural magic in the path of the destructive forces of greed and short-term self-interest that are polluting our planet have been a regular part of peaceful environmental demonstrations from the road protest movement of the 1990s to more recent anti-fracking campaigns, both of which met with considerable success. Globally, we have lent our support to the Dakota Access Pipeline protests in the USA and similar indigenous ecological movements elsewhere in the world. In performing such rites, modern Druids are following a history of ecological awareness going back at least two thousand years, when classical writers tell us that our ancestors honoured the gods in groves of sacred trees. A thousand years later, medieval manuscripts affirm the continuing sanctity of trees and their protected status under ancient laws. Druid revival groups have run tree-planting campaigns since at least the early years of the 20th century. Green Druidry has long roots.

The concept of the land, and the plant and animal life that lives upon it, as sacred, sentient and imbued with spirit is hard-wired into the DNA of Druidry. Every continent and country has a native spirituality that has grown out of the land, sea and sky, trees and herbs, animals and birds, spirits and ancestors of each particular place and its people. In the British Isles and much of Europe the earliest native spirituality for which we have a name is Druidry. Native traditions take on different forms depending on local climate, geography, flora and fauna, changing with the shifting tides of time, people and ideas, yet retaining certain common features. Shamanism, native to Siberia, the Dreamtime of the indigenous peoples of Australia, Bon-Po in Tibet, Wakan among the Lakota of the American plains and other kindred traditions elsewhere all grow out of a deep connection with the natural world. They offer a spiritual framework within which all of life is contained, from birth to death and beyond, into the realms of ancestral spirits. Within this framework, they retain and retell traditional tales and sing songs that provide a backdrop to their belief systems. They offer rites of passage and ways of healing. They give a context in which visionaries, healers, shamans, priests and poets practice their crafts for the benefit of their people, rather than being ostracised as weird or spooky, as such folk often are in post-industrial cultures like ours. Operating through knowledge of, and contact with, the spirits who inhabit the natural world and the gods and ancestors who inhabit other worlds, practitioners of these native spiritualities seek to gain knowledge and invoke aid and protection from these spirits, giving appropriate offerings in return. For our European ancestors, Druidry fulfilled all these roles. For many of us in the 21st century, it still does.

In common with other folk around the world, people of European origins are increasingly looking to revive, restore or renew the ancient native spiritualities of their ancestral homelands for spiritual sustenance and enhanced understanding. During centuries of expansion, exploration and conquest, many Europeans made their homes in other lands, often displacing or destroying indigenous peoples and cultures in the process. Descendants of those same Europeans are now looking to reconnect with the spirits of Nature. Druidry offers ways to do so that do not involve adding insult to the injuries inflicted on indigenous peoples by stealing their spiritual traditions just as our ancestors stole their lands.

As modern Druids, we are actively engaged in the process of rediscovering and renewing the ways of our Druid ancestors, expressing their essence in forms appropriate to our own times. These ancestral traditions are seen as vital means by which we reconnect with the spirits of Nature, our ancestors and the old gods of our lands and peoples, seeking through that reconnection to restore a sense of unity, balance and meaning to our lives and to reclaim personal power in what often seems an increasingly impersonal and disempowering world.

The sense of connection with a long chain of ancestral history is, for some, a strong element in the appeal of Druidry. That said, while we honour our ancestors and draw inspiration from the past, we are not tied to it. The true value of Druidry lies in its ability to help us deal with issues we face in our own lives today. As we shall see in chapter 2, radical redefinitions of Druidry by Druids rescued the tradition from the staid image it had in the 18th and 19th centuries, making it relevant for the 20th and 21st and enabling it to take its place alongside other Pagan traditions such as Wicca and Heathenism. But what is there specific to Druidry that makes it attractive to spiritual seekers?

At the heart of Druidry is the quest for inspiration, known in the British tradition by the Welsh name, *awen* [pronounced AA-wen], and in Irish as *imbas* [pron. Immus] or *dana* (see page 86). We seek it in the beauty of Nature, in personal relationships, music, poetry and song, dreams and visions, active ritual and quiet contemplation, in the wisdom of our ancestors and the old gods. Once our personal sources of *awen* have been found, we learn to work with them to awaken and sustain creativity, expressed through the arts, through how we live our lives and conduct our relationships with the world around us and with its indwelling spirits. *Awen* manifests in increased awareness and understanding and enhanced well-being on many levels. Ultimately, it moves through creativity and knowledge, penetrating to the soul, where it transforms into magic and mystery. Personal growth is part of the process, but Druidry also works with and for our communities, with the wider world and with other worlds beyond.

Druidry, then, offers a holistic approach to life, honouring and celebrating the physical as well as the spiritual. It is a deeply green philosophy, affirming life and seeing all creation as sacred. It is an attitude of mind that fosters respect, understanding and love. It offers reconnection and healing to all aspects of being. We reconnect with the natural world, the cycles of time and processes of change, birth, death and renewal by celebrating the seasons of the Sun and the phases of the Moon and by honouring and working with both the substance and spirit of the mineral, plant and animal worlds. We reconnect with family and friends by gathering together to celebrate festivals and the rites of passage that mark our personal growth and our changing relationships to those around us and to our world. We reconnect with our heritage, honouring our ancestors, their lives, songs, poetry, teachings and beliefs. We reconnect with the land through meditation and ritual at sacred places, whether trees or streams or the ancient shrines and stone circles of our ancestors. Through reawakening these links, we become aware of who we are and what role we have in the great dance of creation. The ultimate goal is to expand our awareness so that we become one with the gods and with the universe.

This book serves as a guide to the Druid path, awakening the reader to the teachings of ancestors, gods and guides and to the spirits of the natural world, of Sun, Moon and stars, tree and leaf, wind and rain, sea and river, fur and feather. The reader will learn to find new and potent relationships with ancestors of blood and spirit, to create and work within sacred space, to attune to the changing patterns of the natural world through celebration of its cycles and, above all, to access and work with the flowing spirit of inspiration and creativity that we call *awen*.

So, to return to our questions: Why is a philosophy rooted in the prehistoric past finding new relevance in our digital age? What is there in the teachings of our ancestors that continues to speak to us across the centuries? A short answer is that Druidry offers us the tools we need to work with and for the natural world and to recreate our world by recreating ourselves.

12

Part One:
The Circle is Unbroken

Chapter 1:
Druidry: Rekindling the Sacred Fires

What is Druidry? The simple answer is that Druidry is what Druids do, which begs the question, what is a Druid? Some friends once tried to define what makes someone a Druid, bearing in mind that there are many different Druid groups in Britain alone, ranging from deep green eco-magicians, through Wiccan-influenced Pagans, wild woodland pixies, otherworld voyagers and psycho-spiritual ritualists, to non-religious friendly societies and Christian cultural organisations. My friends came to the conclusion that there are three things that Druids have in common. One is that they wear white robes, although many don't. Another is that they use a version of Iolo Morganwg's Gorsedd Prayer, a.k.a. the Universal Druid Prayer (see pages 45-6), although many don't. The third is that they perform their ceremonies in daylight, although many don't. Eventually, they concluded that there is only one thing that all Druids have in common; the fact that they call themselves Druids.

If we attempt to define pre-Christian Druids we also run into problems, one being that Druidry has been an oral tradition during much of its existence, so nothing about what early Druids did, said or believed was written down by Druids themselves. There is plenty of evidence for pre-Christian ritual in the archaeological record, much of which may shed light on Druid belief and practice. Although no single inscription or artefact has yet been provably linked to Druids, Julius Caesar wrote (in *The Gallic Wars*, book 6, chapters 13-14, 16-19, 1st century BCE) that Druids were "concerned with divine worship, the due performance of sacrifices, public and private, and the interpretation of ritual questions." If we accept this, then ritual tools and regalia, representations of and inscriptions to gods, shrines, sculptures, figurines, burial practices and the like may well reflect Druidic ideas.

There remains the problem that such archaeological survivals vary widely across the regions in which Druidry is held to have been practised. Of the hundreds of gods named in early inscriptions, most were localised in range, revered by perhaps just a few hundred people in an area of a few square miles. Even those who do seem to cover a wider geographical range may have been understood very differently in, say, Northern England and Southern France. Apparently widespread deities such as Lugos or Dôn may seem to be so simply because their names represent common natural qualities that were widely revered. So the name Lugos, probably meaning 'light' (though some say it means 'oath'), could have indicated a god of the Moon in one area, a Sun god in another. Dôn probably means 'one who flows' (though some say it means 'earth') so her name appears in river names across much of Europe.

The lack of contemporary writings by Druids, coupled with the variety and ambiguity of the archaeological record mean there is no single body of evidence to which we can point and say, "that is authentic, ancient Druidry." That said, as we shall see in chapter 2, we can piece together a few basics from the second or third-hand accounts of classical Greek and Roman writers. They tell us that Druids were part of an educated class or caste among the Iron Age people whose culture dominated most of Europe in the centuries prior to our Common Era. Other members of this caste were bards, who were poets, singers, musicians and storytellers, and *vates*, or ovates, who were philosophers and seers. Druids themselves seem to have combined all these functions as well as being teachers, priests, judges and advisors to tribal rulers. Julius Caesar tells us their period of training lasted up to twenty years, that Druidry originated in Britain, and that "those who want to make a profound study of it generally go to Britain for the purpose."

Given the paucity and ambiguity of early evidence, you may ask how we can hope to create, or recreate, ancient Druidry in the modern era. The truth is, with the possible exception of some of those known as Celtic Reconstructionists, that's not what we are trying to do. Certainly we draw inspiration from the rich and varied past of the tradition, aspects of which are explored throughout this book, but our primary interest is to construct a Druidry relevant to our lives today. Classical Druidry existed in a time when the majority of people were directly involved in agriculture and animal husbandry, when the rapid transport system was the horse, when warfare was carried out at close quarters with spear, sword and shield, and the primary means of transmitting information was the spoken or sung word. Now most of us live in towns and cities, get our food from supermarkets and travel inside machines capable of speeds that would have terrified our ancestors, wars are increasingly fought from computer screens where the faces of the enemy are never seen by those tasked with killing and maiming them, and information is digitally transmitted worldwide in the blink of an eye. Our lives, and the needs and problems arising from them, are radically different from those of our ancestors. We therefore require a different Druidry.

To take just one example, there is every reason to believe that animal sacrifice was a regular component of classical Druidry, as it was of other ancient religions. In the Iron Age most people were intimately involved in the care of animals through farming, hunting and horse-riding. The act of sacrifice was informed by the closeness of the connection between us and the animals involved. We knew them well. We relied on them for sustenance. We not only ate their flesh but made clothing and bedding from their hides, tools and musical instruments from their bones and so on. Now we buy meat shrink-wrapped in neat, pre-prepared packages. Having lost any personal connection with the animal persons we eat, the act of sacrifice would no longer have anything like the same significance it did for our ancestors. Modern Druidry has therefore abandoned it. Instead we sacrifice that which is of most value to us today, often our time and energy, occasionally our own blood.

The Sources of Modern Druidry

The Druidry of today differs from that practised two hundred, let alone two, four, six or eight thousand years ago because, while we draw on the wisdom of our ancestors, we do so in answer to the needs of our own time. That said, modern Druidry is inspired by many sources and archaeology is one. While artefacts with direct, provable links to ancient Druids may be lacking, evidence for ritual activity is abundant and inferences about belief and ritual practice can often be drawn from it. The arrival of literacy following the Roman conquests of Gaul and then Southern Britain means that we have the names of hundreds of native deities, often preserved with accompanying images and linked with Graeco-Roman gods whose narratives survive. So, when we find Sulis-Minerva honoured at the hot springs of Bath in Somerset and the healing shrine that grew up around them, we may gain some understanding of the role of the native British goddess Sulis by reading legends of Minerva, the Roman goddess of wisdom, justice and the arts.

Archaeology also reveals the structure of sacred shrines. During the Iron Age, the period most associated with ancient Druidry, many of these were remarkably similar to those of the Neolithic era two thousand years earlier, consisting of bank-and-ditch earthworks, some circular, some containing arrangements of posts or standing stones aligned on rising or setting points of Sun or Moon. Many contain the remains of sacrificial animal persons, often placed near entrances, another practice surviving from the Neolithic.

Occasional wooden images presumed to represent deities survive, crudely carved but undeniably powerful. The Iron Age example shown here, found at Ballachulish in Scotland in 1880, was carved from a single alder trunk in around 600 BCE. A young female about 5 feet in height, she has quartz pebbles for eyes and originally stood in a wickerwork shrine beside a peaty pool.

Even a few early ritual texts have been discovered and tentatively translated. A Latin inscription dating from the 1st century BCE, found at Rom (Roman Rauranum) in Western France, is an invocation to a native horse goddess whose various names or titles are given in it. Engraved on a thin sheet of lead, it accompanied the sacrifice of a filly and a votive offering of a bronze cauldron. G. S. Olmsted's English translation of it is quoted in full in Peter Berresford Ellis' *A Brief History of the Celts* (Constable & Robinson Ltd., 2003). Demonstrating how archaeology can inspire our practice of Druidry today, I created a chant based on the Rom inscription that can be found online at https://youtu.be/ZS51ysaYoqE

Classical texts are not our only source of information about North European paganism. Early Christian writers fill in some gaps by suggesting penances to be performed by parishioners who maintain pagan practices. In doing so, they naturally have to tell us what those practices are. Dressing as animals to celebrate festivals is one.

As we shall see in chapter 5, the medieval literatures of Wales and Ireland are another valuable source. Although often written, compiled or copied by Christian monks, a number of these texts offer, if not a description of 'authentic ancient Druidry,' then at least fascinating glimpses of what

the medieval Welsh and Irish thought ancient Druidry was like. Since Druids still existed in Ireland, and may have done so in Wales, when the earliest of the texts were written, the image of Druidry they give seems likely to bear some relationship to reality. Many of these texts presumably originated with stories transmitted orally by bards who, as we have seen, were members of the ancient caste that included Druids. We know a fair bit about bards since organised bardic schools survived until the late 18th century and several copies of their text books survive in both Ireland and Wales.

Other sources drawn on by modern Druids are folklore and folk customs. Britain and Ireland have a rich heritage of folk tales, often passed on orally for generations, sometimes written down, whether in medieval manuscripts or the journals of 19th century collectors. Later oral tales can sometimes fill gaps in the manuscript sources, providing additional information about particular characters or variations of their legends. Many folk customs practised in Britain and Ireland today are modern revivals of medieval or early modern ones that had fallen into disuse. Some, such as well-dressing, beating the bounds and some annual pilgrimages in Ireland, may be Christian adaptations of formerly pagan activities. Cornish Midsummer bonfires may be a direct continuation from the pagan past. Others are modern creations, some of which, like the huge annual Beltane celebration in Edinburgh, are self-consciously tapping into both ancient pagan roots and modern Pagan sensibilities. Though the forms of celebration may have changed, there is unequivocal evidence that our ancestors celebrated Midsummer, Midwinter and the quarter days now known in English as Candlemas, May Day, Lammas and Hallowe'en (see pages 74-80).

Where not enough information survives to enable us to properly interpret the sources we've looked at already, we can sometimes supplement it by looking at similar practices in other cultures. So, although there are no surviving texts written by ancient Druids, their beliefs and practices were likened at the time to those of Greek philosophers and Hindu Yogis whose writings have survived. We can therefore look to these to gain some idea of what Druids of the time believed. Knowing from medieval sources that the Irish Fianna were groups of young men living apart from society who were looked upon as wolf warriors, we can look to evidence for wolf warrior societies from Bronze Age archaeology, early Hindu Vedic texts, medieval Scandinavian and early modern Baltic folklore and 19th and 20th century accounts of apparently similar wolf societies in North America.

As modern Druids, we are also blessed (or cursed depending on your point of view) to have inherited the works of other Druid revivalists of the last three hundred years or so. While much of what they wrote is ill-informed and deeply misleading, occasional flashes of inspiration shine through.

Those of us who are modern Pagan Druids also draw inspiration from other modern manifestations of Paganism, notably Wicca and Heathenism. Wicca draws on many of the same sources that we do, including classical Greek and Roman paganism, medieval magical grimoires and the influential Victorian magical society, the Hermetic Order of the Golden Dawn. Modern Heathenism primarily draws on two 13th century Icelandic texts, the *Poetic Edda* and the *Prose Edda*, much as some modern Druids draw on the medieval literatures of Wales and Ireland. Heathenism as a whole tends to take a more 'reconstructionist' approach to this material than do most modern Druids.

Modern Druids also draw inspiration from each other. Given that there are many different Druid groups, often believing and doing markedly different things, many modern Druids explore a variety of voices within the tradition. This may manifest in joining, or training with, more than one group, or just reading works published by members of other groups. So, for example, while the Anglesey Druid Order gets together for teaching and ceremonies on the island from which it is named, some of its members are also members of groups such as the Order of Bards, Ovates and Druids (OBOD) or the British Druid Order (BDO), while books published by Anglesey Order founder, Kristoffer Hughes, are read by interested folk worldwide. Several groups begin their ceremonies by calling for peace, a practice initiated by the Gorsedd of Bards of the Isle of Britain in the 1790s. Many have adopted the practice of chanting *awen* three times introduced by OBOD Chosen Chief, Philip Carr-Gomm, in the 1980s (but see page 89). Several groups have adopted the BDO's understanding of *awen* as the flowing spirit, our emphasis on medieval literature and our 'shamanistic' approach to Druidry.

Finally, there is personal gnosis derived from the ability we all have to make direct connections with spirits of place, of animals, plants, ancestors and the old gods of our lands. *Awen* is the medium through which these connections are mediated. Which brings us neatly to...

Druidry as Native Spirituality

In our Introduction, we defined Druidry as a spirituality native to Britain and Europe, but what does this mean? The religious traditions of indigenous peoples such as First Nations Americans and Aboriginal Australians demonstrate a close connection with the land. A sense of the sacredness of the natural world is one of the defining traits of native spirituality, an animistic view that sees consciousness embodied not only in humans and other animals, but in many plants, springs, streams and rivers, even rocks and mountains. This sense has been largely lost in technological cultures, hence the ease with which such societies plough roads through ancient woodlands, lay oil pipelines across rivers, dump toxic waste in oceans or connive in the destruction of rain forests. Growing protests against the wholesale exploitation of our planet, often channelled through groups like Extinction Rebellion, demonstrate not just an increasing awareness of the malaise that has left us feeling detached from the Earth we walk on and the myriad other sentient, inspirited beings with whom we share it, but a strong desire for reconnection.

For those who live in the British Isles, Druidry offers unique opportunities to rediscover specific connections with our landscape. The roots of Druidry reach deep into the history and prehistory of these islands and into the land herself, singing through her sacred places the songs of the spirits who dwell among her forests, hills, valleys, streams and rivers. As we shall see in chapter 5, many such places are identified in the medieval literature of Wales and Ireland, enabling us to visit them with knowledge of legendary incidents that occurred there in our own 'dreamtime' and to identify beings involved in those events. The British Isles are also rich in places of religious reverence wrought by human hands, from famous monuments such as Avebury and Stonehenge to small woodland shrines, holy wells, ritual shafts and modest burial mounds. One of the tasks of modern bards, ovates and Druids is to seek out such holy places, make new connections with their guardian spirits, recover the songs and traditions surrounding them, and, in doing so, breathe new life into the spirits of place, the old gods and the land.

The same principles apply to Druids living or travelling elsewhere in the world. Druidry allows us to make connections with the indwelling spirits of whatever land we find ourselves in, helping us relate to them with respect and reverence for the spirits themselves and for local people and indigenous traditions. In the USA, for example, we relate to sacred places of the First Nations not as Wannabee Indians, but as Druids.

Working with spirits of the land, of place and of Nature restores a sacred relationship with the world that fuels the vision of Druidry as a green, ecologically aware spirituality. Many Druids see themselves as guardians of the natural world. This is another way in which Druids find natural kinship with other indigenous spiritual traditions.

We work with our ancestors. This too is a feature of indigenous spiritualities around the world. We speak of ancestors of blood and of spirit. Those of blood are our genetic line, from parents and grandparents back through the generations to the earliest humans and beyond. Our ancestors of spirit are those who have walked spiritual paths similar to our own. Through the practice of our tradition, we learn to communicate with our ancestors, learning from them, sharing our understanding with them, listening for their songs and laughter on the wind, honouring their spirits. Though we may wander far from the lands of our ancestors, their songs still sing through our memories, our spirits, our blood and DNA.

Growing out of our work with the ancestors of our land and tradition, the British Druid Order (BDO) pioneered calls for the respectful reburial of ancient human remains in the UK unearthed during archaeological digs. This finds expression in Honouring the Ancient Dead (HAD), an organisation founded by noted writer and former joint chief of the BDO, Emma Restall Orr, which seeks to build bridges between its broadly-based membership and archaeologists and museum curators to promote mutual understanding and rational debate on the issue. See our Resources section for their web address.

Meeting with folk from other indigenous traditions, with elders, teachers and healers, we thus find shared understanding through the common ground of animism, the belief that all things are imbued with spirit, and through the acknowledgement of our ancestors as teachers and guides. Many folk of European ancestry turn to teachers from other cultures, particularly Amerindian, to gain this kind of understanding of the world. Through our teaching and practice of Druidry, we seek to show that Europe has its own, richly powerful spiritual traditions.

If Druidry originated in the British Isles, it was not held within them. By the time Druids came to the attention of the classical world, Druidcraft was practised across much of Europe, from Portugal in the west to Turkey in the east, from Italy in the south to Scotland in the north. Now there are Druids in countries around the world. Most modern Druids are of European ancestry, relating to the tradition in part through their blood line. For them, wherever they may be on the Earth, Druidry provides a way to make connections with the spirits of place, the gods of the region and, through them, with the local people, customs, climate, seasons, flora and fauna. At the same time, Druidry enables them to maintain and draw nourishment from their own ancestral gods and cultural heritage. While it is natural for folk to relate strongly to spiritual traditions linked with their own land and ancestry, such ancestral links are not a requirement for being a Druid. Druidry is a way of being in the world that is open to all who share its fundamental beliefs.

Although much has been achieved over the last forty years, the native traditions of Britain and Europe are still in the process of being rediscovered and redefined after centuries of decay, neglect and abuse. On the plus side, this gives us immense freedom. We have the materials with which to build, provided by archaeology, history, literary and folk traditions, past attempts at revival, and our own sense of the spirits of the tradition, but what we build from them is up to us. Our task is to create something strong and beautiful enough to stand against the destructive currents in the mainstream culture of industrial and post-industrial nations, offering a clear alternative that demonstrates the possibility of walking the Earth in a sacred manner. This telling concept, paraphrased from the book, *Black Elk Speaks* (1932), detailing the world view of an Oglala holy man, has found favour among many spiritual seekers because it has power and resonance for all caring humans. Black Elk himself wished it to be so, saying of the vision that was granted to him, "it is true and it is beautiful, and it is for all men" (Raymond J. DeMaille, *The Sixth Grandfather*, 1984, page xvii). We feel the same about Druidry, though we'd switch 'men' for 'people.'

The religious beliefs and practices of our ancestors continually changed and adapted to reflect changes in the environment and in human understanding. In the process of rediscovering our native spirituality, as in so much else, we are aided and guided by our ancestors, both physical and spiritual, and by the old gods of our lands, who come to us when we call through our songs and prayers, bringing strength and guidance from the spirit worlds. With their help, Druidry is renewing its role as an indigenous spirituality of Britain and Europe, one that honours the natural world, our ancestors, and the old gods in this millennium. In re-creating a spiritual path that responds to the needs of our own times, an authentic modern Druidry, we believe we come as close as possible to recreating the spirit of ancient Druidry. In the British Druid Order we refer to this process as re-kindling the sacred fires of our ancestors.

Having spoken of rekindling the sacred fires of Druidry since the 1990s, I was intrigued two decades later to find a prophecy recorded on a wampum belt passed down for generations among the Anishinabe people of North-eastern America. Called 'The Seven Fires Prophecy,' it tells of seven prophets who came to the Anishinabe to reveal possible futures to them. The prophets of the Fourth Fire warned of "the light-skinned race

21

... wearing the face of death." The prophet of the Sixth Fire told of children being taken away and the ways of the Elders being ignored, resulting in the people losing their purpose, in sickness and grief. Then,

> The Seventh Prophet that came to the people long ago was said to be different from the other prophets. He was young and had a strange light in his eyes. He said, "In the time of the Seventh Fire, New People will emerge. They will retrace their steps to find what was left by the trail. Their steps will take them to the Elders who they will ask to guide them on their journey. But many of the Elders will have fallen asleep. They will awaken to this new time with nothing to offer. Some of the Elders will be silent out of fear. Some of the Elders will be silent because no one will ask anything of them. The New People will have to be careful in how they approach the Elders. The task of the New People will not be easy.
>
> "If the New People will remain strong in their Quest, the Water Drum of the Midewiwin Lodge will again sound its voice. There will be a Rebirth of the Anishinabe Nation and a rekindling of old flames. The Sacred Fire will again be lit. It is at this time that the light skinned race will be given a choice between two roads. If they choose the right road, then the Seventh Fire will light the Eighth and final Fire, an eternal Fire of peace, love, brotherhood and sisterhood. If the light skinned race makes the wrong choice of roads, the destruction which they brought with them in coming to this country will come back at them and cause much suffering and death to all the Earth's people."

(For the full text, search online for 'The Seven Fires Prophecy.')

As modern Druids engaged in the reconstruction of our own tradition, we too are retracing our steps "to find what was left by the trail." The ancestors whose guidance we seek are our "Elders who have fallen asleep." We see our rekindling of the sacred fires of Druidry as our choice of "the right road" and pray to our gods that it may indeed lead to the kindling of the Eighth Fire, ushering in a new era of "peace, love, brotherhood and sisterhood" for all humankind. The climate crisis suggests that not nearly enough of us are currently choosing the right road, even though the consequences of choosing otherwise, spelt out starkly in the last sentence of the prophecy, are increasingly clear to those with eyes to see and hearts to feel.

Which brings us to the role of Druids today. Given the wide diversity of belief and opinion within modern Druidry, I can only offer my own view, but will try to keep it as inclusive as possible.

The Paths of Bard, Ovate & Druid

Most modern Druid groups recognize three main areas of study and practice within Druidry, those of the bard, ovate (Welsh *ofydd*) and Druid (Welsh *Derwydd* or *Dryw*). The bard is a creative artist, a custodian of lore and tradition, a scholar, poet, composer, performer, musician, storyteller, historian, genealogist and mythographer. The key to the way of the bard lies in contacting the inspiring spirit traditionally viewed as flowing from, and gifted by, the gods, in British tradition most especially by the witch-like Ceridwen, described in medieval literature as patroness of bards (pages 113-4). In the Welsh language the spirit of inspiration is called *awen*, which I translated many years ago as 'the flowing spirit.' A possibly more accurate rendition might be 'feminine spirit,' but my earlier translation has spread around the world. Why? Because, as a visionary and spiritual descriptor of what *awen* is and does, it works, which is why medieval Welsh bards often refer to *awen* in liquid terms, notably as a gift from the cauldron of Ceridwen. The bardic path is the subject of chapters 4 and 5.

The ovate explores the roots of things, the philosophy that underpins Druidry and life itself, seeking answers to questions such as; Who are the gods? Who are the spirits of nature? How can we relate to them? What is the nature and destiny of the human spirit? What is the nature of destiny? What happens to the human soul and psyche after death? The ovate seeks to use *awen* to understand the flow of events, past, present and future, by combining mental discipline with the intuitive gifts of the bard. A primary ovate skill is divination, seen in its literal sense as communication with the divine. Allied with this is seership, the visionary ability to perceive other worlds and other times. Another ovate skill is that of healing, the practice of which draws on an understanding of the flow of spirit, the will of the gods and the nature of human destiny. The ovate approach to the world is what ancient Greek and Roman writers referred to as 'natural philosophy.' The ovate path is the subject of chapters 6 and 7.

The skills of the Druid are gained through working as a bard and ovate. The Druid seeks to use the intuition, inspiration and creativity of the bard and the understanding and insight of the ovate to work with *awen* in order to weave ritual, to offer guidance and teaching and to become a fully active participant in the great dance of creation. The Druid is a walker between worlds, whether journeying into spirit worlds or working for reconciliation between opposing groups. The Druid may also practice shape-shifting, whether transforming into spirit animals or changing their interaction with the world in other ways, perhaps again in order to bring about peace and reconciliation but often to bring about healing or discover otherwise hidden knowledge. The Druid is also the teacher of the tradition and early sources refer to Druids as moral philosophers. I am sometimes asked if Druids work magic. How one defines magic is open to debate, but central to it is the ability to work with other levels of reality and with the energies of creation that flow through all of existence. These things a Druid certainly does. A common definition holds that magic is "the art of bringing about changes in conformity with the will." This is not my understanding. For me, rather than seeking to dominate spiritual forces and bend reality to one's will, the Druid seeks to understand the workings of spirits and the flow of natural forces and to work with them in such a way that a desired outcome manifests itself naturally. The Druid path is the subject of chapters 8 and 9.

Put briefly, the bard makes contact with the spirit world, the ovate sees it and the Druid enters it. In practice, however, there is considerable overlap between the work undertaken in these three areas. The Druid continues to utilise skills acquired as a bard and an ovate, the bard may weave ritual and use divination. In my understanding, bard, ovate and Druid are not a rigid ladder of grades but useful descriptions of areas of study and practice within the tradition. Some people are born bards and devote themselves to perfecting their expression of one or more of the bardic arts. This does not make them any less valuable or advanced than, say, a healer devoted to that ovate skill, or a Druid counsellor. The Druid path encourages us to develop and exercise the skill sets we are most drawn to and for which we have the most natural aptitude.

Core Concepts

While defining the entirety of Druidry, whether ancient or modern, presents problems, defining individual Druid groups is perhaps a little easier. We'll look at some of the larger and more influential of them in our next chapter. Those referred to in the early part of it represent what has been called 'the new Druidry,' a re-creation of the tradition which, as we shall see, came to prominence in the 1990s but has roots that go back much further. Below we set out some core concepts that help define this new Druidry. Given here as they appear in the British Druid Order's bardic course, they apply to a greater or lesser extent to most of the groups who espouse this form of Druidry. Based on ancient ideas, they remain relevant to us today, shaping our view of the Druid path and helping to define its place and ours in relation to the wider world of Nature, humankind and spirituality.

1) **Animism**, i.e. the belief that all things are imbued with spirit. This fundamental belief encourages us to be aware of the true, spiritual nature of all things. This awareness encourages us to treat all beings and all things with respect and lies at the heart of the green spiritual environmentalism that is so much a part of modern Druidry. Animism is also found in Buddhism, Islam and Christianity.

2) **Polytheism**, i.e. the belief that there are many gods and goddesses, all worthy of respect and reverence. Among other things, belief in a multiplicity of deities fosters tolerance, allowing us to see other faiths as valid paths to spiritual growth. While we see the ultimate goal of all spiritual paths as being oneness with the universe, we do not see that oneness as a single, male father god or female great goddess. Universal unity is beyond any such limited human conceptions.

3) **Respect for our Ancestors**. We recognise ancestors of spirit as well as those of our direct bloodline. Ancestors of spirit are those who have walked similar spiritual paths before us and with whom we therefore feel close affinity. Respect for our ancestors stems from the fact that so much of who we are is derived from them, both physically and spiritually. We may also find teachers and guides among our ancestors.

4) **Paganism** in its original sense, which is simply that of a spirituality that honours the spirits of the place in which we live. Honouring the spirits of our own locale naturally leads us to honour those of other lands we may travel to. In honouring the spirits of place, we are also honouring the inhabitants of that place, both the living and their ancestors in spirit.

As said, these basic principles help define the British Druid Order but are by no means limited to it. On the contrary, they apply not only to many contemporary Druid groups but to other modern Pagan paths such as Wicca and Heathenism, and also to New Age spirituality, indigenous religions, shamanism, Chinese folk religion, Japanese Shinto and Hinduism. Estimates vary, but these beliefs are shared by roughly one-third of the world's population, thus representing the world's largest faith community. Though numerically exceeding Christianity or Islam, we lack the political clout of either largely because we are so fragmented. Think what we could achieve if we were to all work together.

Which brings us to…

Ethics

For those of us who accept the core tenets of animism, polytheism, respect for our ancestors and paganism, they underlie our ethical approach to the world and our relationships with everything in it. These are summarised in the BDO bardic course as follows:

1) **Ethnicity**. Given its origins and history, Druidry may be of primary interest to those of European ancestry, or who currently live in mainland Europe, Britain or Ireland. Membership of the BDO is, however, open to people of any and all ethnic and cultural backgrounds living anywhere in the world. We do not discriminate on grounds of race, skin colour, ethnicity, hair colour or shoe size and believe it is wholly and utterly wrong to do so. We promote equality and inclusivity.

2) **Gender**. We recognise that gender is not, and never has been, a simple binary consisting solely of male and female. Some are transgender, some non-gendered, others are gay, straight, lesbian, bisexual, transsexual, transvestite, or otherwise queer. The BDO is open to people of any and all genders and sexual orientations. We do not discriminate on the grounds of people's genitalia or what they do with them, so long as they do no harm to others.

3) **Politics**. The BDO supports democracy in its original Greek sense of government of the people, by the people and for the people, with no political parties, representatives being chosen by random ballot and serving for one year. There are currently (2022) no major nations that come close to meeting this definition. The UK, USA and Russia, for example, are best described by another Greek term, plutocracy, i.e. government of, by and for the rich. Plutocracy promotes huge inequality between people that adversely impacts the majority in favour of a tiny minority, affecting health, education, lifestyle, social mobility and every aspect of life. It is also responsible for the ecological crisis we are currently plunging into and must, therefore, be replaced by genuine democracy as soon as possible. As an adjunct to real democracy, we also promote equality of opportunity and of reward.

4) **War & Peace**. As an organisation, we collectively promote a pacifist agenda that calls for an end to all conflicts between people. Once this is achieved, the unbelievably vast sums currently spent on armaments and training people to kill and maim each other can be redirected to more useful ends such as ending world poverty, ensuring clean water, decent

food, good education and health care for all. Following on from this, we support non-violent protest as a means to effect social and political change.

5) **Ecology**. Druidry is often, and with some justification, portrayed as a naturally green spirituality. In the BDO, concern for all beings who inhabit our planet follows on naturally from the first of our core beliefs, Animism. As animists, we recognise the sentience of a wide range of beings, from mushrooms to mountains, hedgehogs to human beings.

Humans are not the only beings with a right to life. In 2010, the government of Bolivia became the first in the modern world to recognise the rights of all beings when it enacted a 'Law of the Rights of Mother Earth.' This inspired a number of indigenous peoples and ecological groups to call for the United Nations to adopt a 'Universal Declaration of the Rights of Mother Earth,' Article 2 of which sets out a series of 'Inherent Rights of Mother Earth' which are in accord with BDO beliefs and practices. I encourage all Druids, Pagans and others who share our core principles to support the adoption of the 'Universal Declaration.' Visit https://www.rightsofmotherearth.com

In pursuit of the aims of the Declaration, the BDO is a founding supporter of the charity, PaganAid, which funds initiatives combining ecological principles with practical assistance for indigenous peoples seeking ways to live well and in harmony with Nature. Visit https://www.paganaid.org

While these ethical statements are drawn, as said, from the bardic course of the BDO, other contemporary Druid groups will be in broad agreement with some or all of them.

Brendan Myers, a professor of philosophy and humanities at CEGEP Heritage College, Quebec, and a leading exponent of the new Druidry, has written an excellent book on pagan ethics called *The Other Side of Virtue: Where our virtues really came from, what they really mean, and where they might be taking us* (O Books, 2008). He sees the failings of the Christian ethical code as rooted in its reliance on obedience to human interpretations of the thought processes of an angry God and fear of divine vengeance from that God. After then addressing the failings of the self-obsessed nihilism that often replaces Christian ethics in Western societies, he writes (pages 14-15, quoted with permission):

> My suggestion for an answer will not be a modification of either Christianity, or modern individualism. Rather, I believe we should assert something like this. The good life involves each person finding within herself the purpose and worth of life. But this activity of self-exploration

27

must not cut people off from sources of meaning beyond themselves. It must not lead the way to nihilism, relativism, apathy, and empty self-centredness. Similarly, we should assert that some values really are 'out there,' beyond the self, and are not a matter of personal opinions and preferences. But we must find a way to assert this without falling back on old models of conformity and obedience. ...

To think philosophically or spiritually is to think in a way that breaks from the previous non-philosophical, non-spiritual way of thinking. To even ask how to begin to think differently is already to think differently. The process is normally initiated by an experience that cuts into the structure of one's ordinary routine, as if from outside. Something must happen that cannot be accommodated by an auto-pilot. Self-knowledge is found, perhaps only found, with an event or situation that *calls one's life into question*. (Emphasis as in the original).

Myers' second paragraph calls to mind a group of texts referred to either as 'the Cauldron of Poesy,' or 'the Three Cauldrons,' which form part of a 16th century manuscript in the library of Trinity College, Dublin (MS H.3.18, pages 53a1-57b5). Here too we find the idea of self-knowledge being gained through extreme events that evoke either sorrow or bliss. My translation of the relevant part reads as follows:

What is ... the source of poetry and every wisdom besides? Not hard. Three cauldrons are in each person from birth; the cauldron of devotion, the cauldron of motion and the cauldron of wisdom. The cauldron of devotion is enchantment-born upright in a person, turned to dispense wisdom upwards in early youth for each generation. The cauldron of motion, however, which comes after it and ... increases in a rush, is born on its side in a person. The cauldron of wisdom is by enchantment born on its lips and bestows learning in every poetic art. ... On its lips is the cauldron of motion until it is turned by sorrow or spiritual bliss.

Question; how many divisions of sorrow are there that turn it? Not hard; there are four. Yearning for home, grief, grinding jealousy, and pilgrimage undertaken for the sake of the deity. *In the midst of life these four occur, and their causes are external.* (My emphasis.)

There are two types of ... bliss which turn the cauldron of wisdom, and these are divine bliss and human bliss. Of human bliss there are four divisions ... (1) rejoicing in the energy of sexuality, and (2) the bliss of wholeness and freedom from care with abundance of food, and being a person seeking mastery of bardcraft, and (3) bliss on account of the principles of divination forged through good work, and (4) bliss from the casting of the nuts of inspiration from the nine hazels of fine fruitfulness at the well of Segais of fair aspect, falling in multitudes, along ram-headed waves of the Boyne they surge upstream, swift as a driven horse, in the middle of the month of Midsummer, one day in every seventh year. Divine bliss, however, comes because of movement towards the cauldron of wisdom which turns it upright, from which there are divine and human seers and commentators who combine grace and application to learning, so that thereafter they have speech of virtue to make miracles, and so that their speech forms precedents and judgements, so that they become the pattern of every desire. Except *that which comes from outside restores this cauldron* whose core is spoken of in the ancient sayings of Nede mac Adna. (My emphasis.)

Many see the three cauldrons texts as an instruction manual for a meditational system embedded in bardic training. The cauldrons themselves seem to represent a concept similar to the three *Tan T'ien* energy centres of Taoist Yoga which, like the cauldrons of devotion, motion and wisdom, are located in the belly, solar plexus and head. Parallels with Kundalini Yoga have also been made based partly on the description of the onset of human bliss as being like 'ram-headed waves' surging upstream. The image of a ram-headed serpent appears repeatedly in Romano-Celtic art, as in the image below from the 1ˢᵗ century BCE Gundestrup cauldron. It has been likened to the Kundalini serpent. Both seem to represent spiritual power. The Kundalini serpent embodies the

feminine cosmic force known as Shakti. As we have seen, Ceridwen's power manifests as *awen*, which may be translated as 'feminine spirit.' The cauldron of devotion is akin to the cauldron of Ceridwen (page 113), both being vessels in which poetic inspiration is brewed.

Translations and analyses of all the 'three cauldrons' texts feature in the BDO bardic course. In them, and in the philosophical and ethical principles arising from them, we see vital keys to recreating ourselves, thereby rekindling the sacred fires of Druidry and remaking our world.

Chapter 2:
Beginnings

In my youth, I used to stare into mirrors. If I stared long enough my own face would fade away to be replaced by that of an old man with a bald head and a wispy white beard. His eyes were white as though he were blind, yet I felt he looked from the mirror into the innermost recesses of my soul. I didn't know who he was but looked forward to those encounters, knowing the old man's presence would always lead me to look deep inside myself and strive towards the realisation of my deepest dreams. It took me years to realise that he was not only the perfect representation of my idea of a Druid, but was my guide, the silent, knowing teacher of my heart, mind and spirit.

When thinking of a Druid, most people probably conjure up a similar picture of an old man with a white beard, usually with a robe to match, perhaps armed with a staff and an enigmatic smile, an age-old wisdom in his ageless eyes. This is the Druid archetype we have inherited, filtered to us through myth and fiction as Merlin, Gandalf or Getafix. But where does this archetype come from, what can we learn from it, and how close is it to the reality of Druidry, either as it is now or as it was in the past?

Look inside yourself. What is *your* image of a Druid? Is he that ancient, white-bearded sage? Is he a wild shaman dressed in animal skins and feathers? Is your Druid a woman? Find the image and hold it in your mind. What does it tell you about your own yearnings, beliefs and aspirations? What does it say to you? Does your Druid have a name, a background, a history, a message or lesson for you? Spend some time in the company of your Druid archetype, then, when you are ready to continue, give thanks for what you have seen, felt and learned.

Aware of your own present image of a Druid, let us now look at some other images of Druidry, both as it is now and as it was.

Honouring Our Ancestors

One of the things that attracts people to Druidry is the sense that it provides a link with the past. For the Druid, the past is not a static thing held fast within the dry and dusty pages of history books, it is a living part of our reality; it is how we became who we are and the blueprint for what we may yet become. The past is a potent source of inspiration, of *awen*. More than that, the past is the realm of our ancestors and, for the Druid, our ancestors are our companions and teachers in this life.

The ancestors of blood who comprise our genetic line are our parents, grandparents, great-grandparents, back ten thousand years to the time after the last Ice Age when people first walked the land of Britain, back three million years to when the first humans walked the plains of Southern Africa, back to the single-celled life forms of three billion years ago. The earth on which we walk, and the sedimentary rocks below the earth, are the remains of our ancestors in this three billion year chain of evolving life. We honour this chain of other lives that have given us the life we have now. To remind ourselves of this connection between the earth we walk on and our ancestors, we might chant to the rhythm of a drum:

Earth and stone, blood and bone, all are one, all are one.

In working with our ancestors, we begin by honouring our parents. Many of us find our own parents harder to relate to than ancestors living a thousand years ago or more. We are simply too close. But whatever problems we may have had in childhood, we give thanks to our parents for the extraordinary gift of life. We recognize that experiences we may find difficult contribute strongly to who we are. Teaching may be harsh or gentle, learning hard or easy and, as the 'Three Cauldrons' texts (pages 28-30) suggest, positive results can often come from negative experiences. Perhaps arguing against your parents helped form your strength of character, hone your mind and increase your independence. Perhaps their behaviour towards you has helped you to form better relationships with others. Perhaps the absence of one or both parents has helped you become self-reliant. Whether your relationship with your parents has been based on love or loathing, look for those things of value that you have learned from them and give thanks from deep within your soul. The healing process has begun...

We honour our grandparents, our great-grandparents and their forebears through the generations in the same way, again giving thanks for the gift of life passed down through the chain of DNA, and for the lessons learned or inheritance gained from them.

We also honour our ancestors of spirit, those who have walked paths similar to our own in previous generations. While some may belong to our bloodline, others may be unrelated in any close genetic sense but will have world-views, beliefs and experiences that link them to us in spirit. Those who follow the Druid path may look to these spiritual ancestors as teachers and guides more than to those of our blood line. We give thanks for what we have gained from them. We shall meet them again many times as our path through Druidry progresses.

The Druid path may lead to strange, far-flung, wondrous places but, like all paths, it begins at our front door. When travelling far afield, many of us find comfort in the thought of home, particularly those of us for whom home is a place of refuge, peace and stability. We, of course, have a part to play in creating that stability, making our home a supportive foundation from which we may branch out and explore, knowing there is that place of safety to which we can return. Our spirituality is foundational to who we are and how we relate to the world, and a well-maintained altar can be the foundation of both home and spirituality.

The Altar

In her home, the Druid will often have an altar on which will be arranged a collection of things reflecting her personal and ancestral history, her interests and beliefs. There may be figures of deities, perhaps of her own land, perhaps from other cultures where there is a strong spiritual link. The altar is the bedrock of one's spirituality, a place in the home where we may commune with the spirits of nature, so elements of the natural world will usually appear on it; feathers, flowers, leaves, bones, stones, nuts, perhaps a bowl of earth or sand and another of water. There will often be an incense burner, incense, herbs, candles. There may be gifts or tokens that friends on the path have given, or mementoes of family, pictures of children, lovers, parents, grandparents. The common link connecting all these things and the reason for their presence on the altar is that they provide inspiration, that spiritual essence we call *awen*.

If you don't have an altar, perhaps you might like to make one. What would you put on it? What do you have already that you find inspiration in? Perhaps a painting that would make a good backdrop, perhaps a stone from a place sacred to our ancestors or special to you. Clear a space on a shelf, in a corner or on a table and think about what you will place there. Gather a few things together and see how they fit. Think about what each one means to you and why. Your altar is a reflection of yourself. What do the things you put on it say about who you are and who you would like to be? Aim to make your altar reflect the very best of yourself and your aspirations. Remember that your altar doesn't have to stay the same any more than you do. If some things that you put there lose or change their meaning, remove them, giving thanks for the inspiration they have given you, and replace them with things that more accurately reflect your growing awareness.

Tending the altar daily provides a regular reminder of the spiritual dimension in our lives, as well as a focus for meditation and prayer, a place to make offerings to our ancestors and our gods. These offerings may be of thought or word, poetry or song, incense, oil or water, food or flowers. Offerings are what we give of ourselves in return for the blessings we are given in life, the teaching, healing and wisdom we receive. By making such offerings each day we weave the patterns of Druidry deeper into the fabric of our lives.

Now, from the present day and the secure foundation of our altar, let us journey back through the rich and varied history of the Druid tradition. Druidry has taken many forms over the centuries and what follows is a necessarily selective look at a past full of curious and colourful characters. People have long found inspiration in the many forms that Druidry has taken, and still do. Let us, then, step back through time seeking out those aspects of the tradition that may inspire us today.

Druids Today

We begin with six snapshots illustrating what it's like to be a Druid. All represent the actual experiences of present-day Druids. They range from the domestic and deeply personal to the universal, from individual rites of passage to communal rites of empowerment.

On a crisp, clear May morning shortly before dawn, she stands by the apple tree in her back garden, cradling her newborn baby in her arms. As the Sun rises, her partner runs his fingers through the dew-wet grass and marks the *awen* symbol of three rays with the fresh dew on the child's forehead, illuminated now by the light of the newborn Sun. As the three rays are marked, the couple speak together the names they have chosen for their firstborn. The words that follow are simple and heartfelt; "May the blessings of Mother Earth and Father Sky be with this little one all the days of his life, and may *awen* flow through him always. In the name of the old gods, so may it be. Hale to the gods and goddesses all! Hale to the ancient ones, spirits most wise! Hale and blessed be! Hale and blessed be! Hale and thrice blessed be!" They then chant the *awen* as the morning Sun begins to warm them and the world around them. From this moment on, the child is known to the gods. Later, he will be introduced to the community at a group ceremony held among the old stones of Avebury. For now though, this rite is enough...

Having been brought up with Druidry, he attended his first Druid

34

ceremony while still a babe in arms. Now, his coming-of-age rite is taking place on Dragon Hill, overlooked by the giant Bronze Age chalk hill figure of the Uffington White Horse. During it, he is repeatedly challenged by the men in the circle in ways that will define his new role in relationship to the community now that he is leaving childhood

behind and is himself becoming a man. He is so focussed on the ceremony that he scarcely notices the wind and rain buffeting the hilltop. After the ceremony, in honour of his new status, his father presents him with the hide of a Black Bear, his spirit animal. It is a few days before his fifteenth birthday. Three years later, wearing the Bear skin over his robe, he stands atop Dragon Hill in a circle of bards, ovates and Druids and declaims, "Spirits of the North, spirits of Earth, Great Bear Mother, we ask your presence in our ceremony this day. We ask your blessings of peace, strength and stability, of nurture, nourishment, protection and guidance. Be with us now O great ones as we bid you hale and welcome!" All in the circle add their greeting, beating drums, shaking rattles and repeating the cry, "Hale and welcome!" This is his life and his faith. It feels right.

She is twenty-two and has never been to a Druid camp before. She is here because she was given a book on Druidry by a friend and it seemed to make sense, echoing her concerns for the world and her deep desire to understand her place in it. She is nervous, not knowing what to expect. She needn't have worried. She is made welcome by an elder who makes her a cup of tea and chats with her for a while, telling her about the camp, the site, what to expect and who to turn to for any help she might need. Having set up her tent, she attends an opening ceremony that lifts her spirits to an unexpected degree. That night, sitting around the central fire, listening to stories and songs, chatting with fellow campers, she suddenly realises, "I've come home." It is a wonderful feeling.

She sits by the fire on the third night of her vigil at a remote stone circle high in the hills of North Wales. The air and her body are still charged from yesterday's dramatic thunderstorm. It is three o'clock in the morning and the valley below is illuminated by a brilliant full Moon. A cloud moves across the valley towards her, taking the shape of a huge Raven. Suddenly she is no longer in her physical body, but looking down on it from outside. Raven swoops, grabbing at her body with its claws, tearing it to pieces and throwing them into the fire, causing cascades of sparks to shower up into the cold night air. Raven then pulls her bones from the fire and she sees they now shine as though made of metal. Raven rebuilds her skeleton from the transmuted bones, pushing it towards and into her spirit form. The fusion of hot metal causes her spirit to dissolve, its particles dispersing into the starry canopy of the sky. Raven, fire, moorland, stone circle, stars, the night and her body cease to exist. After this, there is nothing but darkness. Through this state of nothingness and non-being she-they-it become one with all that has been, is and will be. She awakens next morning back in her physical body. She clears the area, makes sure the fire is out, gathers her gear, thanks the spirits of the place and the old gods of the land and makes her way back down to the valley floor, where her companions wait. She will never be the same again. She is calmer, stronger, more capable, more fully aware of her role in the great dance of creation.

They stand on the lower slopes of Slieve Gullion beside an ancient tomb-shrine, a place of the ancestors, a *Sidhe*-mound, gateway to the Faery realm. "I need to journey," she says, "will you hold me?" He puts his arms around her and, as her spirit departs, her full body weight slumps against him. He knows he must support her, yet is concerned for the well-being of her spirit as well as her physical body. So he sets wards around them both, tells his body to keep doing what it's doing, detaches his own spirit and follows her. They dive into the earth and through dense layers of rock beneath the thin topsoil. Deep underground, they find a massive fissure filled with molten rock, roiling and seething under vast pressure. His poetic mind sees it as a fiery dragon. Her more naturalistic vision sees it for precisely what it is. They return to their bodies. Driving further up the mountain, he stops the car, gets out and places his hands on the damp earth between clumps of heather. He doesn't know why, he just feels compelled to do so. A vision comes of a great blacksmith working at a forge deep within the mountain, pounding a rod of iron on a massive anvil, filling the cavern with crashing waves of sound and great gouts of orange-gold sparks. Later, back at the farmhouse where they're staying, he picks up a book. Opening it at random, he finds a poem by a local bard describing exactly what they had found while journeying by the *Sidhe*-mound. He later learns that ancient legends hold the mountain sacred to Cullan, the smith-god from whom the great Ulster hero Cú Chullain received his name, which translates as 'Hound of Cullan.' Thus the bardic arts support the Druid art of spirit journeying, confirming the truth of their visions. The purpose of their trip, in April 1997, is to find ways to bring peace to a land torn by decades of conflict. With local Druids, they devise a ceremony. A few months later, with prayers for peace, one of those Druids ceremonially deposits a sword into the small lake on the summit of Slieve Gullion as an offering to the old gods. In April 1998, representatives of the Northern Irish community and the British and Irish governments sign the Good Friday Agreement, putting an end to nearly thirty years of armed conflict. While it would be patently absurd to proclaim the actions of these Druids responsible for bringing peace to Northern Ireland, they do offer a fine example of Druidry adding its visionary sense and spiritual power to an already powerful movement for change.

A small group has spent several hours preparing the sacred space within the reconstructed Iron Age roundhouse, tending the central fire and the cauldron of healing herbs bubbling over it, drumming and chanting, communing with the spirits of the place, among whom are many deer people, raising energy, calling forth power. The ceremony is part of a week-long camp devoted to our relationships with animal spirits. A commotion outside alerts the group to the arrival of the others who have been out in the woods, becoming one with their spirit animals. Loud yowls, growls and howls ring out, accompanied by wildly skirling bagpipes. Suddenly, the doors fly open and thirty or so wild ones charge into the roundhouse, cavorting, leaping and crawling around its interior, shrieking, screaming, grunting, howling, eyes wide and wild. Some wear animal hides, others masks brought with them or made earlier in the day. Enhancing the wildness, the drum group raise their rhythm towards an intense crescendo. It is energising, wild, wonderful, magical. After a few minutes, the animal people leave and shed their animal guises before re-entering the roundhouse in their human forms. As they come in, the doorkeepers bless them and sain* them with scented smoke from dried bundles of mugwort, meadowsweet and St. John's wort. Soon, fifty are seated in the roundhouse, their cups being filled with the healing brew from the cauldron. Chanting, singing and drumming continue, further invoking the animal spirits who share with us their power, their *awen*, deeply enriching and enhancing our lives, helping maintain our physical,

psychic and spiritual health and well-being. When the ceremony ends with thanks to those seen and unseen, the spirits of place, our animal companions, ancestors and the old gods, the roundhouse and everyone in it are buzzing with energy and sheer joy, refreshed, renewed, energised and empowered. As ever, the closing words are, "Peace without and peace within, until we meet again. So may it be!"

*'Sain' is an old Scottish term derived from 'sanctifying' and denoting purifying with smoke.

Diverse though these snapshots are, they are united by the fact that those taking part find them deeply meaningful, hugely empowering, even life-transforming. They demonstrate that Druidry works. They represent a type of Druidry taught and practised by groups who see it as a spiritual path. Membership of such spiritual Druid groups is estimated at about 10,000 in the UK alone, plus more than five times that number in the rest of the world. This form of Druidry emerged in the 1960s. Over the next few pages, we look at four groups who espouse it. For their web addresses, see our Resources section.

The Reformed Druids of North America (RDNA)

Longest-established of the new Druid groups is the Reformed Druids of North America (RDNA). It was founded in 1963 by students of Carleton College, Minnesota, who objected to being forced to attend regular Christian ceremonies. On finding that college rules specified only that they had to attend a religious ceremony, they decided to create their own and the RDNA was the result. Starting as a student protest, within a few years, RDNA had branches on college campuses across the United States. The group spawned a number of spin-off groups and now claims a membership of more than 4,500. Its website engagingly describes it as "the oldest and largest Druid organization native to the United States, but perhaps the least well organized."

The Order of Bards, Ovates and Druids (OBOD)

Probably the best known and among the most active and influential of the new spiritual groups is the Order of Bards, Ovates and Druids (OBOD). Based in Britain and Ireland, it has a worldwide membership, being particularly strong in the USA, Australia and the Netherlands. OBOD was founded by Philip Ross Nichols, also known by his craft name, Nuinn, the Irish word for the ash tree. He was a tutor at a private school, a poet and a lifelong Christian, despite which he enjoyed a long friendship with Gerald Brosseau Gardner, the founder of modern Witchcraft or Wicca, the new Pagan religion constructed by Gardner and his coven in the 1940s and 50s. During this period, Nichols and Gardner were both members of the Ancient Druid Order (see below). Both were dissatisfied with that Order's eclectic approach to Druidry, wanting it to embrace more fully the rich literary and folk heritage of the British Isles. One result of their collaboration is the Wheel of the Year, the eightfold festival cycle which is now central to much of modern Paganism and Druidry (pages 74-80). Many ADO members shared their dissatisfaction and joined Nichols when he founded OBOD in 1964.

OBOD held regular ceremonies on Glastonbury Tor in Somerset. During one of these, in 1969, a young man named Philip Carr-Gomm was initiated into the Order. Following Nichols death in 1975, the Order became dormant. Carr-Gomm came into possession of most of its teaching materials and, after his old mentor came to him in a vision, he and his wife, Stephanie, reformed OBOD in 1988. Central to it were distance learning courses largely written by another husband and wife team, John and Caitlin Matthews, who subsequently established a considerable following through their many books on Celtic magic and mysticism. Carr-Gomm's training in, and practice of, psycho-therapy has strongly influenced OBOD's approach to Druidry. A talented writer, he has published several excellent books and substantially rewritten OBOD's courses (see our Resources section).

As well as helping update its image, Carr-Gomm changed the name of the tradition. For at least a couple of centuries, English-speakers had referred to it as Druid*ism*. Seeing -*ism* as an ugly suffix, Carr-Gomm coined the more elegant substitute, Druidry. Many clearly agree, since the new term is now fairly universal.

Carr-Gomm stepped down as Chosen Chief of the Order in 2020, passing the mantle to Eimear Burke, an Irishwoman with a similar background in that she also has an abiding interest in spirituality and trained as a psychologist.

The British Druid Order (BDO)

Another well-known, influential group based in the British Isles but with an international membership is the British Druid Order (BDO). The Mother Grove of the BDO was founded in 1979 in Hastings, Sussex. It grew out of a Wiccan coven formed a few years earlier by Gary Colcombe, who had trained as a High Priest in a coven run by Alex Sanders, known to the popular press as the 'King of the Witches.' Gary invited me to join this new coven. Having discovered Druidry but being unable to find a Druid group to join, I was duly initiated into the coven. Alex Sanders suggested we adopt Ceridwen and Cernunnos as our primary goddess and god. Knowing Ceridwen from the *Story of Taliesin* (page 113), the prospect of encountering her in a ceremonial setting was exciting, if a little concerning. I needn't have worried. Ceridwen was ably embodied by our High Priestess, Pam, who physically glowed in our basement temple when the spirit of the goddess entered her.

The Wiccan *Book of Shadows* we inherited from Sanders contained only the barest bones of the eight festivals of the Wheel of the Year so I was tasked with fleshing them out. I did so from that great collection of Welsh lore and legend, *The Mabinogion* (pages 106-13), introducing more native deities into our rites alongside Ceridwen. By the time the festival cycle was complete, the new ceremonies, along with revisions of others in the *Book of Shadows*, led us to stop calling ourselves a coven, becoming instead the Grove of the Badger. Gary and Ruth Colcombe now run the excellent Celtic Myth Podshow.

I first encountered Druidry in 1974 through a deeply strange book, *The White Goddess*, by Anglo-Irish poet, Robert Graves (Faber & Faber, 1948). At the same time, I was reading *Shamanism: Archaic Techniques of Ecstasy*, by Romanian scholar, Mircea Eliade (Routledge & Kegan Paul, 1964). Reading the two in tandem led me to conclude that Iron Age Druids had been the North-west European equivalent to shamans in other cultures. Hence the BDO has always had a Pagan, shamanistic take on Druidry and this is reflected in the Order's distance learning courses. Those courses combine practicality with a scholarly approach to the tradition firmly rooted in archaeology, medieval literature and folklore while encouraging personal gnosis.

In the early 1990s, the BDO pioneered open, public Druid rites that encouraged multi-faith participation. We also led calls for the respectful reburial of ancient human remains held in museums.

Emma Restall Orr, arguably the world's best known female Druid, was joint chief of the Order between 1995 and 2002. Through public ceremonies, appearances on radio and TV, in newspapers and magazines, and through her books, a wider public was presented for the first time with a deeply feminine and feminist vision of Pagan Druidry. As a result, the gender balance in Druidry shifted swiftly and dramatically. From the patriarchal image it had at the beginning of the 1990s, by the end of that decade more women than men were joining both the BDO and OBOD. Among current BDO course students, 56% identify as female, 39% as male, 5% other. The same gender balance was found across all 'new Druidry' groups in a survey undertaken by Larisa A. White for her book, *World Druidry: A Globalizing Path of Nature Spirituality* (2021).

A Druid Fellowship (ADF)

Ár nDraíocht Féin, also known as A Druid Fellowship (ADF), was founded in the United States in 1983. Its founder, Philip Isaac Bonewits, a prolific writer on magic and Paganism, saw it as offering a more structured and distinctly Pagan Druidry than that found in the RDNA. As with other 'new Druidry' groups, ADF has local groves, an open membership policy and publishes teaching materials. Like the BDO, ADF offers open, public ceremonies.

Dozens more spiritual Druid groups exist in countries around the world, though most last only a few years and few outlive their founders. Most founded since the 1980s are Pagan. All the groups referred to so far represent the new Druidry that emerged in the 1960s and 70s, partly inspired by Wicca. By the late 1970s, some in the new Druidry were also drawing inspiration from indigenous cultures, seeking the roots of Druidry as a shamanistic, native European spiritual tradition. These influences combined with new research into the medieval literature of Wales and Ireland to fuel the ongoing re-creation of Druidry as a magical, holistic, Pagan, earth-ancestor spirituality.

Today's spiritual Druids come from a wide range of backgrounds. Many work in IT, education, the healing professions, the arts, forestry and conservation, while others are college students, lawyers, builders, shop assistants, soldiers or oil rig workers. As with most spiritual traditions, even within established groups there is a wide diversity of belief and practice. At any sizeable Druid gathering you might find, among others, Pagan Druids, Buddhist Druids, Christian Druids and Atheist Druids. It does often seem that the only thing we have in common is that we think of ourselves as Druids. With such diversity, it may seem hard to find a common thread, yet all are responding to their own vision of the Druid archetype.

So, even within the new Druidry there is a diversity that can be quite daunting for those starting out on the path. How, then, do you find the group most compatible with your own vision? For the 21st century seeker, the Worldwide Web is a superb resource. Created by Tim Berners-Lee in 1991, around 5 billion people now have access to the Web. Of course, the sheer quantity of information it contains can be daunting in itself. If, however, you start by searching for the groups named above and in our Resources section, you will find a great deal of information about them and about Druidry in general. Their websites offer links to online resources such as blogs, video channels, podcasts, etc., and to social media where you can interact with fellow seekers and members, all of which should help you get a feel for the group.

Each group's particular take on Druidry gives it an individual style reflected in its ceremonies and the beliefs and activities it promotes among members. Among the most frequently asked questions for those of us who coordinate Druid groups is how our own group differs from others. Shorthand answers can be attempted, but seldom do justice to any of the groups concerned. By far the best way to find out is to carry out your own research. That said, this chapter's journey through time is intended in part to give some idea of where some of today's groups originate and how and why their particular styles of Druidry developed.

In exploring Druidry, many find group ritual helpful, offering a real sense of kinship and community. Those attending a first Druid ceremony often describe a feeling of homecoming. Most Druid rites are small, perhaps a few friends gathered round a fire in a forest at twilight making offerings of bread and mead to the ancestors, spirits of place and our great Mother Earth, sharing the rest among themselves, along with laughter, stories and songs, teaching and ritual. After a few hours they will leave, tired but elated, waking the next day refreshed in spirit for the tasks ahead. By contrast, open ceremonies held at festival times at major sacred sites may attract hundreds. Such rites, small or large, public or private, form only a small part of the life of the modern Druid. As subsequent chapters show, she may practice her craft in many ways, as a healer or counsellor, teacher, artist, writer, poet, parent, clerk or clown, each activity being inspired, informed and underpinned by the understanding of the world and her place in it that comes through Druidry.

Today's Druids being such an eclectic bunch, while some may attend ceremonies wearing robes in colours recommended by the particular group of which they are a member, most wear either their regular street clothes or their 'Sunday best.' Some wear tokens of animal spirits they work with. Some wear clothing based on historical or archaeological models drawn from periods from the Neolithic through to Steam-punk-influenced Edwardian. Most group ceremonies take place in the open air and in circles, usually cast for the occasion, although some modern Druids still like to gather together in ancient stone circles when the opportunity arises. Most modern group ceremonies begin with calls to the elemental spirits of the four cardinal directions. Most rites are celebratory in nature, often taking place at one or other of the eight seasonal festivals celebrated by modern Pagans but with roots in the pagan past (pages 74-80). Another advantage of the Worldwide Web is that it is no longer necessary to even be in the same country to get

together, many Druids meeting for ritual, discussion and teaching in online spaces created for these purposes.

Of course, it's not necessary either to join a group or attend group ceremonies to be a Druid. There are many solitary Druids, either because they have yet to find a group to join, through being too geographically distant from any of them, or through simply not wishing to join one. That's fine, there is much that can be done in your own home to connect you with the Druid path. Now, though, we continue our journey into the past by exploring some longer-established groups.

The Ancient Druid Order

Before the 1990s, the image of the Druid presented in the popular press was of groups of men in white robes standing in a circle at Stonehenge at sunrise on the summer solstice. This annual spectacle was as much a part of the English summer as cricket and cream teas. It seemed to reflect how things had always been; robed figures in the twilight before the dawn, making elaborate ritual then disappearing again until the following year. For many years, the group creating these ceremonies was the Ancient Druid Order (ADO, also known as the Druids of the Universal Bond), founded in 1909 under the influence of the late Victorian and Edwardian interest in spiritualism, orientalism, magic and the occult. A key influence was the Theosophical Society, founded in 1875 by Russian occultist, Helena Petrovna Blavatsky (1831-1891). Adopting its interest in 'ascended masters,' who were almost invariably Asian, some early ADO ceremonies at or near Stonehenge were carried out by English gentlemen oddly dressed in white Druid robes topped by over-sized turbans. The Order inherited a strong thread of pacifism from its founder, George Watson MacGregor Reid (circa 1850-1946). In the 1950s, this led to the creation of a piece of liturgy still heard at many Druid gatherings today during which all in the circle link hands and repeat three times:

> We swear by peace and love to stand
> heart to heart and hand in hand,
> mark, O spirit(s) and hear us now,
> confirming this, our sacred vow.

For obvious reasons, this is often known as the Oath of Peace.

The ADO was also influenced by another great Victorian spiritual organisation, the Hermetic Order of the Golden Dawn. Founded in 1887, the Golden Dawn has continued to exert a powerful influence over many subsequent magical and spiritual groups, including Wicca and Druidry. In the case of the ADO, this was directly acknowledged by their calling their Stonehenge sunrise ceremony 'the Ritual of the Golden Dawn.'

In appearance, and in some of what its members believed and did, the ADO conformed to a stereotype of Druids formed long before they came into existence. Go back another hundred years and we are coming closer to when that image was formulated.

The Gorsedd of Bards of the Isle of Britain

Throughout the 19th century, Druids were represented in the public mind partly by the Gorsedd of Bards of the Isle of Britain. The Gorsedd still appears in early August each year at the National Eisteddfod, that great annual celebration of Welsh language and culture. Members wear robes in three colours: blue for bards, green for ovates and white for Druids, colours later adopted by OBOD. Their ornate ceremonies are held in modern stone circles erected for the purpose in towns where the Eisteddfod is to be held. Ceremonies are conducted in Welsh. Calling for peace, "*Heddwch*!," a sword is unsheathed and then sheathed again to signify that there is peace. Young girls bring garlands of flowers to a central altar stone on which stands the Archdruid. The Hirlas Horn is passed around. The bard who composes the best poem in a traditional metre is presented with a crown.

A pivotal moment of the late 18th century Druid revival took place atop Primrose Hill in London at the summer solstice of 1792. Here we find a small group of London-based Welshmen, led by the slim, frock-coated figure of Edward Williams (1747-1846), a stonemason, failed businessman, talented poet and literary forger. Standing in a circle of pebbles he had gathered on a beach in South Wales and brought with him in his coat pockets, he is called by his bardic name, Iolo Morganwg [pronounced YOLlow mogGANNoog]. As the ceremony gets underway, he makes the call for peace, unsheaths and sheaths a sword and declaims the Gorsedd Prayer:

Grant, O God, thy protection,
and in protection, strength,
and in strength, understanding,
and in understanding, knowledge,
and in knowledge, the knowledge of justice,
and in the knowledge of justice, the love of it,
and in that love, the love of all existences,
and in the love of all existences, the love of God,

45

God and all goodness.

Iolo's prayer is still spoken at the Welsh National Eisteddfod each year. It is also heard during the ceremonies of many other Druid groups, including OBOD and the BDO, although the word God is usually replaced with Spirit or Spirits, Gods, Goddess, or God and Goddess.

Iolo (right) claimed to have discovered the rites, rules and regulations of the Gorsedd in ancient Welsh manuscripts. For a hundred and fifty years after his death, many believed him. Then, in the 1950s, a young scholar going through Iolo's papers found draft versions of the supposedly ancient manuscripts, all in Iolo's own handwriting. Virtually the whole of Iolo's complex system of bardic and Druidic lore turned out to be his own invention. As a result, many now dismiss Iolo as at best a romantic, at worst an outright fraud. Nevertheless, when Iolo turned his hand to forging medieval Welsh poetry he was able to pass off his own verses as the work of Dafydd ap Gwilym, arguably Wales' greatest medieval bard. When published, Iolo's fakes actually became more popular than Dafydd's originals. Iolo clearly had talent, even genius. Given his penchant for forgery, it is ironic that the motto he gave his Gorsedd is *Y Gwir yn Erbyn y Byd*, 'The Truth Against the World.'

As a child, Iolo had been inspired by his mother's tales of times past, when every Welsh noble family had its household bard. As an adult, he found inspiration in visits to the great stone circles of Avebury and Stonehenge. Not only did his inspirations lead to the foundation of the Welsh Gorsedd and all it does to promote and preserve Welsh language and culture, but Iolo also inspired the foundation of the National Library of Wales and the University of Wales. Members of the Gorsedd include former Archbishop of Canterbury, Rowan Williams and the late Queen Elizabeth II, though some say she forfeited her membership by failing to learn Welsh. Since the first edition of this book was published, the Centre for Advanced Welsh & Celtic Studies at the University of Wales has undertaken a major project on Iolo Morganwg and his place in the 18th century Romantic movement, publishing a number of books on the man and his work that have gone some way towards rehabilitating his reputation in his native land and beyond.

The Ancient Order of Druids

On the wall of a London pub, near where the poet and artist William Blake lived in Poland Street, is a plaque inscribed, "In this Old King's Arms Tavern the Ancient Order of Druids was revived 28th November 1781." By a curious coincidence, this happens to be the date of Blake's 24th birthday. The formation of the Ancient Order of Druids (AOD) thus preceded Iolo's Gorsedd by eleven years.

Little is known of the AOD's founders, who seem to have been London merchants. The Order was inspired by English Freemasons, whose first Grand Lodge meeting took place in another London pub, the Goose and Gridiron in St. Paul's Churchyard, on Midsummer's Day, 24th June 1717. As in Freemasonry, the AOD collected subscriptions to be given to members in need. Both groups met in lodges into which only men were admitted and both shared a fondness for ceremonial regalia, badges of office and the like. AOD lodges were usually located in pubs and one of their main aims was bringing men together to drink and sing popular songs. This naturally made the Order itself popular and lodges soon sprang up in Australia, New Zealand, the USA and elsewhere. The Order even proved attractive to the landed gentry and minor members of the royal family. Photographs of the AOD meeting in large numbers at Stonehenge in 1905 show many members wearing false white 'Santa Claus' beards and long white, hooded robes, holding staves topped with brass sickles. Sir Edmund Antrobus, then owner of the henge and the

land around it, was initiated into the Order at that ceremony. Other famous photos show a young Winston Churchill being inducted into the Order at Blenheim Palace in 1908 (right). Again, many AOD members are sporting false white beards.

Men-only lodges and false beards make the AOD seem quaintly archaic, but in other respects they were quite forward-thinking. On a visit to one of their lodges, I noticed a framed poster on the wall promoting a tree-planting campaign they ran in the early 1900s. An AOD offshoot, the Ancient Order of Druids in America (AODA) has undergone a radical shift of emphasis in recent decades and now operates very much on the model of the new Druidry as an ecologically engaged, green spirituality, taught and practised through the three paths of bard, ovate and Druid, with *awen* at its core. The current Grand Archdruid, Dana O'Driscoll, is a permaculture designer and an OBOD-trained Druid.

Druids, Antiquarians & Artists

Iolo's imaginative creation of his bardic order and the slightly earlier formation of the AOD were both responses to a popular public fascination with Druids that began in the 17th century. Wiltshire-born antiquarian John Aubrey (1626-1697) was the first to link Druids with prehistoric stone circles such as Stonehenge. He was followed by an eccentric Christian minister from Lincolnshire, William Stukeley (1687-1765), who, like Aubrey before him, visited Stonehenge and Avebury. Stukeley turned his garden into a Druid grove, filled his sermons with references to Druids and signed his letters, 'Chyndonax of Mount Haemus, Druid.' He saw Druidry as a patriarchal religion brought to Britain after the Biblical Flood and portrayed Druids as proto-Christians practising what he called Natural Religion.

Aubrey and Stukeley's ideas were taken up by a number of poets, including William Wordsworth (1770-1850). Like many of his contemporaries, Wordsworth had an ambivalent attitude towards Druids. On the one hand, he saw them in the light of classical references to Druid involvement in human sacrifice, especially Julius Caesar's notorious description of giant wicker-work figures in which captive warriors and criminals were burnt to death. On the other, he accepted that the bards of Wales, Scotland and Ireland maintained a proud poetic tradition that had formerly been part of the ancient Druids' craft. Hence, in the 1850 edition of his 'Prelude,' he wrote:

Lo again
The Desert visible by dismal flames;
It is the sacrificial altar, fed
With living men - how deep the groans! the voice
Of those that crowd the giant wicker thrills
The monumental hillocks, and the pomp
Is for both worlds, the living and the dead.
… where'er I turned,

Beheld long-bearded teachers, with white wands
Uplifted, pointing to the starry sky,
Alternately, and plain below, while breath
Of music swayed their motions, and the waste
Rejoiced with them and me in those sweet sounds.

The visionary poet, artist and mystic, William Blake (1757-1827), also wrote of Druids. Blake (right) not only saw them as proto-Christians, he identified Biblical figures such as Noah and Abraham as Druids. Unlike Stukeley and Wordsworth, however, Blake despised all organised religions and their priesthoods, including Druids, referring to them in his 'Milton' (1804) as "Satan's Druid sons," and to Stonehenge, then widely perceived as a Druid temple, as "a building of eternal death: whose proportions are eternal despair." Despite which, and despite their not having been founded until 1909, the Ancient Druid Order claimed Blake as one of their past Archdruids. Intriguingly, Blake may have attended one of the Primrose Hill ceremonies held either by the Ancient Order of Druids or by Iolo's Gorsedd. He apparently told an acquaintance,

I have conversed with the Spiritual Sun - I saw him on Primrose Hill. He said 'Do you take me for the Greek Apollo?' 'No,' I said, 'that (Blake pointed to the sky) that is the Greek Apollo - He is Satan.'

Many contemporary artists, including two of England's finest, Joseph Mallord William Turner (1775-1851) and John Constable (1776-1837), produced paintings and drawings of Stonehenge. Through the work of these poets and artists, the image of the Druid returned to the mainstream of British culture for the first time since the Roman era. It was an image largely derived from classical descriptions of Druids as white-robed sages, merged with images of Biblical patriarchs to create the idea of Druids as monotheistic priests of a patriarchal religion that worshipped one god through the image of the Sun, thus paving the way for the coming of Christianity. This solar vision of Druidry is encapsulated in Iolo Morganwg's proclamation that no Druid rite could be performed except "... in the face of the Sun; the Eye of Enlightenment."

Bardic Schools & Druid Survivals

Until the early 18th century, bardic schools existed in Scotland. A century earlier, there had been similar institutions in Ireland and Wales. They represented a direct survival from the Druidry of the remote past, when bards and Druids were members of the educated class among the Iron Age peoples of Europe in the centuries before our Common Era. Late medieval bardic schools in Ireland seem to have consisted of a central stone building with two or three floors, with students living in small, beehive-shaped stone huts nearby. Each school had its chief poet, or *Ollamh* (pronounced Ollave). Students were expected to commit huge quantities of poetry to memory, along with the lore and legends of their ancestors and the genealogies of important families. Their predecessors in the time of Julius Caesar seem to have done much the same. Bards in Britain and Ireland studied grammar, composition and music. Representations of medieval bards show them wearing long tunics and playing triangular harps (right). Surviving texts indicate that most of what we now refer to as their poems were actually songs that bards sang while accompanying themselves on the harp, or while another bard played for them. This is clearly expressed in a group of early 14th century Welsh triads devoted to music (my translation):

> There are three chief crafts, namely: the craft of the string, the craft of wind, and the craft of the tongue.
> There are three chief crafts of wind, namely: organ, and pipes, and the craft of the bagpipe.
> There are three chief crafts of the string, namely: the craft of the *crwth* (a type of bowed lyre), the craft of the harp, and the craft of the *timpán* (probably a long-necked lute with a drum-like soundbox).
> There are three chief crafts of the tongue: composing poetry, and good singing, and singing with the harp.

Triads such as these were used as teaching and memory aids in the bardic schools of Britain and Ireland. As with the above, each consists of an initial statement of a common theme followed by three phrases or short paragraphs related to it. Many triads refer to specific individuals, animals, places, etc. though some are more general or deal with abstract concepts. Several refer to traditional tales, mythical histories and legends like those we'll look at in chapter 5. Medieval bards being tasked with remembering large numbers of these as well as songs, grouping them together in triads would have made recalling them much easier.

As well as studying grammar, poetic forms and music, late medieval and early modern bards crafted poems in praise of their aristocratic patrons and satires that could destroy the reputation of those who mistreated them. They also practised a curious method of connecting with *awen* through a kind of sensory deprivation (pages 91-2). In Ireland, they also studied the Ogham alphabet and various forms of divination (pages 128-36).

Despite centuries of Christian missionary activity, Druids continued to advise Irish kings until at least the 10th century CE while verses attributed to the great bard, Taliesin, refer to him as a Druid active in Wales in the 13th century. This was the period when tales of pagan gods and heroes were being committed to writing in Britain and Ireland, often by Christian monks. In Ireland, these portray Druids as royal counsellors, poets, magicians, healers, diviners, interpreters of dreams and omens, able to prophesy the future, raise magic mists, brew cauldrons with miraculous healing properties, raise the dead, affect the weather, change themselves and others into birds or animals and bring down tyrants with their curses. In short, they are an altogether wilder, more magical breed than the romantic Druid revivalists of the 18th century would have us believe. One Irish tale features a Druid named Mog Ruith [pronounced Moy Rooth] donning a feathered cloak and rising into the sky on the smoke from a fire. He has the ability to change his physical shape, manipulate the weather, alter water-courses, hurl lethal fire-balls and perform other feats that have caused many to liken him to more recent 'shamans' in other cultures.

In the late medieval period, Druid-like functions were attributed to Merlin in tales of King Arthur and his knights (pages 114-6).

Classical Druids

Go back another thousand years and we find the first written records of Druids. The few surviving descriptions of Druids offered by Greek and Roman writers of the last few centuries BCE and the first few centuries CE inspired the antiquarians of the 17th century who, in turn, inspired 18th century Druid revivalists. Among the most influential was the Greek historian, Pliny the Elder (23 or 24-79 CE). His *Natural History* (Book 16, chapter 95) gives a vivid account of Druid beliefs and of a particular rite taking place in a forest glade:

> The Druids ... held nothing more sacred than the mistletoe and the tree that bears it, always supposing that tree to be the oak. But they choose groves formed of oaks for the sake of the tree alone, and they never perform any of their rites except in the presence of a branch of it ... In fact they think that everything that grows on it has been sent from heaven and is a proof that the tree was chosen by the god himself. The mistletoe, however, is found but rarely upon the oak; and when found, is gathered with due religious ceremony, if possible on the sixth day of the Moon (for it is by the Moon that they measure their months and years, and also their ages of thirty years). They choose this day because the Moon, though not yet in the middle of her course, has already considerable influence. They call the mistletoe by a name meaning, in their language, the all-healing. Having made preparation for sacrifice and a banquet beneath the trees, they bring thither two white bulls, whose horns are bound then for the first time. Clad in a white robe, the priest ascends the tree and cuts the mistletoe with a golden sickle, and it is received by others in a white cloak. Then they kill the victims, praying that god will render this gift of his propitious to those to whom he has granted it.

While this made a deep impression on Druid revivalists of the 17th, 18th and 19th centuries, it describes a rite Pliny himself did not witness. Even assuming his account is accurate, the rite was conducted in Southern France and may not have occurred anywhere else. On the oak, the word Druid may derive from the Proto-Indo-European words, *deru-*, meaning 'tree,' especially the oak, and, by extension, 'strong, steadfast, true,' and -*wid*, 'to know, or see.' The first element of *Derwydd*, one of the Welsh words for Druid, is *derw*, 'oak.' On the other hand, medieval evidence suggests that the primary sacred tree of Ireland may not have been the oak but the yew, with ash a close second. Pliny has his Druid dressed in white while among other classical writers, Strabo refers to them dressed in red robes trimmed with gold and Tacitus to women who may have been Druids wearing black robes (page 56).

That said, present day Druids recognise some aspects of Pliny's description as relevant to our own practice. These include his presentation of Druidry as a magical belief system; honouring the passage of time and the cycles of nature through the phases of the Moon; concern with the healing properties of herbs and with the spirits resident in trees, plants and animals. Modern Druids do not, however, sacrifice animals since we are not trying to revive Druidry as it may have been two thousand years ago, when food was scarce and death from famine, disease or warfare was an ever-present threat. For most of us, life is very different now. Druidry is a living tradition. As times change and human consciousness evolves, Druidry also changes and evolves, renewing its relevance for each new generation.

What else do we know about ancient Druids? In the 1st century BCE, the Greek historian Diodorus Siculus gave the following account of the Druids of his time:

> And there are among them [i.e. the Gauls, the people who inhabited a country with borders roughly equivalent to those of modern France] composers of verses whom they call bards; these singing to instruments similar to a lyre, applaud some, while they vituperate others. They have philosophers and theologians who are held in much honour and are called Druids; they have soothsayers [vates] too of great renown who tell the future by watching the flight of birds and by the observation of the entrails of victims; and every one waits upon their word. ... It is a custom of the Gauls that no one performs a sacrifice without the assistance of a philosopher [i.e. a Druid], for they say that offerings to the gods ought only to be made through the mediation of these men, who are learned in the divine nature and, so to speak, familiar with it, and it is through their agency that the blessings of the gods should properly be sought. It is not only in times of peace, but in war also, that these seers have authority, and the incantations of the bards have effect on friends and foes alike. Often when the combatants are ranged face to face, and swords are drawn and spears bristling, these men come between the armies and stay the battle, just as wild beasts are sometimes held spellbound. Thus even among the most savage barbarians anger yields to wisdom, and Mars is shamed before the Muses.

Diodorus introduces us to the three main areas of Druid practice, those of the bard, ovate and Druid. Each awakens different areas of the self and offers different ways of seeing and being in the world. As we saw earlier, the path of the bard focuses on finding personal sources of inspiration and awakening creativity; the path of the ovate focuses on healing, awareness and understanding processes of change within ourselves and the world; the path of the Druid seeks to work with those processes of change in order to take a more active part in the continuing dance of creation. Modern Druids still act as priests, though nowadays the sacrifices we assist with tend to be of such things as time, poetry, seasonal fruits and flowers, bread and mead. Diodorus' final two sentences provide inspiration to many of today's Druid pacifists and peace campaigners.

Pliny and others tell us that ancient Druids conducted rites in forest groves, though this practice may not have been common before Roman attempts to suppress the activities of Druids began in the 1st century BCE. Druids at that time had a concept of sacred space called the *nemeton*, an area marked off for ritual use, often surrounded by a bank and ditch earthwork. Sometimes, small temples or shrines were built within the sacred area. Shrines were often wooden structures, though some were of stone, occasionally of bone. Some were square or rectangular, others circular. Many *nemetonae* contained ritual pits into which offerings were placed. Some held wooden posts or standing stones aligned on sunset or sunrise at significant times of year.

Classical writers tell us that Druids used sacred herbs and trees in their rites and practised divination from the behaviour of birds and the movement of stars. Some rites featured music and dancing. Ritual and religion were not the only areas in which Druids, ovates and bards operated. They were also judges and lawyers, historians, teachers, doctors, singers, musicians. In fact, every aspect of life that required extensive formal education seems to have been their province.

Despite which, at school in Britain in the 1960s, I was taught that our ancestors prior to the arrival of Roman civilisation in the 1st century CE were ignorant savages living in caves. This could not be further from the truth. Our Iron Age ancestors lived in roundhouses on family farms or in

hilltop towns and villages then known as *oppida*, now as hill-forts, of which the most spectacular is Maiden Castle in Dorset. Its name derives from the Celtic *Mai dun*, meaning 'great hill,' and its massive earthwork ramparts enclose an area of 47 acres (19 hectares). Inhabited since the Neolithic, in the late Iron Age it was the chief *oppida* of the Durotriges tribe. It seems likely that *oppida* were inhabited primarily by regional rulers, their war-bands and retinues, prominent among the latter being Druids and bards.

Druids advised rulers and oversaw the spiritual well-being of all. In some *oppida*, a roundhouse set aside for sacred purposes seems to have been located near the centre of the settlement with a broad, well-worn path leading to it. External signs would presumably have indicated its status, its wooden door-posts perhaps bearing carved and painted representations of gods, its walls painted with symbolic designs or incidents concerning those deities. Ceremonies held within, by the light of the central fire, may have included rites of cleansing and healing, divination, blessings and the swearing of sacred oaths to the gods. One such recorded in the early Roman period says simply "I swear by the gods my people swear by." This phrase recurs in the medieval literature of Ireland, notably in 'The Cattle Raid of Cooley' (page 118-9).

Social cohesion was maintained by regular feasting during which bards would sing and recount legends of gods and heroes. During this classical era, circa 900 BCE to 400 CE, bards wore thigh-length tunics, diamond-patterned like a diagonal tartan, with trousers of matching material and belts that sat low on the waist. They played lyres of varying sizes, the most common number of strings probably being seven, as was the case in ancient Greece.

A group of 1st century BCE bronze figurines from Neuvy-en-Sullias in central France includes several animals and a number of naked dancers, both male and female, accompanied by a male bard (right) whose lyre has unfortunately not survived. The celebratory nature of dance suggests a joyous seasonal festival. That music and dance were common features of celebrations is confirmed by other images of lyre-playing bards and dancers like those on decorated pots found in Austria, dating from the 8th century BCE. A bearded man in a loose, calf-length robe (previous page) completes the Neuvy group. In his left hand, he holds something against his solar plexus while his right is extended in a gesture of benediction. One of the two largest human figures in the group, surely he must be a Druid giving his blessing to the celebration?

As well as such celebratory rites, the Druidry of this period had what is, from our viewpoint, a darker side, probably including human as well as animal sacrifice. This was a time when the warriors among whom

Druids lived and worked were head-hunters, preserving the heads of their enemies as trophies. Severed heads decorated some *nemetonae*. We are now a very long way from the romantic 18th century image of white robed sages, or perhaps not, since Greek writers refer to Druids of this era as natural philosophers, astronomers, orators, judges, skilled diplomats and inspired prophets. It was these writers whose work most inspired the 18th century Druid revival. While Druids of this period worked closely with death, they held a strong belief in life beyond it, so strong that death was celebrated as a liberation and a rebirth. They also believed in the transmigration of the soul, a belief held by many Druids today.

Tacitus (circa 56-120), writing of Roman legions attacking the island of Anglesey in 61 CE, gives us perhaps our most graphic and tragic account of ancient Druids in action:

> On the shore stood the opposing army with its dense array of armed warriors, while between the ranks dashed women, in black attire like the Furies, with hair dishevelled, waving brands. All around, the Druids, lifting up their hands to heaven, and pouring forth dreadful imprecations, scared our soldiers by the unfamiliar sight, so that, as if their limbs were paralysed, they stood motionless, and exposed to wounds. Then urged by their general's appeals and mutual encouragements not to quail before a troop of frenzied women, they bore the standards onwards, smote down all resistance, and wrapped the foe in the flames of his own brands. A force was next set over the conquered, and their groves, devoted to inhuman superstitions, were destroyed. (*Annals*, Book XIV)

Here we see Druids hurling spells against an opposing army much as they do in the literature of Ireland recorded more than a thousand years later. While we learned from Diodorus Siculus that members of the Druid caste acted as bringers of peace, and Julius Caesar wrote that Druids did not carry weapons or pay war taxes, it is understandable that they might turn their magic against an enemy clearly intent on their destruction.

Tacitus' account has been used to suggest that Druidry ended abruptly and completely in 61 CE. Tacitus himself says nothing of the sort. Some tribes in southern Britain allied themselves with Rome and it seems highly unlikely that Roman authorities would eradicate the Druids of these tribes. As teachers, judges, counsellors and priests, Druids were, after all, vital to the functioning of their societies. In the wake of the Boudiccan rebellion of 60-61 CE, some native shrines were destroyed in areas that had supported her, but most were rebuilt shortly afterwards and probably continued to be staffed by local priests, i.e. Druids. In areas that did not support the rebellion, there was no destruction of shrines and religious life continued as before. In England and Wales, this meant replacing some native shrines with Roman-style ones and linking native deities with Roman gods who were seen as equivalent to them. So, at the hot springs in Bath, Somerset, the local goddess Sulis had the name of the Roman goddess Minerva added to her own. Scotland and Ireland, and their Druids, remained beyond Roman control.

And what of the women in black who played such a wild role in the ritual directed against the legions on the shores of Anglesey? Perhaps they were devotees of a battle goddess like the Irish Morrigan, whose name means 'Great Queen' and who often takes the form of a raven or crow upon the battlefield. A British goddess equivalent to her may be Rhiannon, whose name has the same meaning and who, like the Morrigan, is associated with magical birds and horses. Rhiannon acts as a horse (page 107), the Morrigan shape-shifts into one (page 117). Shape-shifting is a common trait amongst the gods of many cultures.

Druid Roots & Celtic Identity

The origins of Druidry are lost in prehistory. The earliest records place Druids among the Iron Age peoples of Europe who are identified by modern historians as 'Celts.' This term derives from a Greek geographer, Hecataeus of Miletus, who refers to a people living in and around the city of Massilia (modern Marseilles) on the Mediterranean coast of Gaul (modern France) in the 6th century BCE as *Keltoi*. A century later, another Greek historian, Herodotus, uses the same word to refer to people living around the headwaters of the River Danube in the Black Forest in the South-western corner of what is now Germany, and also in the far west of Europe on the Iberian Peninsula (modern Spain and Portugal). We do not know if the people referred to by either writer called themselves *Keltoi*, or whether this was a name given to them by others, nor do we know what the word originally meant. A brief trawl of the internet reveals possible derivations of *Keltoi* from Indo-European roots variously said to mean 'to hide,' 'to heat,' 'to impel,' 'stain,' 'blemish,' 'fight,' 'war,' 'strike' or 'beat.' Other suggested meanings include 'heroes,' 'strangers,' 'hidden ones,' 'secret people,' 'tall ones,' or 'barbarians.' Given such a wide range of possibilities, it's safe to say that no one actually knows.

In the following centuries, Greeks and Romans applied the name *Keltoi* to most of the peoples living in Europe, from the Danube in the East to the Iberian Peninsula in the West, the Mediterranean coast of France in the South to the English Channel in the North. The Roman version of the name was *Celtae*. However, the peoples of a large part of this area were also known to Greeks and Romans as *Galli*, Gauls. We don't know if any of them called themselves either *Galli* or *Celtae*. Iron Age Europe, Britain and Ireland were divided into tribal territories and it seems likely that people saw themselves primarily as members of individual tribes rather than as part of any wider, pan-European cultural group. Hence they would have thought of themselves as Atrebates, Belgae, Brigantes, Cornovii, Durotriges, Regnii, Silures, Votadini and so on, rather than Celts or Gauls. Some tribal names occur on both sides of the English Channel. As we saw earlier, Greeks and Romans referred to the people of the British Isles neither as *Galli* nor *Celtae*, but as *Pretani*, 'painted people.' This gives us the name *Britannia* for both the Roman province and its tutelary goddess, and the modern designation, Britain. Welsh *Prydain* [PRUDine] remains close to the original. If Caesar is right that Druidry originated in these isles, it developed among the *Pretani*, whose name appears in pre-Roman Britain as *Coritani*, in Scotland as *Picti* and in medieval Ireland as *Cruithne*.

In the late 17th century a Welsh scholar named Edward Llwyd (1660-1709) identified a group of languages that includes Breton, Cornish, Irish, Manx, Scots Gaelic and Welsh as being related. He dubbed this language group 'Celtic,' because, as we have seen, that's what Greek and Roman writers called various early peoples of north-western Europe. Those who spoke these languages in Llwyd's time did not, however, think of themselves as Celts, but as Breton, Cornish, Irish, Manx, Scottish or Welsh. Since the 20th century, the countries in which the speakers of these languages live have sometimes been referred to as Europe's 'Celtic Fringe.'

In his book, *Facing the Ocean: The Atlantic and its Peoples* (Oxford University Press, 2001, pages 296-7), the archaeologist, Colin Renfrew, suggests that a language he calls 'Atlantic Celtic' developed "from the early third millennium BC." Elsewhere, he suggests that the Indo-European culture out of which the language, lifestyle and religion of the Celts developed may have spread across Europe at around the time of the very first megalithic tomb-shrines, around eight thousand years ago (*Before Civilisation*, Cambridge University Press, 1979). Recent studies suggest that a substantial amount of the DNA of the peoples of Wales, Scotland and Ireland derives from the first hunter-gatherers who re-populated these lands after the last Ice Age, twelve thousand years ago. Perhaps they brought with them the first seeds of what was to become Druidry.

In the mid-19th century, beside a lake near Hallstatt in Austria, archaeologists began to unearth artefacts of a previously unknown Iron Age culture. Recalling what Herodotus had called the inhabitants of this region, they called this culture 'Celtic.' Again, it is unlikely that the people who, 2,500 years earlier, had buried those artefacts with the bodies of their dead thought of themselves as Celts.

'Celtic,' then, is a name applied by Greek and Roman writers to a diverse group of European peoples, a 17th century designation for a group of languages, and a 19th century one for a group of archaeological artefacts and the cultures that produced them. It is not an ethnicity. Early Graeco-Roman writers refer to Celts as tall, blonde-haired and blue-eyed. The stereotypical Welsh person of today is shortish with dark hair and brown eyes. The similarly stereotypical Scot is red-haired. DNA studies show that the inhabitants of the 'Celtic fringe' countries differ greatly from region to region, and even within regions. The people of north Wales, for example, are as genetically different from those of south Wales as people from central and southern England are from those of northern England and Scotland, while Cornish people are much closer genetically to other English groups than to either Welsh or Scots.

The Iron Age culture archaeologists came to call Celtic developed in central Europe early in the first millennium BCE. If Julius Caesar's informants are right and Druidry originated in Britain, then it must have existed here in the Bronze Age, a period spanning from around 2200 to 800 BCE. It would thus have preceded the arrival of Iron Age Celtic culture in circa 800 BCE by several centuries, perhaps millennia. If Colin Renfrew is right, then the Bronze Age inhabitants of Britain and much of Europe were already speaking a proto-Celtic language.

It is reasonable to assume that wherever Druidry developed, it did so over thousands of years, with origins long pre-dating the emergence of Celtic Iron Age culture. From the archaeological record it is clear that many ritual practices of Iron Age Britain were common a thousand years earlier among the Bronze Age builders of the great stone circles, and even a thousand years earlier still, among the Neolithic folk who built megalithic tomb-shrines like that of Maes Howe in the Orkneys and Newgrange in Ireland. Marking out sacred space with earthwork banks and ditches, making ritual offerings in pits or shafts and erecting standing stones or wooden posts aligned on the rising or setting of the Sun or Moon at particular times of year are all common practices from at least 3500 BCE to at least 400 CE.

From the 17th century to the middle of the 20th, it was widely held that Druids built Stonehenge and the other great stone monuments of prehistoric Britain and Ireland. Then it was decided that Druids belonged among the Celts, and that Celtic culture didn't emerge in

Europe until around 900 BCE, reaching Britain a century later, more than a thousand years after Stonehenge had ceased to be a major ceremonial centre. According to this theory, Celtic culture, including Druidry, came to Britain with waves of Iron Age invaders from the Continent. This invasion theory has largely been abandoned in favour of an understanding that most prehistoric people tended to stay where their ancestors had always lived, absorbing innovations in culture, language and religion through trade links and inter-marriage more than invasion or mass displacement. Taken alongside Caesar's statement that Druidry originated in Britain, we might once again see Druids as the builders of Stonehenge or, if not themselves the builders, then at least their direct physical and spiritual descendants.

As in the Iron Age, our Bronze Age ancestors lived in roundhouses and seem to have had a tribal structure sustained by feasting and ritual, much of which was centred on stone circles. Stone circles had their origins in the preceding Neolithic era, the earlier part of which saw the building of chambered stone tomb-shrines. In all these periods of prehistory, most people lived in more-or-less comfortable, weather-proof homes furnished with beds and chests of drawers. Their clothes were mainly of well-woven wool or linen. They made good quality leather and beautiful, intricate metalwork. They kept domestic animals and grew food crops. In other words, these were people who lived, loved and laughed much as we do. They were also pagans.

What does that mean? Well, in the early Neolithic, at least for some, it meant gathering around fires lit in the forecourts of chambered tomb-shrines that incorporate huge stone slabs weighing many tons. The bodies of some of the dead were exposed on wooden platforms or buried until their bones were cleaned of flesh. Their skulls and larger bones were then placed in the tomb-shrines as objects of reverence, some being periodically brought out to take part in the ceremonial feasts held in the forecourts. Clearly these bones were those of revered ancestors and yet, from time to time, the tombs were emptied of their contents, the remains disposed of and new burials brought in to take their place. The implication is that after a time in the chambers the spirits of the ancestors were deemed to have left the bones entirely and entered into the fabric of the tomb-shrine, finding a permanent home in the stone and earth structure. This would certainly explain why many modern Druids visiting these ancient tomb-shrines continue to experience the presence of the ancestors long after any trace of their bones has been removed by tomb-robbers, antiquarians or archaeologists.

The age of tomb-shrines began around 4500 BCE and continued until around 1000 BCE. The nature of these structures, whose dark interiors were commonly accessed by crawling through a narrow entrance, suggests that they were regarded as home to deities of the earth and the Underworld as well as the human ancestors whose remains were placed in them, perhaps especially of an Earth Mother whose body may have been represented by the great earthen mounds with which the chambers were covered. If so, then the interiors may have been seen as wombs from which ancestors might be reborn into another life following the death of the physical body. The passageways inside some tomb-shrines are aligned on sunrise or sunset at significant times of year such as equinoctial sunrise at the West Kennett Long Barrow in Wiltshire (above), midwinter sunrise at Newgrange and midwinter sunset at Maes Howe.

In the later Neolithic and early Bronze Age, many tomb-shrines fell out of use and were blocked off, as was West Kennett. Around 3300 BCE, the ceremonial focus began to shift from the dark, enclosed spaces of the tomb-shrines towards stone circles that were open to the sky and were eventually built across much of Britain and Ireland. They too were often aligned on astronomical phenomena occurring at specific times of the year. Most famous is Stonehenge (below), aligned on both the

61

midsummer sunrise and midwinter sunset. Others are aligned on solar events at other times of the year or on the rising and setting of the Moon, of individual bright stars or significant groups of stars. They strongly suggest a shift of ceremonial focus from gods of the earth to gods of the sky, perhaps embodied in the Sun, Moon and stars. Astronomical alignments also have the practical benefit of allowing advanced planning of the agricultural year with its cycles of sowing, growing and harvesting and of moving domestic animals between winter and summer pastures.

In both the Neolithic and Bronze Age, it seems likely that the erection of these great stone (megalithic) structures and their subsequent ceremonial use was overseen by religious specialists. Our first historical evidence for the existence of such specialists is in the writings of classical Greeks and Romans who refer to them as Druids. Were they called that in the Megalithic era? Who knows?

If we seek the earliest potential roots of Druidry, the trail we must follow is recorded in our DNA, the basic building blocks of life. In combination with the archaeology of language as well as artefacts, this suggests that almost all prehistoric and present-day religions originate with a family of nomads travelling across the Central Asian Steppes around 40,000 years ago, following the great herds of wild horses, cattle and mammoths they relied on for food, clothing and shelter. They brought together the basic elements of what anthropologists now call shamanism, i.e. direct communication with other-than-human beings including rocks, mountains, springs and water-courses, clouds, Sun, Moon and stars, plants and animals; the concept of a sky-world above us and an underworld below; journeying between these worlds, often enabled through rhythmic, repetitive drumming; and creating ceremonies to appease, or ensure the cooperation of, other-than-human beings, usually for healing and protection or knowledge of hidden things.

The spread of these shamanistic beliefs and practices eventually led to the emergence of winter ceremonies centred on wolf spirits. Evidence for these is found in cultures from the Black Sea region of Russia during the Bronze Age, circa 2000 BCE, through early Vedic India, circa 1200 BCE, ancient Greece and Rome, early medieval Ireland, Wales and Scandinavia, to indigenous peoples of North America at the present day. These ceremonies were traditionally organised around groups of young wolf warriors who lived together for several years apart from their families. Members of the group were initiated during winter rites, the primary function of which was to invoke healing and protection for individuals and their communities through ritual, dance, music, chanting and feasting. The

Irish Fianna were such a group (page 119). As well as training in combat skills, they were expected to master the bardic art of poetry and commit to memory groups of native tales, particularly those associated with ancient sacred sites. There is evidence for the existence of similar wolf warrior societies in Wales, Cornwall and Brittany. The Romano-British god, Apollo Cunomaglos, whose name is inscribed on a 3rd century CE altar from Nettleton Shrub in Wiltshire, may have been the tutelary deity of such a group. A Greek form of the god Apollo is called *Lykaios*, 'of the Wolves.' The name of the British Cunomaglos is thus best interpreted as meaning 'Wolf Lord.' The name of Maelgwn, who ruled North Wales in the early 6th century CE from his royal court on Anglesey, has the same meaning.

Archaic, shamanistic beliefs and practices survived into the medieval era and beyond. Many of the practices described by Isobel Gowdie, a Scotswoman accused of witchcraft in 1662, bear a remarkable resemblance to those of 'shamans' in other cultures and recur in folklore collected during the 19th century and even the 20th. They include magical flight, communication with spirits, animal transformations and the ability to cause harm by striking people or animals with 'Elf-shot,' which often took the physical form of prehistoric flint arrow-heads. Nor are archaic beliefs and practices entirely left behind by mainstream society in the 21st century. How many people still consult astrological forecasts on a daily basis, often now on phone apps? How many of us still drop coins in wells and fountains whilst making a wish, cross our fingers or touch wood to ward off potential harm or wish upon the first star of the evening? Most of us still decorate our houses with greenery at Midwinter. Many of us attend celebrations marking the changing seasons like those referred to in our next chapter.

Despite the 17th and 18th century 'Age of Enlightenment' and the 19th and 20th century promotion of scientific rationalism, the same kind of magical thinking that gave rise to 'shamanism' among our ancestors 40,000 years ago remains strong in us today. Nor is such magical thinking necessarily a bad thing. The human brain is hardwired to find meaning in the world. Studies have shown that those who employ some magical thinking tend to be more self-confident and optimistic while those who employ no magical thinking are more prone to depression and less able to experience pleasure. Magical thinking may also be essential for creativity, enabling us to see patterns and make associations that more 'rational' thinkers fail to perceive. Taking magical thinking to extremes can result in delusions, causing us, for example, to fall prey to wild conspiracy theories, but abandoning it altogether seems to make us, and our world, duller. For Druids, as I trust this book shows, magical thinking is pretty much an essential tool of the trade. As with most things though, moderation is crucial in its application.

This is illustrated by a story told by Michael Harner, an American anthropologist who created a popular form of 'global shamanism' in the 1980s and 90s. As described in his *The Way of the Shaman* (1982, pages 2-10), he was investigating shamanism in the Amazon rainforest in 1961 when one of his indigenous contacts gave him a hallucinogenic drink. During the resulting trip, he was contacted by huge, whale-like creatures with little wings who told him they came from space and were the originators of life on Earth, continuing to exist within all life forms. They further claimed to be the true masters of humans and all other living beings. Astonished by the implications of this cosmic revelation, Harner couldn't wait to tell the Conibo shaman who had given him the drug. Finding the blind shaman in his hut, Harner excitedly recounted the amazing revelations the creatures had given him. The old man's response was to grin and say, "Oh, they're always saying that. But they are only the Masters of Outer Darkness." Harner, doubtless still in thrall to the extreme magical thinking the drug had plunged him into, chose to take this response as proof that what he had seen and been told was 'real.' A more obvious interpretation is that the old man was telling Harner not to take anything those guys told him too seriously, his point being that just because a spirit tells you something doesn't mean it's true. A large part of Druid training consists of learning how to differentiate between the real and the vividly imagined, how to apply rationality to the seemingly irrational so as to avoid falling into the trap of delusion.

In exploring the barest outlines of Druidry's long history and prehistory in this chapter, our journey has taken us from the age of the microchip to the age of stone tools. Did you encounter your archetypal Druid along the way? In which stage of the developing story of the tradition do you feel most at home? What does that tell you about who you are and what your expectations and desires might be?

Having made our journey through the past, we bring ourselves back consciously to the present, aware of who we are and of our surroundings. When we are fully back in the here and now, we give thanks to our ancestors of blood and of spirit for all that we have learned, for all the rich heritage of tradition and teaching that we inherit from them.

Hale, O Druid ancestors!

Hale and blessed be!

Chapter 3:
The Sacred Circle

When undertaking a journey through any landscape that is new to us, a good map is always useful. Even the increasingly ubiquitous satellite navigation system is based on maps. In Druidry, one of the foremost maps we use to help us navigate the journey of our lives is the sacred circle. At its centre is the axis, the point of perfect balance, stillness and security. Around its rim are all the elements of life and the cycles of time. Because we are all different, we paint our maps in different colours, yet the basic structure of the map remains the same. This chapter describes that structure, showing how to tailor the map to your own needs and use it to assess where you have been, locate where you are now and plan future stages of your life's journey.

As we move further into our understanding of Druidry, we become aware that what we do operates on many levels. Symbol, psyche and soul are woven together within the sacred circle. Having no beginning and no end, the circle symbolizes eternity. This symbolism is evoked when we exchange rings during the marriage rite. We invoke the same symbolism when we draw the sacred circle around ourselves, creating the space in which we enter meditation or make ceremony. As the circle is eternal, so, when we are within it, we place ourselves beyond the normal constraints of time and space. The edge of the circle is a boundary, enclosing that which is within, setting it apart from that which is without. It symbolizes protection, strength of purpose, unity and perfection. As well as a boundary, the perimeter of the circle represents a journey through the cycles of time, of Sun, Moon and stars, of birth, life, death and decay, of the zodiac and the horizon.

The Aura: Circle of the Self

At its most fundamental, the sacred circle is simply the area in which our bodies are centred. We each have an aura, or energy field within and around our bodies. Psychics see the aura as an area of coloured light surrounding and interpenetrating the body. The size, strength and colour of the aura change according to physical health, emotional, spiritual or psychic well-being.

In cultures around the world, from ancient times to the present day, the reality of the aura has been accepted among psychics, mystics and healers. In 1939, it appeared to enter the realm of science when an Armenian electrical engineer, Professor Semyon Davidovitch Kirlian, and his wife, Valentina, photographed it. The couple developed a device that surrounds living objects with high-frequency electrical currents and captured the resulting effect on film. Their technique revealed multi-coloured clouds, flares and sparks forming brilliant patterns of light. These seemed to confirm experimentally what seers through the ages had maintained about the properties of the aura and how it is affected by disease and other factors. Various attempts have been made to debunk the Kirlian phenomenon, but when my friend, Mike Bloxham, and I conducted experiments with it in the 1970s we found a dramatic effect among people who identified themselves as healers. When asked to consciously 'turn on' their healing power, all were able to produce bright flares of light from their fingertips that we captured on film, an effect non-healers were unable to replicate.

Not only humans but all living things have an aura. Even apparently inanimate objects such as rocks have an aura. As we saw in chapter 1, a central tenet of BDO Druidry is animism, the belief that spirits exist within all things. The aura seems to represent a kind of interface, a means of passing information between spirit and physical matter. Through the medium of the aura, we communicate with everything in our environment. When our own aura comes into contact with another, an interweaving takes place through which messages are passed. For most of us, most of the time, this is an entirely unconscious process, but in Druidry we seek to enhance our ability to communicate. To do this we seek to increase our awareness of the processes involved.

We commonly use only a portion of the capacity of our senses to receive data and of our minds to process it. There are good reasons for this. If our senses were constantly operating at their maximum potential, we would be so flooded with incoming sensations that our ability to function would be seriously impaired. If every sound, vision, taste and touch were heightened to maximum intensity, our ability to process them would be so overwhelmed that simple acts like driving a car, making a shopping list or even walking would become difficult, if not impossible. States of extremely heightened awareness do, however, occur naturally in most people. The psychologist Abraham Maslow (1908-1970) called them 'peak experiences' and believed them to represent a register of psychological well-being: the more peak experiences, the healthier the individual. These states are immensely liberating and invigorating, opening the mind to endless vistas of possibility. In our practice of Druidry, we seek to access such states of heightened awareness. One stage in this process is to increase awareness of our own personal sacred circle, our auric energy field.

Sensing the Aura

If you relax into awareness of yourself while you are in the midst of a crowd, it is not hard to become aware of how you react to people close to you, even though they may not be physically touching to you or talking to you, or even conscious of your presence. You may feel drawn to some, uncomfortable about others. Much of this instinctive reaction is accounted for by non-verbal, usually unconscious signals. Our reactions to people rely heavily on gesture, facial expression, the way they stand, dress or move. But beyond these responses, we communicate on a deeper level, spirit to spirit, again usually unconsciously. We do this largely through the sensations that filter through to us when our own aura makes contact with another.

A simple exercise that can be carried out either alone or in a group will help to develop awareness. Sit comfortably with your body balanced, back straight, shoulders relaxed, head centred over your spine and fully supported by it. Become aware of your physical body, feeling the points at which you touch the floor, then move your awareness slowly upwards. As you do so, allow your mind to focus on each part of your body, feeling its presence and the sensations flowing from it as fully as you can. If you sense any discomfort, move until you find the position in which you feel most comfortable. If you find stress or tension in your muscles, allow yourself to become conscious of it then consciously let it go, allowing your body to relax. When you are satisfied that your whole body is comfortable and supported, hold that sensation for a while, feeling yourself centred within your body. Be aware of your breathing, which should be effortless, slow and even.

When you are centred and relaxed, allow your awareness to move beyond your physical body to the area immediately around it, within a few inches of your skin. Working again from the ground up, feel any blockages or areas of discomfort in the auric energy close to your body, just as you did with your physical body. If you come across such problem areas, consciously release the tension in them as you did with your physical body. When you have scanned and processed this part of your aura, move your consciousness outward again. Feel the edge of your auric field, seeking the point where your own energy interacts with the energy fields of the people and things around you. Become aware of the sensations produced by the interaction, whether they are pleasant or unpleasant, weak or strong, attractive or repellent. When you feel you have explored these sensations long enough, re-focus your awareness within your body. Be aware of its living, breathing physicality, of your self-awareness centred within it, and of your solid presence in relation to your surroundings.

As with any spiritual work undertaken in Druidry, you may complete this exercise by giving thanks to your gods and guides, ancestors and spirits of place for what you have gained from it.

This exercise helps to develop awareness of different layers of reality, how they interact with each other, how we affect them and they affect us. It can be performed anywhere and any time, requiring only a little space, a little time and enough peace, inner and outer, to allow you to focus without too much distraction. As with most things in life, the more commitment you bring to it, the more you will gain from it.

Casting the Circle

The sacred circle is a safe space, set apart from the distractions of everyday life, within which we may explore ourselves, develop our potential and work through processes of change in our lives. The centre of the circle is the eye of the storm, the point of balance, the fixed axis around which everything revolves. It is this central point that defines the circle. The perimeter of the circle is the interface between the sacred space we create and the rest of creation beyond. Exploring the perimeter from within our sacred circle allows us to work through events in our lives and relationships from a place of safety.

The circle can be formed in many ways, from just imagining its existence to marking it with chalk, charcoal, leaves, sticks, sand, stones, earth or whatever else comes to hand and feels appropriate. Often it is simply drawn in the air with the hand or index finger. The circle is usually cast sunwise (i.e. clockwise), beginning and ending in the east, the quarter from which the Sun rises. Others prefer to cast the circle from the north, the quarter that represents the element of earth, feeling that this helps to ground their circle and themselves. As important as the physical act is the intention behind it. When drawing a sacred circle, we need to be aware of what it means.

Weaving the Web

Each of us exists at the centre of a web of energy that links us to the rest of creation. Our Scandinavian ancestors called this the Web of

Wyrd, conceiving it as the interwoven threads of fate or destiny that link all things in the universe. Similar concepts seem to lie behind the Welsh term, *Tynged*, and the Irish *Díach*, both meaning 'destiny, fate.'

Often, when we wish for perfect security within our circle, as we draw it, we deliberately and consciously cut the threads that link us to the world beyond. This strengthens the circle, preventing anything that might distract from our purpose from entering in, and, just as importantly, preventing our own psychic energy from leaking out. If this cutting is done, it is essential that the links are restored before the circle is closed otherwise we may find that our relationships with the world are damaged. The process of restoring the threads is referred to as re-weaving the web. Both cutting and re-weaving are done with the hands, with clarity of intention. To reinforce the intention, some use the exposed blade of a ceremonial knife or sword for the cutting, though still using the hands for re-weaving. A ceremonial blade is one dedicated for use in ritual and not used for any other purpose. When we make group rituals, we weave together the threads of all those within the circle, strengthening the spirit of the group. Some see these processes as purely symbolic, others hold the web to be as objectively real as the clothes we wear or the houses we live in. Others argue that it doesn't matter which view we hold, since symbolic actions affect the psyche and the psyche in turn affects our physical well-being and our relationships. In Druidry, experience is more important than belief.

The perimeter of the circle is the screen on which the dramas of our lives are played out against the backdrop of existence. As we move around the circle, we experience different aspects of ourselves, past, present and potential, different areas of relationship, tension or release. The journey around the circle is a process of learning about ourselves and our place in the world. Before we begin the journey, we need to populate our circle with images and ideas, to map out the storyboard of our lives.

The Cardinal Directions

We begin this process with the four cardinal directions: East, South, West, and North. These are our main reference points. They have many potential meanings, and, as in so much of Druidry, rules are fluid rather than fixed, individual rather than collective. There are, however, basic areas of agreement. For example, most Druids will attribute the four classical elements to the four directions in the same way: Air in the East, Fire in the South, Water in the West and Earth in the North. To these we may add a fifth, Spirit in the Centre.

East

East is the quarter of sunrise and of spring, of birth, childhood, youthful energy and enthusiasm, awakenings and new beginnings. It is associated with the element of Air, with clarity of thought and vision, lightness of being. In the animal kingdom its associations are naturally with birds, particularly those who sing vigorously at dawn such as the blackbird, those known for clarity of vision such as the hawk or eagle, or those associated with springtime such as the cuckoo. Mythologically the East is linked with gods of the air, sunrise and spring. In Irish myth, Lugh [pronounced Loo] of the Long Arm, the young god of light comes from the East. His British equivalent is Lleu Llaw Gyffes [pronounced ᶜʰthlay ᶜʰthlow G'FFess], 'Lleu of the Steady Hand.' Lugh and Lleu, and the earlier form, Lugos, all mean 'light' (or 'oath' according to others). Lugh/Lleu's primary weapon is a magical spear that never misses its mark, perhaps symbolic of the first shaft of sunlight at dawn. The Spear of Lugh is one of the four treasures that the old gods of Ireland, the

Winter - North - Midnight

Stone of Destiny
Earth
Bear or Bull

Autumn
West
Sunset

Cauldron
Water
Salmon of
Wisdom

Spirit
Centre

Spear
Air
Eagle or
Hawk

Spring
East
Sunrise

Stag or Wolf
Fire
Sword of Nuada

Summer - South - Midday

Tuatha Dé Danann [pron. Too-uhu day darnun], 'Clan of the Goddess Anu,' brought with them from their island home on the world's rim.

South

South is the quarter of summer warmth and midday Sun, of power and strength, associated with the element of Fire, with passion, energy and desire. Animals that express these qualities might include the rutting stag, the wild boar, the fox, the hunting wolf or wild cat. Otherworld creatures associated with the element of fire include the dragon, phoenix and salamander. In Irish tradition, the magical weapon of the South is the Sword of Nuada [NOOuduh], another of the treasures of the old gods. A British equivalent might be Caledfwlch [kal-ED-voolkh], 'hard cleaver,' the original Welsh name of King Arthur's sword, now better known as Excalibur. Nuada's name, like that of his British counterpart, Nudd [Neethe], means 'cloud,' or 'mist.' Before Nuada lost a hand in battle, he was king of the gods. After the healer god, Dian Cécht [Deeuhn kecht with the 'ch' as in Scottish loch or German Bach], replaced his lost hand with one of silver, his place as ruler was taken by Lugh, the young god of light. Lugh/Lleu reaches the height of his power at Midsummer.

West

West is the region of autumn and the setting Sun, of maturity and the wisdom that comes with age and experience. Its element is Water, linked with the emotions, fluidity, mutability and the otherworld that lies beyond the western ocean. Its animals are those that dwell in or near water; the heron, swan, turtle, otter, frog, dolphin or whale. By far the most commonly invoked in Druidry, however, is the salmon of wisdom. Irish legend tells of the Well of Connla, said by some to be the source of the River Shannon, while others say it is the source of all the sacred rivers of Ireland. Around it grow nine hazel trees bearing nuts that contain all wisdom. The nuts fall into the well and are eaten by salmon. Anyone lucky enough to catch and eat one of these fish gains knowledge of things past, present and future. In Irish tradition, the magical treasure of the West is the Cauldron of the Dagda, the father of the gods. His cauldron is inexhaustible and everyone who comes to it finds exactly what they need. Those who bathe in it have their wounds healed, and it can restore the dead to life. In Welsh tradition, the prime magical vessel is the Cauldron of Inspiration (*awen*) in which the goddess Ceridwen brews the broth that gives the gifts of poetry, prophecy and shape-shifting (page 113).

North

North is the place of dark night and winter cold, of old age, death and decay, dormancy and hibernation, the quarter from which Sun and Moon never shine. Its element is Earth, its qualities include physicality, solidity, stability and endurance. Its animals include the bear, bull, badger, sow, raven, crow, owl and bat. In Irish tradition, its magical treasure is the *Lia Fail* [pron. Leeuh foil], the Stone of Destiny, the ancient coronation stone of the high kings of Ireland that used to cry out in recognition of the true monarch. Goddesses associated with the North include the Irish trinity of Badb [Baav], Macha and the Morrigan, who transform themselves into crows or ravens to choose those who would die in battle and to feast on their corpses. In British tradition, a god associated with the North is Gwyn ap Nudd [Gwinn app Neethe], 'White son of Cloud,' the horseman who, accompanied by his white, red-eared hounds, leads the Wild Hunt of the souls of the dead through the night on their journey to the otherworld of Annwn [ANNoon].

Making Your Own Map

While the attributions given here are fairly common, they are by no means universal. Some see the Sword of Nuada as being associated with the element of Air in the East. Since Nuada and his Welsh counterpart, Nudd, both have names meaning 'mist or cloud' this seems perfectly reasonable. The Spear of Lugh is then associated with the South, quarter of Fire. Since Lugh/Lleu is a lord of light who shines like the noonday Sun while his Spear is described as fiery, this again seems reasonable.

Some of the suggested attributions may be inappropriate to you. If, for example, you live on the east coast of Scotland, looking out across the wild North Sea, it might not make much sense for you to attribute the element of Water to the West. Similarly, if you live in Western Australia, it would defy logic to place cold, dark winter in the North when that is the direction from which the Sun shines at noon. Since these words first appeared in print, Gordon Cooper, a Druid from America's Pacific Northwest, has given a name to the notion of creating a practice tailored to your own locale and its ecosystem. He calls it 'Wild-crafting Druidry.' It's a good name, and searching for it online will bring up useful articles on its practice. Working with the sacred circle then, you should develop your own associations. Your map will become much more effective as you construct it in ways that have meaning for you.

From the centre of your sacred circle face each of the four cardinal points in turn, thinking about what they mean to you personally. Perhaps you have suffered painful burns. If so, you might associate the South with pain. Or your feeling about the element of Fire might have more to do with the warmth of hearth and home. Feelings may intermingle. Fear of drowning may give negative associations with Water, but you might also love the sight and sound of waterfalls. You might relate the element of Earth to strength and stability or darkness, claustrophobia or your dislike of winter cold. Establishing a personal map of such correspondences makes your sacred circle uniquely your own.

Working with the Circle

Once you are familiar with the meanings associated with the four directions you can begin to work with them. Having cast your circle as described above, move to each of the cardinal points in turn and see how your feelings change as you align yourself with the elemental and other qualities of each quarter. You might feel uncomfortable in one quarter, secure in another, enlivened in another. Analysing these positive and negative responses can offer insight into your present state of being. Lacking clarity? The answer may lie with the clear light of dawn in the East. Lacking energy? If so, you might need to attune yourself with the element of Fire in the South. Stressed? Perhaps you need to bathe in the cool waters of the West. Feeling insecure? Maybe you need the stability of the element of Earth in the North.

There are many ways to connect with the elemental powers of the quarters. Facing the appropriate direction and consciously opening yourself to its gifts can be simple and effective. You might choose an animal associated with the quarter and awaken its attributes in yourself, perhaps through imitating its actions and cries. Don't feel embarrassed, no one is watching! Exploration is the key. Being attuned to your own responses as you move around the circle will lead you to find your own ways of working with and within it.

We call to the powers of the quarters as we make our sacred circle. When we do this, we invite into our ritual space those qualities and energies we feel we need or that are appropriate to the work we are doing. So, for example, a call to the North might go like this:

> Spirits of Earth, I call to you. Brown Bull of the North, I ask for your strength and determination. Great Bear Mother, I ask for your nurturing warmth, your protectiveness. Raven of Winter and dark night, I ask for your hidden wisdom. May these gifts of the powers of the North be present in this circle, that those gathered here may know them. Spirits of

the North, spirits of Earth, I bid you hale and welcome!

For calls to each of the quarters, see chapter 8 (pages 154-5). As ever, the ritual texts given in this book are merely suggestions. Your rites will be more potent if the words you use are your own, clearly expressing your own understanding and intention.

The Wheel of the Year

Through the links we make with the four cardinal points, we anchor our circle within the world, aware of its place in the web of relationships of which each of us is the centre. Quartering the circle gives us the symbol known as the Celtic cross. Building on this fourfold foundation we further sub-divide the circle by adding the cross-quarters to our map. This gives us the image of an eight-spoked wheel. Taking the perimeter of the circle to represent the cycle of the Sun through the year, the points at which the spokes meet the rim mark the eight major festivals celebrated in modern Druidry. In celebrating these festivals within the sacred circle, we align ourselves with the cycles of the natural world reflected in the changing seasons.

In Wales, the solstices and equinoxes are designated as 'Alban,' probably from *âl ban* [pronounced AL-ban], 'birth of the quarter,' i.e. the quarter of the year, equivalent to a season. Many modern Druids and Celtic Pagans translate *Alban* as 'light,' but the usual Welsh words for light are *golau, lleufer* or *llewych*. Our suggested derivation from *âl*, 'giving birth,' and *ban*, 'quarter,' not only seems more viable linguistically but also makes better sense.

Midwinter – *Alban Arthan*

Our journey around the wheel's rim begins at the North, the dark of the Moon, midnight, Midwinter. In Wales, Midwinter is called *Alban Arthan* [pron. Al-ban ARTH-ann], 'Birth of the Bear Quarter.' Arthan may be from the legendary King Arthur but is more likely from *Arctos*, an old Celtic word for 'bear,' from which the name Arthur is also derived. This relates the festival to *Ursa Major*, the Great Bear, also known as the Plough, the most prominent constellation in the Northern night sky.

The winter solstice, falling on or about December 21st, is the shortest day of the year. The literal meaning of solstice is 'Sun's standstill,' when the Sun's rising position on the horizon appears to remain the same for about five days. Our ancestors celebrated Midwinter a few days after the solstice, in a night-long vigil that began at sunset on

'Mothers' Night,' December 24ᵗʰ, climaxing at dawn on December 25ᵗʰ, the first morning when the position of sunrise begins to move northward again, thereby offering the first sign of a coming end to winter's cold and the longed for rebirth of vegetation and warmth that spring and summer will bring. Our ancestors therefore saw this Midwinter sunrise as representing the rebirth of the Sun. In wealthier nations, most of us take for granted the easy availability of food and luxuries such as double-glazing and central heating. It's easy to forget that, for our ancestors, winter brought the very real threat of starvation and death. No wonder the rebirth of the Sun was greeted with celebration.

The Egyptian god Horus, the Babylonian Baal, Persian Mithras and Greek Adonis were all born on December 25ᵗʰ. The Irish god of light, Lugh of the Long Arm, was born inside the prehistoric tomb-shrine of Newgrange where, on the morning of the winter solstice, a shaft of sunlight illuminates the innermost chamber of the tomb. In the collection of Welsh legends called *The Mabinogion* we hear of Mabon, 'Child,' son of Modron, 'Mother,' being stolen from his mother's arms when three nights old. Through such tales we glimpse what Midwinter meant to our

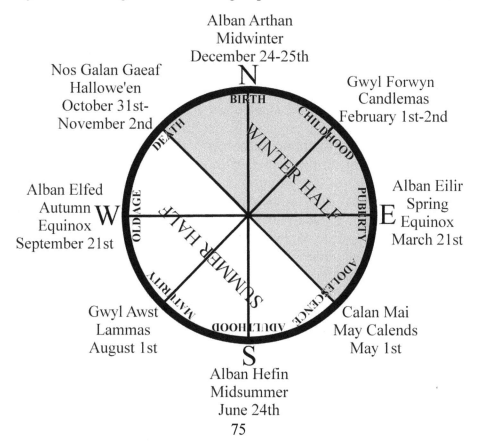

75

ancestors: a time of new birth emerging in the midst of death and decay, of consciousness emerging from the dark comfort of the womb, open to a flood of new experiences, yet helpless and reliant on others for protection and nourishment. In particular, as newborn children, we rely on our mothers. The nurturing arms of the mother, the comfort and security of the womb, are associated with the North, where the Great Bear of the winter constellation hibernates with her young. The father god of one of the pantheons whose stories feature in the *Mabinogion* is Math, whose name derives from *matu*, another early Celtic word meaning 'bear.' Our ancestors viewed death as a return to the womb of Mother Earth. In the North, then, we find both the end of life and its new beginning.

Candlemas – *Gwyl Forwyn*

Moving sunwise (clockwise) around the circle, we come to the North-East, where the elements of Earth and Air combine. This marks the first of the cross-quarter days, Candlemas, falling on February 1st and 2nd. It is celebrated as *Imbolc* in Ireland and as *Gwyl Forwyn* [pron. Gwul VORwin], the 'Feast of the Maiden,' or *Gwyl Fair*, the 'Feast of Mary,' in Wales. It marks the time when ewes begin to lactate and the first wild flowers appear, heralding the coming spring. It is traditionally a celebration of lights, candles being lit to illuminate churches and homes. As at the other quarter days, offerings of food and drink, particularly milk, are put out for the Faery folk or poured over standing stones. In Scottish folklore, Candlemas is when the white Serpent of Bride emerges from underground where it has spent the winter months, a potent image of life returning to the land. Bride, Brigid or Brigit is an ancient goddess of fertility, childbirth, poetry, smithcraft and brewing. After the coming of Christianity, she remained so popular that the church co-opted her as a saint with the same name, making her midwife to the Virgin Mary. In Wales she is honoured as Saint Ffraid.

The child born at Midwinter has now grown, but remains reliant on its mother and father for nourishment and protection. The child begins to recognize boundaries and differences between itself and the world, the first step towards independence of thought and being.

Spring Equinox – *Alban Eilir*

East marks the spring equinox, which falls on or about March 21st. In Welsh it is *Alban Eilir* [Al-ban EYE-leer], 'the Birth of the Spring Quarter.' The word *Eilir* may have been coined by Iolo Morganwg from Welsh, *eil*, 'interweaving' and *ir*, 'fresh, or green.' The Sun is now just entering the zodiacal sign of Aries, the Ram. On the morning of the equinox, the Sun rises directly in the east. The literal meaning of equinox is 'equal night,' because day and night are of equal length at this time. It is therefore a time of balance between the long nights of winter and the long days of summer. Balance is a temporary state, however, and is about to tip in favour of summer.

In human life, this is when the child begins to develop as an individual independent of its parents, still wide-eyed with wonderment but no longer content just to observe. Creating its own circle of friends, forming its own interests and tastes, the child is now eager to experience all that the world has to offer.

May Day – *Calan Mai*

Moving sunwise again, at the South-East we come to the second cross-quarter day, May 1st, May Day. In Ireland, this is celebrated as *Beltaine*, said by some to mean 'the fires of [the god] Bel,' and in Wales as *Calan Mai* [KAL-ann my), 'May Calends.' In folk festivals held at this time, twin fires were lit on hilltops and cattle were driven between them to protect them from disease. Brands from the fires were carried around fields to ensure growth and around houses and barns to protect them through the coming year. In Britain and elsewhere May Day has traditionally been celebrated by choosing a young girl to be Queen of the May, decking churches with seasonal flowers and dancing around Maypoles. Everywhere it is celebrated, it is seen as the first day of summer and the end of winter.

In some folk celebrations a battle is enacted between the forces of winter, sometimes led by a man dressed as a woman, and those of summer, often led by the May Queen or her consort. May Eve is a traditional time for young men and women to go to the greenwood to make love. At dawn, women used to bathe their faces in May morning dew to renew, enhance or preserve their youth and beauty. I've done so myself, albeit with limited success. Young people gather May flowers, particularly hawthorn (also known as May) blossom if it is out, for use in the revels of the day. Thorny twigs bedecked with blossom, known as May gads, were brandished by young folk who tried to whack each other with them. The old expression, "Ne'er shed a clout 'til may be out," sensibly advises us not to discard our winter clothes until the May blossom is in bloom.

On our circle, the South-East is the midpoint between the elements of Air and Fire, a volatile mix appropriate to this celebration of youthful vigour. It is here that we experience the sexual awakening that marks the leaving behind of childhood and the beginnings of adulthood. For many, it is a time of wild excitement, but also of great tension as we struggle to come to terms with a host of new sensations. It is a time of change and upheaval, shot through with the passionate energy of youth.

Midsummer – *Alban Hefin*

As the wheel turns we come to the South, the place of Midsummer, called *Alban Hefin* [Al-ban HEVin] in Wales, the 'Birth of the Summer Quarter,' *hefin* being Welsh for 'summer.' The summer solstice falls on or about June 21st when, as at Midwinter, the Sun's rising position remains still for about five days. Midsummer's Day falls a few days later, on June 24th, when the sunrise position begins to move southward again. All across Europe and throughout recorded history up until the 18th century Druid revival, Midsummer has been celebrated on Midsummer's Day and not on the day of the solstice. As at Beltaine, Midsummer is traditionally marked by hilltop fires. In less safety-conscious times, wheels were set on fire and rolled downhill. How well they burned, how far and fast they rolled and how high they bounced indicated the fortunes of the community through the coming year. The ancient, pan-European tradition of lighting such fires on Midsummer's Eve, June 23rd, survives on the Cornish peninsula.

At the South of the circle, the adolescent has become fully adult, retaining the energy of youth, but now with the strength of body and will to transform desire into action. Strong desire and the energy to achieve can be very attractive, but can also lead to conflict. In the fiery South, conflict may be welcomed for the opportunity it offers to display strength, courage, dominance and determination. Yet if conflict is unconstrained or misdirected, great harm can ensue. At the pivotal point of the solstice, the power is too wild, hence the celebration of Midsummer a few days later when energies have cooled enough to allow us to focus more clearly on the true power of the season, the celebration of strength, light and life, imbuing all into the growing crops in the fields, the pasturing animals, our families and wider communities.

Lammas – *Gwyl Awst*

Moving on to the South-West, we come to the point where Fire and Water meet. The festival of this cross-quarter day is called Lammas in England, from the Anglo-Saxon *Hlafmas*, 'Loaf-mass,' and is celebrated on August 1st. In Ireland it is called *Lughnasad*, the 'Festival of Lugh.' In Wales it is *Gwyl Awst* [Gwul owst], the 'August Feast.' It is a celebration of the first fruits of the harvest, a time to give thanks for the magical conjunction of earth, air, rain and Sun that gives us the food we eat. Our ancestors feasted at this time both in thanksgiving and in honour of the hard work of the harvest. Lammas is a traditional time for pilgrimages to sacred sites, at some of which our ancestors organised Lammastide games and races, giving young hot-heads a chance to let off steam while they entertained, and were cheered on by, the rest of the community. Lammas is also a traditional time for celebrating marriages. This reflects the idea of youthful passions giving way to maturity, to thoughts of settling down and raising a family.

At this point in the cycle, the flaming passion of the hero begins to cool a little as the youthful desire for action is tempered by the beginnings of wisdom. Our focus shifts away from pure self-interest and we begin to develop an understanding of the needs of others, a sense of compassion and community. For our ancestors, harvest was a time for united, communal effort, coming together for the benefit of all.

Autumn Equinox – *Alban Elfed*

In the West we reach the fall of the year, the autumn equinox, on or about September 21st. In Wales it is called *Alban Elfed* [Al-ban ELLved], 'Birth of the Ripe Quarter.' *Elfed* seems to have been coined by Welsh antiquarian, William Owen Pughe (1759-1835), from *el*, 'spirit' and *med*, 'ripe.' As at the spring equinox, day and night are of equal length and we are at a point of balance. Now, though, the balance is about to tip from summer, the season of growth, into winter, the time of dormancy and decay. The harvest is gathered in and stored against the coming cold, trees and hedgerows are heavy with fruit. The work of harvest largely done, there is time to rest, reflect, celebrate and give thanks, and to prepare for the cold months ahead.

In the cycle of our lives, we have achieved the wisdom of age. The struggle is past and we can rest and take stock, deciding which aspects of ourselves have real and lasting value and which we no longer need. In the terminology of the harvest, we separate the wheat from the chaff.

Hallowe'en – *Nos Galan Gaeaf*

The wheel rolls on, bringing us to the North-West, the festival of Hallowe'en, known in Ireland as *Samhain*, 'Summer's end,' and in Wales as *Nos Galan Gaeaf* [Noss GAL-ann GYE-av], the 'Night of Winter Calends.' It falls on October 31st and celebrations traditionally run through to November 2nd. It represents the conjunction of the elements of Water and Earth. As at May Day, its opposite on the wheel of the year, Hallowe'en fires were lit on hilltops and cattle were driven between them for protection and blessing. In parts of Wales, when the fires died down, everyone would run home helter-skelter while the cry went up: "*Adre, adre, am y cynta, Hwch Ddu Gwta gipio'r ola,*" 'Home, home, be the first, the Tailless Black Sow take the last!' Another version links the Black Sow with a *Ladi Wen heb ddim pen*, 'headless White Lady,' presumably a harsh winter spirit akin to the Gaelic *Cailleach*, 'Hag.' Dwelling most of the year on remote mountain-tops, she descends at the beginning of winter, bringing frost, ice and snow with her. At this time of year, our ancestors brought their herds down from high summer pastures, slaughtering excess livestock they were unable to feed through the winter.

Of all nights of the year, Hallowe'en is when ghoulies, gheesties and long leggity beasties are out in greatest force. Witches fly the night sky on broomsticks, making their way to the greatest Sabbat of the year. Gwyn ap Nudd or his Saxon counterpart, Woden, rides the night at the head of the Wild Hunt, leading the souls of the dead towards their long rest. Our ancestors placed lighted candles in their windows to welcome home the spirits of the dead, putting out offerings of food and setting places at table for relatives who had died. It was a trickster night when pranks were played on neighbours, with animal disguises and cross-dressing adding to the playful chaos. Why? Because this, along with May Day, is one of the great thresholds of the year. Hallowe'en marks the gateway between summer and winter. On this night, the gateways between the worlds of flesh and of spirit are wide open. Through the games, tricks and disguises that mark the festival, our ancestors faced the darkness with humour, imagination and courage.

In the cycle of our lives, the North-West represents old age and death. Now we sense the coming darkness, aware at last of our own mortality. We make our final decisions about what we are content to leave behind, what we will carry with us into the darkness. Aware of our frailty and the long road that lies ahead, we know we must choose only those things we value most.

The final part of our journey brings us back to where we began: the womb-like peace of the North from which we are reborn to begin the cycle anew. So the whole of life is encompassed within the sacred circle.

The timing of festivals has altered over the millennia during which they have been celebrated. There is some evidence that they originally took place on the nearest full Moon to the dates given above, a practice first recorded in the ancient Middle East more than 4,000 years ago.

Some time after the adoption of Christianity, this changed to the nearest Sunday to the full Moon nearest the festival date. This is still how the date of Easter is calculated in the Western Church. As modern Druids, we often have to time group celebrations to fit in with the working week while celebrating the given dates, or nearest full Moon, at home.

Walking the Circle

In marking out the circle around us, and in cutting the threads that link us to the world beyond its edge, we make the circle a place of perfect safety. By walking its rim with clear intention, we find those parts of our life where we experience pain, sorrow, joy, clarity, fear, jealousy, inspiration, anger, peace, disillusion, love, embarrassment, hatred, kindness. Through reliving these experiences within the safety of the circle, we learn about ourselves, our weaknesses and strengths, hopes and fears, our sources of inspiration and those things that hold us back.

There are life experiences and negative self-images that can keep us from fulfilling our potential. The sacred circle offers the opportunity to work through these blockages. Often, the simple act of facing such problem areas in our psyche within the circle offers its own solutions. Other blockages might require more work to overcome. As with our experience of the four elements, walking the eightfold wheel with awareness, attuned to our own feelings and responses, can often present new answers to difficulties in our lives.

Once a problem area has been recognised, cast your circle as described earlier, sunwise from East to East. When it is cast, go to each quarter in turn, beginning at the East and moving clockwise to South, West and North, returning again to the East. At each quarter, invite into the circle those positive qualities you feel you most need. Then go to the centre of the circle and centre yourself using the 'Sensing the Aura' exercise given earlier (pages 67-8).

From the centre, try to locate where your problem lies on the rim of the circle. A problem with male dominance might lie in the South. An emotional problem might surface in the West, a sexual problem in the South-East, social interactions in the South-West. Once you have found where on the circle your problem lies, move to that place and let yourself go as deeply as you can into the problem, feeling how it affects you personally. If this is uncomfortable, remember you are within the safety of sacred space, that you have full control over what you invite into your circle and what you allow to leave it. Try not to dismiss the discomfort or ignore it, but really feel it. Ask your guides, whether you

81

view them as aspects of your psyche or self-existent beings, to help you discover the root causes of the problem. When you feel you have understood all that you can about the nature of the problem and its causes within yourself, think about how it affects others around you.

When you have immersed yourself in all aspects of the problem, you are ready to look for solutions. Often these can be found by moving around the circle to the next stage of the cycle. So, if your problem is with male dominance in the South, the solution may lie in the maturity and sense of community that emerges in the South-West. If the answer doesn't emerge through moving around the circle, it may be found by looking across the circle to the opposite point on the perimeter. So, if the problem is that you are lost in emotional turmoil, the West is the place of emotion. Its opposite is the East, the quarter of Air, the mind, clarity and new beginnings.

When you have located where you think the best solution to your problem might be, walk the circle to that point. When you reach it, allow yourself to dive into your feelings again, imagining how you might put the solution into action and what results it might have for yourself and those around you. You may find a clear certainty that your chosen course of action is the right one. Or you may not. If you have doubts after exploring all the possibilities here, go back and start again. Return to the point where you located the problem and immerse yourself in it again. Then look for other possible solutions. Having found where they lie on the circle, go there and test out your new ideas. Repeat the process as many times as necessary until you are sure you have found what you need to do to move your life forward.

This exercise is about locating areas of tension, then finding the point of release that will free you to move on. Used well, with focus and understanding, it is one of the most powerful tools in Druidry.

Having created a sacred circle, it must always be closed when the work within it is done. If a circle is not consciously closed, the psyche can remain tied to the processes undergone in the circle, failing to return fully into relationship with the world beyond its rim.

Before closing the circle, give thanks to the ancestors, your gods and guides, for all that you have learned and experienced. Go to each quarter again, beginning in the North, moving counter-clockwise through West, South and East, ending back in the North. Give thanks for the elemental qualities you called forth at the beginning of the rite. Suggested forms of words for each of the quarters are given in chapter 8 (page 163). Again, it is better if you speak your own words, clearly reflecting your own feelings, so the following example is given solely for guidance:

> Spirits of the North, spirits of Earth, Brown Bull, Bear Mother, Raven of Winter, I thank you for the gifts of strength, security and wisdom you have brought to this circle. May they remain with us as we now bid you hale and farewell!

Then close the circle by erasing it, either physically or in imagination, depending on how it was made. As before, begin at the North and move counter-clockwise through West, South and East, ending at the North. If you began by 'cutting the threads' as described earlier, you should now consciously re-weave them as you go around the circle. As you close the circle, be aware of coming back fully and consciously into the everyday world. Finally, give thanks to the spirits of place, thanking them for accepting your presence.

The rite is now ended.

May there be peace without and peace within, until we meet again.

So may it be.

Part Two:
Inspiration & Creativity: the Path of the Bard

Chapter 4:
Flowing Spirit, Feminine Spirit

At the heart of Druid practice is the quest for the spirit of inspiration and creativity that is called *awen* in the British tradition. It is the food and drink of the soul, giving strength to the body, courage to the heart, knowledge, wisdom and insight to the mind, ecstasy to the spirit. *Awen* is a feminine noun variously translated as 'muse,' 'genius,' 'inspiration,' 'poetic furore' or 'poetic frenzy.' As mentioned earlier, a Victorian Welsh-English dictionary persuaded me that *awen* is made up of the words *aw*, 'flowing,' and *en*, 'spirit,' giving it the literal meaning of 'flowing spirit.' This translation has since spread around the world, aided by the publication of the first edition of this book. Though subsequent research has shown *aw* to be linguistically dubious, references to *awen* in medieval Welsh literature show that it was thought of as liquid and it does flow from one person or thing to another across time and space as do, for example, the poems of Taliesin and the stories collected together in the *Mabinogion* that were first written down a thousand years ago and continue to inspire us today. That said, a more accurate translation of *awen* may be 'feminine spirit.' As we shall see, this also works.

Following another idea from Iolo Morganwg, *awen* is often represented by the symbol of three rays of light, as in the version opposite, used by the British Druid Order.

The idea of *awen* has fascinated me since first encountering it in the poetry of medieval Welsh bards. The *Story of Taliesin*, first recorded in the 16th century, helped me realise just how central *awen* is to the understanding and practice of Druidry. In it, as we shall see in chapter 5, a child named Gwion Bach, 'Little Innocent,' inadvertently drinks three drops from a cauldron of inspiration (*awen*) brewed by Ceridwen, witch-like wife of an otherwise obscure character named Tegid Voel, 'Beautiful Bald One.' Through these magical drops, Gwion gains the three gifts of poetry, prophecy and shape-shifting, ultimately being reborn as Taliesin, Primary Chief Bard of Britain. These gifts define the three areas of Druid practice: poetry for the bard, prophecy for the ovate and shape-shifting for the Druid. Like *Shakti*, the feminine creative power in Hindu tradition, *awen* may be seen as the active power of creation. Like *Shakti*, it is an energy that takes many forms, in British tradition manifesting especially through Ceridwen as is its chief source and primary agent.

Awen is closely associated with Ceridwen and her cauldron in both poetry and prose. Her name is said by some to translate as 'Crooked Woman' or 'Bent White One,' though 'White (or Pure) Craft' may be a viable alternative. Medieval Welsh bards called her the ruler, or patroness, of their order. In Ireland, a close equivalent to *awen* is *dana*, variously translated as 'a gift, a treasure, a spiritual offering or gift, art, science, calling or the art of poetry.' *Dana* is seen as a gift of the goddess Brighid, described in one 9th century text as "a poet and a goddess worshipped by poets on account of the generous protection afforded them by her." Dana, Ana, or Anu is also the name of a goddess. An Irish term, *áes dána*, meaning 'people of skill,' applies to craftspeople in general and especially to bards (Irish *filid*), but also to the pagan Irish pantheon, the Tuatha Dé Danann, 'Clan of the Goddess Anu.' Its Welsh equivalent is *wyr keluydon* [modernised as *gwyr celfyddon*, pron. gwir KELLV'thon], meaning 'people of skill,' 'experts,' and also 'enchanters, magicians.'

Another Irish term, *imbas* [pron. immus], means 'great knowledge, poetic talent, inspiration, foreknowledge, or magic lore,' a group of meanings also close to those of *awen*. One of three methods of divination taught to students in the eighth year of their studies in Irish bardic schools is called *imbas forosnai*. *For-osna* means 'lights up, illumines,' so *imbas forosnai* is '*imbas* that illuminates.' Since the name of the inspired bard Taliesin means 'radiant brow,' this suggests that *awen* also manifests as light. Irish bards occasionally refer to inspiration as a 'fire in the head.' As we have seen, Welsh bards primarily regard it as a liquid, though some have likened it to breath or bread, two fundamentals of life. Most see it as a substance we can reach out and grasp, drink or otherwise imbibe, if only we try.

In our culture we tend to see inspiration as a force beyond our understanding or control that falls randomly on lucky individuals at rare and unpredictable times, enabling them to create music, art and literature or some new scientific process. To the Druid bard, inspiration, *awen*, is a power we can learn to access more-or-less at will. With this in mind, we begin our journey towards understanding its power and potential...

Sensing Awen

To begin to understand the flow of *awen*, we should first learn to sense its presence. One way to do this is to become fully aware of the physical and psychic sensations the products of other people's *awen* engender in us. The poet Robert Graves (1895-1985), for example, said that true poetry made the hairs on the back of his neck stand up. There are pieces of music that produce a similar effect on me. A Van Gogh painting in a gallery in Amsterdam produced a feeling that my body had become weightless and insubstantial. Some ancient sacred sites produce a tingling in my palms like static electricity while others generate a sensation of heat and tautness in my solar plexus. Some people become short of breath, others find their heart rate slows or speeds up. Our responses to the presence of the inspiring spirit are as different as we are from each other and may vary in us from moment to moment. Sometimes we respond with simple awe. There are many ways in which we may recognize the presence of *awen*.

To explore your own responses, immerse yourself in whatever art form you find most inspirational: a painting, a chamber concert, a rock gig, a forest, hilltop or sacred site, a favourite piece of music, a poem or passage from a novel, a film. While immersed in the experience, look for the physical and psychic reactions that are your personal response to the spirit of *awen* as inspiration. Be aware of how you feel before and after the experience. If you are left feeling elated, open, free, connected, pleasantly intoxicated or high, rising on a good day towards ecstasy and beyond then the chances are you have had a genuine encounter with *awen*. If, on the other hand, you feel deflated, dispirited, bored or confused, maybe you should consider changing your taste!

In Druidry there are many ways in which we seek to bring *awen* into our lives. The arts are a rich source, the natural world another. Again, our responses are individual. The sight, sound and scent of the sea are intoxicating to some, while some find their deepest inspiration in the quiet depths of a forest, others on a high hilltop or in the midst of a thunderstorm. Some bloom under the heat of the summer Sun, others respond more powerfully to the changing faces of the cool Moon. Some find enchantment in the colourful flash of a kingfisher, others in the patient solitude of the heron, the ghostly, silent flight of the hunting barn owl, the soaring freedom of the mountain eagle. Some revel in the self-satisfied purr of a contented cat, others find their soul's reflection in the lone wanderings or pack protectiveness of the wolf, the strength of bison or bear, the regal authority of the stag, the quick movements of the roebuck. Trees too can inspire: the dark and ancient wisdom of the yew, the epic grandeur of tall pines, the strength and stability of the oak, the fluid flexibility of willow, the prickly beauty of May or blackthorn. Leaves, flowers, the colour and texture of dark loam or golden sand, the quicksilver of moonlight on water, the tumbling roar of a waterfall, the gentle burble of a woodland stream, the flicker of firelight, the ever-changing shapes of clouds, summer rain or winter snows. All these can be potent sources of inspiration, creating the same kinds of physical, psychological and spiritual responses that we find in art.

We recognize and honour our sources of inspiration in various ways in ceremonies, perhaps saying something like this after a circle is cast:

> The circle is unbroken,
> the ancestors awoken.
> May the songs of the Earth
> and of her people ring true.
> Hale to the spirits of this place:
> of root and branch, tooth and claw,
> fur and feather, of earth and sea and sky.
> Hale and welcome!

If these words sound familiar, it may be that you heard them spoken during the closing ceremony of the London 2012 Paralympics.

Chanting Awen

Early bards sought to understand the nature of *awen* in order to be able to access and use it, sometimes describing the means they employed in verse. Frank Olding's translation of 'The Hostile Confederacy,' a poem attributed to the bard Taliesin, contains the lines:

> I sing *awen*,
> I bring it forth from the deep,
> the river that encircles the world:
> I know its size and strength,
> I know where it ebbs,
> I know how it flows,
> I know how it courses,
> I know how it retreats.

In modern Druidry, both in shared ritual and personal practice, we often invoke *awen* simply by chanting the word itself. As in 'The Hostile

Confederacy,' we sing *awen*. The intonation is often pitched low, producing a distinct vibration deep in the belly. Raising the pitch takes the vibration up into the chest or head. Experimentation will establish what works best for you under what circumstances. The sound of each letter is extended for as long as breath will allow.

Often, the chant will be made within the environs of a sacred circle. In group ceremonies we chant to draw inspiration into the circle and those within it, enabling each individual to give and receive more fully, strongly and clearly within the context of the rite being performed. Making the chant as a group has the effect of pooling the inspiration of all those present, creating a spiritual cauldron of inspiration from which all may drink. In personal practice we may chant the *awen* when we have particular need of inspiration, either for some creative project or to find the answer to a particular problem.

Often, the *awen* is chanted either three times or in multiples of three. The three-fold *awen* chant was introduced into modern Druidry by Philip Carr-Gomm, Chosen Chief of the Order of Bards, Ovates and Druids (OBOD) from 1987 to 2020. However, since poems recorded in 13th century manuscripts refer to singing *awen*, it seems Philip was updating a far earlier practice, inspired by his own *awen*. Sometimes, in what has come to be known as a 'rolling *awen*,' the chant will simply run on until it ends naturally. In groups, it is not necessary for everyone to chant in unison. Indeed, the quality of the sound may seem richer and more multi-textured if different voices start and end at different times. The rolling *awen* was, I believe, introduced (or re-introduced?) by Emma Restall Orr (Bobcat) and myself while we were joint chiefs of the British Druid Order between 1995 and 2002.

Seeking Awen

Here's an exercise you might like to try. Its purpose is to help you identify personal sources of inspiration and perhaps find some new things to add to your altar.

Cast your circle as described in the previous chapter. You might like to light a candle on your altar or burn some incense. Experimentation will show what you need to do to create an atmosphere conducive to spiritual practice. Settle down before the altar. Sit comfortably, spine straight and supporting your head well. Now focus clearly on the intention of the rite which, in this case, is to increase your knowledge of yourself and your sources of inspiration. Take a couple of deep, slow breaths and let them out again slowly. Following the third intake of breath begin the *awen* chant, chanting the word three times. The sound of the chant is:

Aaaaaaaaa-oooooooo-eeeeeeeee-nnnnnnnnn.

('a' as in father, 'oo' as in Moon, 'e' as in when)

As you chant, be aware with all your senses of the physical, psychic and spiritual effects the process has on you. When you have completed the chant, sit still for a few moments, allowing the resonance of the sound to permeate yourself and the space around you.

When you are ready, get up and open a gateway in your circle. You can do this by putting the palms of your hands together, sliding them into the rim of your circle and then moving them apart, as if parting a pair of curtains. Alternatively, you may draw a doorway in the air. Step through and then close the gateway you have made. This may seem a curious process but it has the effect of maintaining the 'seal' of your sacred space. It is also a physical reminder that the space you have created is sacred and therefore worthy of respect.

Now go out into the world and look for some small, portable object that inspires you. Don't look too consciously or too hard, like Sherlock Holmes with his magnifying glass. Act from the belly, not the head. Be open, free from preconceptions. Go wherever instinct takes you and find whatever you are led to by it. When you have found something, bring it back with you. Open your circle again as described above before entering it, close it behind you and resume your place before the altar.

Now hold the object you brought back in your hand and focus on it, allowing your mind to wander down whatever avenues of thought are awakened by it. If you find yourself drifting off into thoughts of whether you let the cat out or what price lemons are this week, use the physical presence of the object to bring you back to focus. Examine every aspect of it: its texture, shape, colour, smell, taste. What thoughts, sensations, feelings and impressions do these things evoke in you? After following each chain of association as far as it will go, return again to the object. In this way you will expand your knowledge of the object itself, of yourself and your responses to it, of the sources of your inspiration and, if you allow the meditation to carry you far enough, of the structure and meaning of the universe.

Every material object is composed of molecules, atoms and sub-atomic particles. Between these particles is the space through which flow energies that cause them to move in the patterned dance that gives substance its structure, determining whether the basic building blocks of existence manifest as wood or water, silk or stone. This web of energies, mirroring the Web of Wyrd, links all things together. Through it, the infinitely small relates to the infinitely huge, the energies flowing out from each individual pebble, flower or grain of sand to every other, and then reaching out from the Earth to touch the Moon and Sun, and beyond them the stars and distant galaxies, on to the very edge of the universe where time and space cease to exist, just as they do here, at the centre of the sacred circle...

When the object of your meditation has taken you as far as it can, it is time to give thanks for what you have learned and close the circle. You should know by this time whether your object is something to make space for on your altar. If it is, take an offering back to the place where you found it and offer it, with thanks, to the spirit of the place. Offerings should be such that they will leave no trace after a few hours or days: food that birds or animals may eat, drink that will soak into the earth, flowers that will rot down, releasing nutrients into the soil.

If you decide not to keep the object, take it back to the place where you found it and replace it carefully. You may leave an offering for the spirit of the place, or you may give the object itself, and the time and effort it has taken to take it back, as your offering.

Poetry & the Cell of Song

For medieval bards, poetry and song were the foremost ways by which their *awen* was made manifest. The same can be true for us today. Among other things, poetry represents a heightened, intensified use of language in which every word is considered not only for its standard meaning, but for potential multiple meanings, as well as for its sound in conjunction with the words before and after it and within the context of the poem as a whole. It is, in essence, a kind of verbal meditation.

A traditional method of awakening the flow of *awen* practised in the bardic schools of Ireland is described in some detail in *The Memoirs of the Marquis of Clanricarde* (1604-1657), published in 1722. The same practice is referred to more briefly in Martin Martin's *A Description of the Western Isles of Scotland* (1703). In Wales, a 1382 'Elegy for the Sons of Tudur ap Gronwy,' by Iolo Goch ('Red Iolo,' circa 1320-1398) speaks of:

The dark island, cell of song,
So once was called Anglesey of the verdant landscape.

The word translated here as 'song,' *cerdd* [pron. care-th], also means 'poem, art of poetry, music, craft, art,' so 'cell of bardcraft' would be an equally viable translation. *Cerdd* has the secondary meaning of 'journey, voyage.' Anglesey has a long history as a centre of pagan spirituality, from late Neolithic tomb-shrines through to deposits of Iron Age metal-work in the 1st century CE. As we saw in chapter 2 (page 56), the Roman historian, Tacitus, referred to it as an island devoted to the practice of Druidry or, as he put it, "inhuman superstitions."

Bards undertaking the 'cell of song' were given a subject on which to compose a poem and then shut up alone in dark, windowless cells in complete silence for a day and a night. All that time they would lay on their beds, often with their heads swathed in cloth to enhance their state of sensory deprivation. In the silent darkness, removed from all distraction, the mind roams free, entering a state between dream and waking where associations that normal consciousness would miss or dismiss may be pursued along paths of imaginative thought to remote, often wildly illogical conclusions – *cerdd* in all its multiple meanings. The normal sensory defences crumble as the hours go by, enabling the *awen* to flow free.

After twenty-four hours, the bards were brought candles and wrote down the poems they had incubated in the womb-like darkness of their cells. The class then reassembled and the poems were offered for assessment. The quality of the verses gave their tutors a clear indication of the extent to which each bard had connected with the *awen*. This is one reason why, in Druidry, we use our inspiration to create; so that our inspiration can be judged by others through the quality of our creations. This can be a scary process, but it encourages us to constantly refine and improve what we do. Also, the products of our creativity are the offerings we give in exchange for the inspiration we receive. So the flow of *awen* is maintained.

For present-day bards, long, solitary train journeys can be a useful, if gentler, version of the cell of song. As in the traditional technique, they can leave the mind with little to do but wander, a circumstance ideal for the creation of poetry. Focusing on the noise of the train on the tracks can effectively block out most distracting sounds while the speed at which scenery goes by makes it impossible to focus on it as a potential source of distraction. Sadly, many of us now ruin these creative opportunities by focusing our attention on distractions we carry with us, like mobile phones, notepads or laptops. Next time you find yourself on a train, forego these distractions, free your mind and ask the *awen* to flow. Carry pen or pencil and paper with you to record the results. Very old school, I know, but offering no additional distractions like social media or checking emails.

As a non-driver, I travel quite long distances on buses. Like trains, these can also provide a 'cell of song lite.' One day I was reading a book while travelling across Salisbury Plain on the number 2 bus. The plain is quite flat, giving the impression of the sky being huge. Most of the plain is a patchwork of fields divided by hedges, ridges, streams or ditches. It is a managed, tamed, humanised landscape. But on that day, the autumn sky was its own patchwork, with pale patches of blue between clouds, some white, some dark and heavy with rain, and curtain-like rays from a hidden Sun breaking through beneath the clouds. The wild sky offered a dramatic contrast with the controlled, manicured fields below, and the drama in the heavens seemed to affect those fields, making even them seem wilder. For a while I tried to keep reading my book, but the scene outside kept nagging me for poetry. Eventually I gave up, took out my notebook and pen and jotted down the following:

Across the Plain
Human patterns of well-tended fields
may still seem wild beneath a scudding sky
dark grey, blue, white, riven by a hidden sun
well-tempered human nature yields
when elder days of autumn come

'Across the Plain' was originally intended as the beginning of the first line, but immediately struck me as a simple, straight-forward title. In the first two lines, I tried to capture the essence of the feelings described in the preceding paragraph in as few carefully-chosen words as possible. I then realised I needed to describe the 'scudding sky' in a way that would convey my visual impression of it, and that called forth the third line. With poetry, there is always a sense that it needs form and structure. Of course, one of the mainstays of poetry is rhyme, hence the next line, which rhymes with the first. It wasn't only about finding a rhyme though. I also wanted to liken the controlled, organised nature of much of human life to the organisation of nature represented by the fields of the opening line. A bonus resulting from rhyming these two lines is that it emphasises the likening of their subjects to one another.

With the last line, I wanted to give a sense of autumn, the time when the poem arrived, but also express how the vision of this human-formed landscape beneath such a wild sky reminded me of a time before the landscape was managed by humans, when it would have been as randomly-patterned as the sky above it. The words, 'elder days of autumn,' have other connotations too, of autumn being the elder part of the year. In the Druidic understanding of time, autumn relates to human maturity, when a measure of wisdom has been gained, and before we wilt into old age. That's where I was in life when I wrote the verse.

There are technical things I could note about it. The number of syllables per line is 9/11/11/8/8, the rhyme scheme is A B C A C, in which 'A' is a full and 'C' a partial rhyme ('fields/yields,' 'sun/come'). There are internal rhymes too: 'may/grey/days,' 'wild/white,' 'riven/hidden.' Line 2 uses the ancient poetic technique of alliteration: 'still seem,' 'scudding sky.' I had no rhyme scheme or structure in mind at all when I began to write. My sole concern was to catch the inspiration of the fleeting moment as elegantly as I could. My knowledge of verse structure came into play at an unconscious level while thinking about how to form the lines, but such considerations were secondary to what it was I wanted to say. I was trying to give voice to a feeling, aware that it would soon pass from experience, and then from memory, unless quickly caught on the page. I knew that I could always come back to the words and re-shape them, whereas I would never have the exact feeling of that moment again.

When these few lines were written I had no idea where they were going. They still seem more like a raw sketch than a finished thing. They might form the basis of a song one day, in which case I might need to alter the rhyme scheme and tighten up the rhythm. They might be the start of a longer poem, in which case I might create more verses using the same rhyme scheme, or pull out individual lines and build new verses around them. They could stay just as they are. They might sit forgotten until, years from now, I dig out that notebook and find them again. I could decide they're crap and do nothing with them. The point is, I took that moment of inspiration, that *awen*, that came to me on the bus and took a first step towards making something from it. The worth of that something has yet to be determined, but, in writing those few lines, I took the *awen* to me rather than letting it slip away. Bardic training holds that the *awen* we receive should be honoured by using it to create, so that we can pass it on to others through our creation, thereby maintaining the *awen*'s flow. Such is the prime duty of the bard. I have now used these lines both here and in the British Druid Order's bardic course. Perhaps that honours their *awen* enough. Time will tell.

Though the words 'poem' and 'poetry' are used throughout this piece, it's worth remembering that most surviving medieval bardic poetry was actually designed to be sung, reminding us that music is another core art associated with the bardic path.

Throughout my lifetime, poetry has undergone periodic revivals as a popular art form. In the 1950s, this happened when a group who came to be known collectively as the Beat Poets began performing their work in jazz clubs in the USA. Prominent among them were Gregory Corso, Lawrence Ferlinghetti and Allen Ginsburg, whose long poem, *Howl*, remains an incredibly powerful piece of art. The 60s saw a similar loose confederation emerge in the UK known as the Liverpool Poets. They included Adrian Henri, Brian Patten and Roger McGough. McGough in particular merged his poetry with music, notably in the group, Scaffold. The 70s saw the emergence of Punk Poets such as Attila the Stockbroker and John Cooper Clarke, who also blended poetry with music. Subsequent decades have seen the periodic re-emergence of performance poetry, again often in concert with musicians. Prominent exponents include Linton Kwesi Johnson, Selina Godden, Lemn Sissay, John Hegley, Kae Tempest and Benjamin Zephaniah. Druid and performance poet, Liv Torc, coordinates poetry stages at large music festivals in the UK. There is still a substantial popular audience for poetry if it is presented well and connects with people's lived experience.

Live performance has the advantage of offering instant feedback. A useful aid in traditional bardic performances was the Branch of Peace. Consisting of a small wooden or metal branch strung with bells, it was shaken by bards to draw attention to the fact that they were about to sing, play or begin to tell a tale. In the medieval era, audiences knew to fall silent when the Branch was sounded, which was especially useful when we recall that most bardic performances took place in mead halls where alcohol would have been imbibed. Today, in a local pub or club, audiences may need a little retraining...

Creative Dreaming

Dreams can be a fruitful source of inspiration that may be translated into poetry, painting, story or song. The world of dreams is an alternate reality and the otherworld most of us enter most frequently. Unlike other otherworlds, it takes no more than laying your head on a pillow for a while to gain admittance to it. Dreaming is like having a free cinema pass every night of the week and most of us don't value it half as much as we should. Robert Graves memorably described dreams as "the finest entertainment known and given rag-cheap."

As in the Cell of Song, sleep frees the mind from its normal constraints, allowing messages to come through that would otherwise be blocked. Many dreams are simply the mind's way of sifting and processing data received during waking life. Others may carry recollections of past lives, intimations of the future or messages from our ancestors, gods and guides. Either way, the dream world often produces rich, strange imagery that can be woven into expressions of creativity. Dreams inspire not only poets and artists, but many scientists find insights and visions in them that help solve problems in their work. Keeping a dream diary at your bedside and writing down your dreams on waking each morning will enable you to recall more and more of your dreams. A dream diary will also allow you to review long-forgotten dreams weeks, months or years later, at which time their meanings may be much clearer to you than they were at the time.

Our greatest contemporary bard, Robin Williamson, formerly of The Incredible String Band and the Merry Band, has produced an entire, very fine album all the lyrics of which are taken directly from his own dream diaries. Appropriately entitled *Dream Journals, 1967-77* (Pig's Whisker Music, 1997), in the opening track, 'Foreword,' Robin says,

> Many songs I wrote back then were based in whole or in part on these notes, written down morning by morning. When resting my head night by night wherever fate had cast me, I'd close my eyes and resume the inner journey.

Robin being my favourite singer-songwriter of all time, a multi-talented, multi-instrumental musician, award-winning harper and magical storyteller worthy, like Taliesin before him, of the title Primary Chief Bard of Britain, I'm more than happy to follow his lead.

Dream well then, dear reader, dream on and dream strong!

Chapter 5:
Ancestral Voices

Our ancestors communicate with us in many ways, not least through the songs and poetry, legend and lore bequeathed to us by previous generations of bards. As we walk the path of Druidry, we encounter many doorways through which we can enter the realms of the ancestors, worlds of spirit, magical otherworlds that exist, eternal and ever-changing, alongside our own and in which many things are possible. The stories, songs and poetry of our ancestors offer such doorways. Through the magic of their words we find ourselves connected, heart, mind and soul, with the *awen*, the flowing, feminine spirit of those who created them.

The stories and songs of our ancestors are the stock-in-trade of the bard. As a triad recorded in a 16th century text called 'The Five Books of Poetry' says, "Three things pertain to the poet: poetry, memory, and traditional lore." For our ancestors, bards were keepers of tradition, re-modelling history into tales that teach and inspire, capable of both holding and moving an audience. In this way, history is transformed into the myths and legends that inform our sense of personal and cultural identity, providing the backdrop to our existence, our beliefs, our sense of self, our connection with the past and the sacred land in which we dwell. Stories and songs are our teachers. Those we hear as children help shape our lives, teaching us about social interactions, alerting us to dangers, awakening us to a sense of magic and wonder, allowing us to work through our deepest hopes and fears in the safe environment of hearth and home. Stories are thus vital to our development as individuals. As adults, they can teach us about right behaviour, the beliefs of our ancestors, other worlds and their inhabitants and the nature of the gods.

In traditional bardic performances, story, song and poetry are often combined. In the medieval era, two bards would often work together, one speaking, chanting or singing while another accompanied on that archetypal bardic instrument, the harp. The bardic, or Celtic harp seems to have appeared about 1,500 years ago in Scotland, ultimately replacing the lyre, depictions of which first appear around 2,800 years ago in Iron Age Central Europe. The music of these instruments was regarded as having spiritual qualities that linked musicians and listeners with the otherworlds of the Faery folk, the ancestors and the old gods of our lands. Skilled players were expected to master the 'three noble strains,' musical modes that were able to evoke laughter, sorrow or sleep.

The ability to alter consciousness is a large part of the magic of the bard. Performing ancient tales and ancestral songs in sacred space, either as part of a seasonal ceremony or as a ceremony in themselves, makes creating such alterations in consciousness that much easier for those taking part, or simply observing, to be drawn into the world the bard creates, or rather recreates, which is that of our ancestors, the Faery folk and the old gods. Through performance, the bard evokes that world, becoming a bridge between it and our world, breathing new life into the beings and events referred to.

To illustrate the magical use of bardic story and song, here are a few verses from my rendering of an 8th century Irish song, 'The Islands of the Blest.' Composed 1,300 years ago, they give a vivid impression of our ancestors' vision of the otherworld to which the soul travels after death as a blessed realm that lies beyond the western ocean. They form part of 'The Voyage of Bran,' a story of a type known as *immrama* or 'voyages.' 'The Voyage of Bran' illustrates the three primary functions of sacred storytelling; to entertain, to inform, and to act as a bridge between worlds. Verses like those below may have been sung at the bedside of those who were dying, providing guidance for their souls' journey to the Islands of the Earthly Paradise. They may have been sung by the 'soul friend' (Irish *anam cara*) of the person preparing for that great journey between worlds that we refer to as death, in truth not an ending but a liberation of the spirit from the cares of this world as we move into the worlds of wonder that wait for us beyond.

At the beginning of 'The Voyage …' Bran, an Irish king, is visited in his hall by a strangely dressed, beautiful woman who sings to him of Emain [pron. Evin], her otherworld home:

> I bring a branch of Emain's apple tree,
> alike in form to those you know.
> Twigs of white silver upon it grow
> and buds of crystal blossom fair to see.
>
> There is an island far beyond this land,
> around which glisten white sea-horses.
> Against its shores they flow in their white courses,
> upon four pillars strong that island stands.
>
> An ancient tree there is in flower,
> whereon bright birds each hour call.

98

In sweetest harmony they all
combine to sing the passing of each hour.

No sorrow known, nor grieving there,
no sickness, death or suffering.
Such is the life of fair Emain,
a life that in this world is all too rare.

A host then comes across the shining sea
and row their craft most skilfully to land,
to where shining stones in circles stand,
from which arise a music sweet and free.

Through ages long unto the gathered throng
they sing a song that sorrow never stained;
a hundred voices, all in chorus reigned,
in praise of life and life's eternal song.

Emain of many shapes beside the sea,
whether it be far or it be near,
women in bright colours wander here,
surrounded by the clear and shining sea.

And if you hear the sweet voice of the stones
and songbirds of the Peaceful Land,
those women will walk close at hand;
no one who comes need walk alone.

Other songs and poems recall other-than-human transformations, suggesting that *awen* can awaken the bard to heightened states of awareness where consciousness merges with the universe and everything in it. So, in Frank Olding's translation of part of *Kat Godeu*, 'The Battle of the Trees,' from the early 14th century *Book of Taliesin*, now in the National Library of Wales, the bard Taliesin sings:

I was in many forms
before I was freed from restraint.
I was a slender, mottled sword
forged by a skilful hand.
I was a droplet in the air,
I was the stars' radiant light.
I was a word in script,
In my prime I was a book.
I was a lantern's light
for a year and a half together.
I was a bridge that spanned
sixty estuaries.

I was a path, I was an eagle,
I was a coracle on the sea.
I was the effervescence in a drink,
I was a drop of rain in a shower.
I was a sword in the hand,
I was a shield in battle.
I was a ringing harp-string,
under nine years' enchantment,
and foam upon the water.
I was a fire's sparking tinder,
I was a tree in a forest fire,
I am not one who does not sing:
I have sung since boyhood.

We may envisage a young bard sitting cross-legged in the doorway of a stone beehive hut on the west coast of Anglesey, looking out over the sea towards the setting Sun, chanting these words to rekindle that sense of oneness with all creation that this part of the poem seeks to evoke. The expression of universal consciousness contained in these lines is found elsewhere in the medieval poetry of Wales and Ireland, reminding us why, among our forebears, bards were regarded with the kind of awe and reverence reserved in other cultures for priests, shamans, medicine folk or wise women and men. Even in our own day, a kind of mystical aura still attaches to the creative arts, a sense that those who practice them are connected to some inner source that sets them apart from the rest of humanity. We recognize this source as *awen*.

Many Blessings

Among our ancestors, a visit from a bard was held to convey blessings on a house, its inhabitants, their crops and livestock. If the bard was treated with sufficient hospitality, he might compose a poem of praise to the hosts that would ensure their good name and that of their family for generations to come. Contrariwise, if the hosts proved mean or spiteful, a bardic satire could ruin them.

The traditional tales memorised and told by bards were themselves believed to bestow blessings on the teller and the hearer. Saint Patrick, patron saint of Ireland, is said to have ordered that no one should sleep or talk during the telling of one tale, 'The Fosterage of the Three Methers,' (methers are communal drinking vessels for mead) and promised those who listened to it success in children, love and marriage, in legal matters and hunting, protection to seafarers, peace in banqueting halls and freedom for those held captive. The recitation of such tales is clearly more than mere story-telling; it is a magical rite and a religious mystery, the blessings offered being the same as those otherwise conferred by prayer or sacrifice to the gods and reminiscent of those promised to one who recites or listens to Hindu sacred tales such as the *Ramayana*. Transcending simple storytelling, they become prayers because, as in the Aboriginal traditions of Australia, telling these old tales and singing these songs brings new life to the spirits, gods and ancestors referred to in them, restoring them to us as living, breathing entities so that, as Robin Williamson sings in 'Mythic Times,' a song from his 1977 album, *Journey's Edge*, "these are the mythic times, when gods and heroes live."

The power of ancient tales has impacted my life many times and in many ways. Visiting a Neolithic burial mound in Wiltshire that pagan Anglo-Saxons had named after the god, Woden, I was relating the bare bones of his Norse avatar Odin's quest for wisdom, as recorded in the 13th century in a poem called *Hávamál*, 'Words of the High One,' when the story reached out and pulled me in. The Sun setting behind the mound cast into deep shadow a hollow at its eastern end caused by tomb robbers. Standing at its lip, I spoke of Odin's sacrifice of himself to himself as he hung for nine nights on the World Tree, pierced with his own spear. Below him yawned the cosmic chasm of Ginnungagap, into which he reached to retrieve the secret of Runes. Grasping them caused such pain that he screamed aloud. As I related this, the letters of the Runic alphabet formed in the shadowy hollow below me, swirling together into a golden whirlpool. Reaching down to grasp them, they burned the palm of my hand. Stepping back, I looked round for my companions and there above us loomed the tall figure of Woden, gazing steadily at me with his one good eye from beneath the broad brim of his hat, two great ravens perched on his shoulders, two huge wolves standing at his side. That encounter changed my spirituality and impacted my life in many strange, unpredictable ways, the effects of which continue to resonate nearly three decades later. This is just one example among many which show that these ancient tales do indeed retain real power.

Tales of the Gods

Tellers of traditional tales sometimes speak of being aware of previous generations of storytellers standing behind them while they recount the old stories. By allowing ourselves to be open to these spirits of our predecessors, we can learn more about the stories, perhaps recovering parts that have been lost.

The class of stories referred to as myths can reveal the nature of the gods, their births, their powers, how they relate to humankind, and how we may relate to them. Sadly, the term 'myth' has also come to mean something untrue or fanciful. For our ancestors, these tales represented greater truths taking place on a heightened plane of reality. This is the sense we need to recover if we are to unlock the full potential of these legends to inform and transform our lives.

Since they often identify places and times linked to particular deities, stories of the old gods can suggest where and when rites in their honour should be performed. So the Irish goddess Brighid is associated with, among others, a sanctuary in County Kildare where a perpetual flame burned in her honour, and Tober Breda, a holy well in County Cork. A Christian saint named Brigit took over the role of her pagan predecessor and her feast day of February 1st- 2nd, the old Irish festival of *Imbolc*, known in Wales as *Gwyl Forwyn*, 'Feast of the Maiden,' and in England as Candlemas. The Christianised goddess is known in Wales as Ffraid. Ceridwen, patroness of bards, is primarily associated with Lake Bala in north Wales. She gave birth to the great bard Taliesin on October 31st (Welsh *Nos Galan Gaeaf*, Irish *Samhain*, English Hallowe'en) according to some, or April 29th, the eve of May Day (Welsh *Calan Mai*, Irish *Beltaine*) according to others. His rebirth from the coracle in which she cast him into the sea occurred at the mouth of the River Conwy in North Wales or, according to others, on the shores of Cardigan Bay in West Wales, between Dyfi and Aberystwyth.

One of the great joys of our medieval literature is that it is full of such references to identifiable times and places linked with legendary characters. This enables us to visit the places where the events occurred, often at the very time of year when they happened, thereby absorbing more of their power from the magical conjunction of time and place that initially gave rise to the legends.

Cycles of the Sun

Many surviving Celtic myths seem to trace the life cycle of a god of light from birth at Midwinter, through to the height of his strength at Midsummer and his death at Hallowe'en. The events of this cycle are usually driven by the relationship of the god to one or more goddesses. One example is the Welsh legend of Lleu Llaw Gyffes which forms part of the tale of 'Math, son of Mathonwy,' featured in the collection of medieval Welsh legends known as the *Mabinogion*. This tells how Arianrhod [pron. Arry-ANN-hrod], 'Silver Wheel,' gives birth to Lleu ('Light') and his twin brother, Dylan eil Ton, ('Ocean son of Wave') as she steps over a staff held by the shadowy enchanter, Math ('Bear'). Since Lleu embodies light, his birth most likely takes place close to *Alban Arthan*, 'Birth of the Bear Quarter,' at Midwinter, December 25th, when the Sun has passed its lowest point at the winter solstice and been reborn, as shown by its rising position on the horizon beginning to move north again.

Lleu is taken by Gwydion ap Dôn [GWUDDY-onn app DAWN], the archetypal Druid of Welsh tradition, whose name may be loosely translated as 'Lord of the Wildwood.' Gwydion finds a nurse to suckle the boy, who grows with supernatural speed. Gwydion then takes the child to Arianrhod, who lays a curse on him that he shall never have a name unless she herself gives one to him. Gwydion and Lleu disguise themselves as shoe-makers and return to Arianrhod's castle in a boat. When Lleu throws a needle through the leg of a wren, Arianrhod comments, "the light-haired one has a steady hand," thus giving the child his name, Lleu Llaw Gyffes, 'Light of the Steady Hand.' This brings us to *Gwyl Forwyn*, Candlemas (February 1st-2nd), a festival associated with light and with the suckling of young lambs.

Having been tricked into naming Lleu, Arianrhod says that he will never bear arms unless she herself arms him. Gwydion and Lleu then disguise themselves as bards and Gwydion entertains the goddess and her court with his story-telling. Next morning Gwydion magically creates the sound of an army surrounding the castle, causing Arianrhod to arm all her guests, including Lleu. The arming of the young god seems appropriate to the spring equinox (Welsh *Alban Eilir*, 'Birth of the Spring Quarter,' around March 21st), when day and night are of equal length but the Sun is beginning to grow in strength.

Enraged at having been tricked a second time, Arianrhod proclaims that Lleu shall never have a wife born of woman. Gwydion and Math then use their magic to create a wife for Lleu from flowers of oak, broom and meadowsweet, naming her Blodeuwedd, meaning 'Flower-face.' This takes us to *Calan Mai*, 'May Calends' (Irish *Beltaine*, May Day, May 1st), when young maidens are traditionally bedecked with flowers and choose young men to companion them in May Day revels. Blodeuwedd seems a fitting archetype for the Queen of the May.

Lleu is given an area of land on which to set up his court. This takes us to *Alban Hefin*, 'Birth of the Summer Quarter,' Midsummer, when the Sun is at its height and the god reaches the peak of his powers, reigning over the land in glory. The marriage of Lleu and Blodeuwedd is appropriate to the next festival in the cycle, *Gwyl Awst* (Irish *Lughnasad*,

Lammas, August 1st), a traditional time for the celebration of weddings or handfastings in Celtic countries.

One day, while Lleu is absent, Blodeuwedd sees a huntsman, Goronwy, pursue and kill a stag. She invites him to her castle where they feast and then sleep together. This takes us to the harvest festival of *Alban Elfed*, 'Birth of the Ripe Quarter' (on or about September 21st), the autumn equinox, when day and night are again of equal length, but the Sun's power begins to wane towards Midwinter. It is also the height of the hunting season in the British Isles.

Blodeuwedd and Goronwy conspire to kill Lleu with a magical spear. This brings us to *Nos Galan Gaeaf*, 'the Night of Winter Calends' (English Hallowe'en, Irish *Samhain*, October 31st-November 2nd). At this time the gates between this world and the realm of the ancestors stand open and the souls of the dead ride the night with the Wild Huntsman and his pack of baying, red-eared hounds. The reign of the lord of light comes to an end and that of the dark lord of winter begins.

As Lleu dies, his spirit leaves his body in the form of an eagle, ancient symbol of sovereignty. The eagle rests in an oak tree where it is found by Gwydion who is led to the spot by a sow. The sow represents the goddess in her dark, winter aspect (page 80). Gwydion charms the eagle down from the oak tree with the following spell:

> Oak that grows between two plains;
> Darkened is the sky and hill.
> Shall I not know him by his wounds,
> That this is Lleu?
>
> Oak that grows in an upland plain,
> Is it not wetted by the rain? Has it not been soaked
> By nine score tempests?
> It bears in its branches Lleu Llaw Gyffes.
>
> Oak that grows beneath the steep;
> Stately and majestic is its aspect.
> Shall I not address it thus,
> That Lleu may come to my lap?

Thus enchanted, the eagle descends from the tree and Gwydion touches it with his staff, restoring Lleu to human shape. This magical resurrection brings us back to Midwinter. Perhaps Lleu is embodied in the white berries of mistletoe, deemed especially sacred when found growing on an oak tree (page 52).

Gwydion and Lleu then pursue Blodeuwedd into the mountains,

where she is transformed into an owl by Gwydion, a fitting end for a goddess who has turned her back on her husband, the lord of light, to align herself with the dark lord of winter. This may have occurred at *Gwyl Forwyn*, some folk celebrations of which include a mock battle between the forces of summer and winter.

Goronwy is pursued to the banks of the river where Lleu himself had been slain. Goronwy shields himself with a standing stone, but Lleu casts a magical spear, piercing both the stone and Goronwy. The stone may still exist in the form of *Llech Ronw*, 'the Stone of Gronw,' a holed stone slab that stands beside the Afon Bryn Saeth in Blaenau Ffestiniog, North Wales. The slaying of Goronwy presumably takes place at *Calan Mai*, the traditional end of the year's winter half. May Eve marks the end of the hunting season for red deer stags in the UK.

A conflict between summer and winter is mentioned in the Welsh tale of Culhwch and Olwen [pron. KILL-hooch and OLL-when], where Creiddylad [Cry-THE-lad] 'Fresh Flowing,' daughter of the god Lludd [ᶜʰthleethe], is betrothed to Gwythyr ap Greidawl [GWUTHur app GR-EYE-Dowl], 'Anger, son of Scorcher,' an appropriate name for a fiery Sun god. However, Gwyn ap Nudd, 'White, son of Cloud, or Mist,' clearly a winter god, carries Creiddylad away. King Arthur is called upon to make peace between them and gives judgement that the maiden should remain in her father's house, and that Gwyn and Gwythyr should fight for her every first of May until the day of doom, and that whichever of them should then be the victor should have the maiden.

This has clear parallels with the Greek myth of Persephone, also known as Kore, 'the Maiden,' which tells how she is taken by Hades, dark Lord of the Underworld. This results in the death and decay of vegetation in the upper world until the god Hermes travels to the Underworld and persuades Hades to give up Persephone for part of the year. Her return to the upper world was celebrated in ancient Greece on February 1st. Her descent into the Underworld was annually re-enacted as part of the Greater Eleusian Mysteries over a nine day period around the autumn equinox, when the harvest had been gathered in and new seed was being sown in the earth. Similar rites would presumably have been celebrated among Iron Age Celts in honour of their own deities.

An Irish legend preserves what may be a ritual dialogue from such a celebratory rite. The pagan gods of Ireland, the Tuatha Dé Danann, the 'Clan of the goddess Anu,' are feasting on the sacred hill of Tara when a young man, Lugh Lamhfada [pron. Loo l-ow-varda], 'Light of the Long Arm,' comes to the door of the hall. The door-keeper challenges him, asking his name and his profession, "for no one is admitted here unless he is master of some craft." "I am a carpenter," says Lugh. "We have no need of a carpenter," says the door-keeper, "We already have a very good one; his name is Luchtaine." "I am an excellent smith," says Lugh. "We do not need one. We have a very good smith; his name is Goibniu [pron. Goyvnoo]." "I am a professional warrior." "We have no need of one. Ogma is our champion."

The exchange continues, with Lugh stating that he is "a harpist," "a warrior renowned for skilfulness rather than mere strength," "a poet and story-teller," "a Druid," "a physician," "a cup-bearer," and "a worker in bronze." The doorkeeper replies that they already have someone within who has each of these skills. Lugh then tells him to ask the king "if he has with him a man who is master of all these crafts at once, for, if he has, there is no need for me to come to Tara." Lugh is invited in and hailed as *Ioldanach*, 'Master of All Arts.'

A similar ritual exchange occurs in the tale of Culhwch and Olwen. In this instance, the court is not that of the gods, but of King Arthur, and the feast takes place on January 1st, New Year's Day. Speeches like these may have been part of ritual dramas performed at great public ceremonies. The modern concept of theatre originated in divine dramas staged at religious festivals in ancient Greece. Such performances were more than mere play-acting. The actors were seen as living embodiments of the gods and goddesses they portrayed, and as channels for their power. The enactment of a myth recreates it for the audience, renewing its spiritual power, re-awakening the gods, restoring their energy to the land and people. Herein lies the true potency of the bardic tradition.

In Britain and Ireland, we are peculiarly blessed with an abundance of ancient myths, legends and legendary histories, recorded in manuscripts mainly dating from the 12th century or later but containing material that must be rooted several centuries earlier since it tells of the activities of the pagan gods of our ancestors. What follows is a brief guide to this treasure trove of inspiration.

The *Mabinogion*

In the British story-telling tradition, one source towers above all others; the medieval Welsh collection known as the *Mabinogion*. This title is actually a scribal error by an early copyist who failed to realise that *Mabinogi* is already a plural, making the plural ending, '*on*,' redundant. This error was perpetuated by Lady Charlotte Guest, the first translator of the whole collection into English. Her hugely successful translation was originally published in seven volumes between 1838 and 1845 under the title, *The Mabinogion*, and the name has stuck ever since, so we shall use it here. The more correct *Mabinogi*, meaning something like 'Youthful Tales,' may be equivalent to the category of Irish bardic stories known as *Macgnimartha*, 'Youthful Exploits.' The name may indicate that these were tales told to the young, or perhaps stories from the youth of the world.

The tales that comprise the *Mabinogion* were probably first written down in the 12ᵗʰ century, possibly in South-west Wales by a gathering of bards called together by a warrior princess named Gwenllian (circa 1100-1136), as part of an increased interest in preserving native traditions spurred by the threat of Anglo-Norman invasion. They may have been compiled specifically for her eight children. The two primary manuscripts in which they are found are the *White Book of Rhydderch* (circa 1375) and the *Red Book of Hergest* (circa 1400).

Strictly speaking, the term *Mabinogion* applies only to the first four of the eleven tales commonly linked together under this title. Collectively known as the Four Branches, these are 'Pwyll Prince of Dyfed,' 'Brân the Blessed, son of Llyr,' 'Manawyddan son of Llyr,' and 'Math son of Mathonwy.'

The Four Branches

In the First Branch, Pwyll [pron. POOL^{ch}th], ruler of the kingdom of Dyfed [DOVE-edd] in South Wales, changes places with Arawn, Lord of the Underworld of Annwn [ANNoon], and fights a battle against a rival Underworld lord in his stead. He triumphs, earning Arawn's lasting friendship, which is demonstrated by the gift of a herd of pigs, creatures previously unknown in the upper world of the living. Pwyll marries a magical horsewoman called Rhiannon [hRree-ANN-on], 'Great Queen.' They have a child, Pryderi [pry-DERRy], born on May Eve on the same night as a mare gives birth to a foal. The child being stolen (as is the foal), Rhiannon is accused of killing him and punished by being made to act as a horse, carrying visitors to the court on her back. The family are eventually reunited and Pryderi is given the foal. Her obvious horse connections have led many to see Rhiannon as a euphemised horse goddess, perhaps related to the widespread Romano-Celtic goddess, Epona. The ancient sanctity of horses in Britain is graphically demonstrated in the flowing lines of the Uffington White Horse, a chalk hill figure first carved into the flanks of a steep escarpment during the Bronze Age and preserved ever since by regular scourings undertaken by local people in the Vale of the White

Horse in Oxfordshire.

The Second Branch tells how Branwen, 'White Raven,' daughter of the sea god Llyr, is wedded to Matholwch [Math-OL-ooch], king of Ireland. Her brother, the giant Bendigaid Frân [BenDY-Guide Vran], 'Blessed Raven,' gives Matholwch a magic cauldron that can restore the dead to life. Matholwch takes Branwen to Ireland, where he mistreats her and forces her to work as a kitchen maid. She asks a bird to carry news of her mistreatment to Brân, who wades across the Irish sea towing a fleet of warships behind him. Branwen is rescued, but all except seven of the Welsh force are killed and Brân himself mortally wounded. The seven who escape include Pryderi, the sea god Manawyddan [Man-awe-WU-THan] and the bard, Taliesin. They return to Wales and Brân asks that his head be cut off and buried in the White Mount, where the Tower of London now stands, to protect Britain from invasion. Having cut off Brân's head, the seven feast for a year at Harlech, where the head continues to speak with them and their sorrows are soothed by the three birds of Rhiannon who sing to them each day. As said, Brân means 'Raven,' and a flock of ravens are still kept in the Tower of London. A late recorded tradition has it that should they leave the Tower the country will fall to invasion. Ravens are extremely intelligent and have a long reputation as oracular birds. Their frequent ritual burial in Iron Age and Romano-British contexts suggests the intriguing possibility that they may have been companions to Druids.

In the Third Branch, Pwyll having been killed, Manawyddan marries Rhiannon, thereby gaining sovereignty over Dyfed. The land then falls under a spell that causes all of its inhabitants and their houses to vanish, except for the central characters in the tale. Rhiannon and her son Pryderi enter a magical *caer* or 'fortification,' where they find a golden cauldron beside a fountain. When they touch the cauldron, both they and the *caer* disappear. Manawyddan restores Rhiannon, Pryderi and the land of Dyfed by capturing a mouse who is, in fact, the wife of the enchanter who caused their disappearance, threatening to hang her if he does not remove his spell.

The Fourth Branch, arguably the strangest of the group, tells how the enchanter Gwydion and his brother Gilfaethwy abuse their magic arts to obtain from Pryderi the pigs that the Lord of Annwn had sent to him from the Otherworld. Pryderi pursues them across Wales until he is slain by Gwydion. With Gwydion's connivance, Gilfaethwy rapes Goewin, the foot-holder of Math, lord of Gwynedd in North Wales. Math's foot-holder must be a virgin. When Goewin tells Math what has happened, he punishes Gwydion and Gilfaethwy by using his magic staff to transform them into three pairs of animals, each for a year, during which they mate together and produce three sons, Bleiddwn, Hyddwn, Hychddwn Hir, whose names translate as 'Wolf Cub,' 'Stag,' and 'Tall Dark Boar.' Goewin tells Math he must find someone to take her place. Math chooses Arianrhod, and so begins the cycle outlined earlier (pages 102-5), of Lleu Llaw Gyffes and his flower-bride, Blodeuwedd, at the end of which Lleu becomes lord of Gwynedd and Blodeuwedd is changed into an owl.

The remaining seven tales that make up the *Mabinogion* are known as the Four Independent Native Tales, and the Three Romances.

The Four Independent Native Tales

The first of the Independent Native Tales, 'The Dream of Macsen Wledig,' recalls a historical 4th century Roman general, Magnus Maximus ('Macsen'), who, in 383 CE, was proclaimed Emperor by the troops under his command in Britain. Taking most of his army to the continent, he defeated the existing Emperor, Gratian, in battle near Paris. After marching on Rome, Magnus was recognised as Emperor of the western Roman Empire, ruling Britain, Gaul, Spain and Africa from his capital at Trier in France. In the story, Macsen pursues a woman called Helen of the Hosts, whom he first encounters in a dream. He finds her in a castle on the isle of Anglesey and marries her. Some believe Helen may originally have been a pagan British goddess. Both she and Macsen have been claimed as ancestors by various Welsh dynasties. The historical Magnus was defeated in battle and executed in 388 CE.

'The Story of Lludd and Llevelys' [pron. [ch]lleethe and [ch]llev-ELLis] tells of two brothers, rulers of Britain and France respectively, during whose time three plagues fall upon Britain. The first is caused by a strange race called the Coranians, the second by a conflict between two dragons, and the third by a powerful giant. Through the wise advice of his brother, Lludd defeats all three. Known as Lludd Llaw Ereint [[ch]llow EReyent], 'Lludd of the Silver Hand,' Lludd is believed to have originally been Nudd, equivalent to Nuada Airgetlam, 'Nuada of the Silver Hand,' warrior king of the Irish gods, the Tuatha Dé Danann. Nudd and Nuada have both been linked with the Romano-British god, Nodens or Nodons, whose name in inscriptions is often linked with that of Mars, the Roman god of war.

'Culhwch and Olwen' is a deliciously strange, archaic tale that tells how a fate is laid on the young Culhwch by his step-mother that he will never have a wife unless it be Olwen, daughter of a fearsome, one-eyed giant called Yspaddaden Penkawr [Isspa-THADun PENkowr], whose name means 'Hawthorn, Chief Giant.' Culhwch asks his cousin,

King Arthur, to help him win Olwen. Culhwch and six knights find Yspaddaden's castle. Olwen comes to meet them, and "four white trefoils sprung up wherever she trod. And therefore she was called Olwen, 'White Track'." Yspaddaden casts three spears at the knights, who throw them back, wounding the giant in the leg, chest, and eye. Yspaddaden then agrees to part with his daughter if Culhwch can complete a number of tasks. One is to hunt down a huge wild boar, the Twrch Trwyth. This requires locating and releasing an imprisoned youth, the great huntsman, Mabon ap Modron, 'Child, son of Mother.' Many connect Mabon with a Romano-British god, Maponus or Maponos, whose cult is centred on northern England and southern Scotland. An image on an altar (RIB 583) from Lancashire shows him as a young man armed with a bow, his name linked with that of the Roman Apollo. Culhwch and his companions seek out the oldest animals in the world, an ousel (blackbird), a stag, an owl, an eagle, and finally a salmon who shows them the castle where Mabon is imprisoned. Arthur's warriors attack the castle and release him. As they pursue the boar across Britain, it kills many knights before they finally overtake it. They return to Yspaddaden, laden with all the magical treasures he had asked Culhwch to obtain, and the giant finally gives up Olwen. This strange, darkly magical tale ends with the son of Yspaddaden's herdsman cutting off the giant's head and placing it on a stake atop the castle.

The last of the Independent Native Tales is 'The Dream of Rhonabwy [Hrronn-AB-wee].' This tells how Rhonabwy and his companions seek shelter one night in a strange hall, the interior of which is gloomy, filthy and inhabited only by a toothless crone. Rhonabwy sleeps on a yellow ox-hide on a raised dais for three nights and three days, during which he has a vision of King Arthur playing a board game called *gwyddbwyll* [GWUTHbool^{ch}th], 'wooden wisdom,' with Owein [O-Wine], son of Urien Rheged [OORry-enn hREGGed]. As the two men play, their game is paralleled by a conflict between Arthur's knights and a group of ravens belonging to Owein. The presence of ravens suggests that *gwyddbwyll* is a Welsh equivalent to an Irish game called *brandub*, 'black raven.' Both games seem to have had ritual significance and may have been used for divination. Other sources suggest that bull or ox-hides were wrapped around bards seeking oracular visions during sleep.

The Three Romances

The first of the Three Romances is 'The Lady of the Fountain,' another early Arthurian tale featuring Owein ap Urien. A knight named

Cynon tells how a man takes him to a castle inhabited by twenty-four women. The man directs Cynon to go at daybreak to a grassy mound where he will find a black giant armed with a huge iron club and surrounded by animals. Cynon finds the giant, who summons thousands of animals to him by striking a stag, causing him to cry out. The animals bow down to the giant as if to their master. The giant directs Cynon to a magical fountain beneath a tree. The knight goes to the fountain, fills a silver vessel he finds there with water, throws it over a stone and a great storm erupts, stripping the leaves from the tree. When the storm abates, hundreds of birds come and perch in the bare branches, singing. A black knight on a black horse appears, defeats Cynon, and sends him back the way he came. Owein repeats Cynon's adventure except that he defeats the black knight and pursues him to a great city. The black knight, who is lord of the city, dies and Owein sees his widow, the Lady of the Fountain, mourning her loss. He falls in love with her, marries her and takes the place of the black knight, defending the fountain that marks the border of her realm. After a while he returns to Arthur's court promising to return, but forgets to do so. When he finally recalls the Lady he flees into the forest in shame and lives among wild animals, passing through further conflicts and adventures before eventually winning her back and returning with her to Arthur's court. The fountain seems to stand on the border between our world and a Faery otherworld. Owein is able to cross over into that otherworld after defeating the fountain's guardian.

The romance of 'Peredur son of Efrawg' is a kind of British *Don Quixote*, dealing with the adventures of an innocent abroad in ways that are both humorous and oddly pagan. Having been raised with no knowledge of weapons, horsemanship or other knightly skills, Peredur nevertheless takes himself to King Arthur's court to be ordained a knight. Arthur's knights make fun of him and the old nag he rides. Cei, one of Arthur's men, sends him out to fight a knight who has insulted Arthur's wife, Gwenhwyfar (Guinevere), promising that if Peredur wins he will be made a knight. He does win but refuses to enter the court until he avenges the blows Cei struck two dwarfs who had greeted Peredur kindly. Peredur rides off, defeating many other knights in Arthur's name before ending up at the court of nine witches who teach him skill with weapons and horses. Peredur then fights and defeats Cei and returns to Arthur's court. There, he falls in love with a woman called Angharad Golden-hand, who fails to return his love. Vowing that he will not speak until she comes to love him, he rides out again from the court. He encounters and subdues a race of pagan giants and a huge serpent before returning, defeating another

111

mysterious knight, and finally winning the love of Angharad. One day, while hunting a stag in the forest, Peredur comes to a hall where he encounters a one-eyed giant whose missing eye was lost fighting a black serpent that lives in a barrow mound. Peredur sets out for the mound and slays the serpent, stopping off on the way at another castle of women who have a magic cauldron from which the dead emerge alive and killing a monster called Addanc who dwells in a cave with a standing stone at its entrance. Peredur returns once more to Arthur's court, where a hideous hag comes to him and sets him off on yet another adventure, to seek out a Castle of Wonders where he will gain wisdom. The tale ends in an appropriately weird and dark way, with Peredur slaying the nine witches who had previously been his teachers.

The third romance, that of 'Gereint [GER-eye-nt] son of Erbin,' tells how Arthur and his knights go hunting for a white stag. Throughout the *Mabinogion*, white animals are seen to be otherworldly, often providing a link between the everyday world and other realities. Gereint and Gwenhwyfar are left behind and see a woman on a white horse accompanied by a giant knight and a dwarf. Gereint follows this curious trio and reaches a castle where he is shown hospitality by an elderly couple and their beautiful daughter, Enid. The old man arms Gereint, who defeats the giant. Gereint marries Enid but comes to believe, quite wrongly, that she loves another. The two set out on horseback. Gereint orders Enid to be silent but each time she hears knights plotting to attack him she breaks her silence to warn him. He slays several groups of knights, receiving many wounds himself. He fights three giants, the third striking him a blow which opens up all his previous wounds. He is carried, apparently dying, to a castle. The lord of the castle strikes Enid, causing her to cry out. At this, Gereint finally realises that Enid truly loves him and rises up, killing the lord and terrifying the rest of the castle's inhabitants who think he has risen from the dead. Gereint is healed, but hears of a 'hedge of mist' behind which enchanted games are held and from which none have ever returned. Riding into the mist, he finds himself in an orchard where a hunting-horn hangs from an apple-tree and a solitary maiden sits on one of a pair of golden thrones. Gereint sits in the other although the maiden warns him that the chieftain who owns it will be angry. The chieftain arrives and challenges Gereint, who defeats him. The chieftain asks for mercy which Gereint grants provided he causes the magical mist to disappear and puts an end to the deadly games. The chieftain tells Gereint to sound the hunting-horn and when he does the mist disperses and he is reunited with Enid. They return to his lands in Cornwall, where Gereint rules prosperously for the rest of his days. It seems likely that the orchard within the hedge of mist is another otherworldly location or Faery realm.

These tales, then, are full of wonder and weirdness, magic and marvels, often with what appear to be pagan motifs. Some feature prominent mounds on which heroes experience strange visions, as do their Irish equivalents when seated on, or entering into, *sidhe* [pron. Shee] mounds, *sidhe* being the Faery folk, among whom the pagan gods of Ireland seem to form an aristocratic elite. The *Mabinogion* stories suggest that similar associations were made in medieval Wales. Also in common with some Irish tales, the use of magic by Math, Gwydion and others echoes the powers attributed to Druids.

The Story of Taliesin

A Welsh legend of particular significance for British Druid bards is the previously mentioned *Hanes* ('Story of') *Taliesin,* telling of the witch-like Ceridwen, her husband, Tegid Foel, 'Beautiful Bald One,' and their children; Creirwy [CRYER-wee], 'Jewel Egg(?),' and Afagddu [AvAGGthee], 'Utter Darkness,' also known as Morfran [MORE-vran], 'Cormorant.' Afagddu is so ugly that Ceridwen decides to make him all-wise to compensate. She therefore brews a magic cauldron of inspiration (*awen*) that has to boil for a year and a day. While she gathers herbs for the brew, she leaves an old blind man called Morda and a child named Gwion Bach, 'Little Innocent,' looking after the cauldron. On the last day, three drops of the potion splash onto Gwion's hand and he puts it to his mouth, thereby gaining the gifts of poetry, prophecy, and shape-shifting. The rest of the brew is rendered not only useless but poisonous and the cauldron bursts apart. On her return, Ceridwen flies into a rage, pursuing Gwion as they go through a series of transformations in which he becomes a hare, she a greyhound, he a fish, she an otter, he a small bird, she a hawk. Eventually, Gwion becomes a grain of wheat and is eaten by Ceridwen in the shape of a black hen. Nine months later she gives birth, puts the baby in a leather bag or, more likely, a coracle, and casts him into the sea. Next morning he is found by a prince named Elphin who has the vessel opened. It is remarked that the baby has a radiant brow, so he is named Taliesin, meaning 'Radiant Brow.' The infant immediately creates his first poem and soon becomes Primary Chief Bard, first to the Court of Elphin, then to the whole of Britain.

This tale has been interpreted as a series of initiations into the roles of bard, ovate and Druid, to whom the gifts of poetry, prophecy and shape-shifting are central. Hence the centrality of the idea of Ceridwen's cauldron as the primary source of inspiration, of *awen*. Elements of the story appear in some of the poems found in the early 14th century *Book of Taliesin*.

Welsh bard, archaeologist and friend of the BDO, Frank Olding, is currently (August, 2022) working on a book containing new translations of all the poems attributed to Taliesin and the stories about him.

Arthur, Merlin & the Matter of Britain

Another major category of British bardic tales consists of those relating to King Arthur and his knights, their stories being collectively known as the Matter of Britain. Arthur may have been a historical warlord of western Britain in the 6th century CE who fought successfully against the Saxon invaders who had then gained control of the southern and eastern parts of the country. The oldest tales concerning Arthur are those contained in the *Mabinogion* and in early British bardic poetry. In a later tale, the young Arthur becomes king by pulling a sword from a stone. In another, the magical sword, Excalibur, is given to him by the Lady of the Lake who may be another incarnation of the archaic goddess of Sovereignty. Arthur marries Guinevere, the Gwenhwyfar of the *Mabinogion*, and brings together the Knights of the Round Table, an Arthurian equivalent to Finn mac Cool's legendary Irish war-band, the Fianna (page 119). Both Arthur and Finn are said to be sleeping in caves, awaiting their countries' greatest need before they reawaken.

Many of the best-known Arthurian tales appear in later texts, but some are roughly contemporary with the *Mabinogion*, like those concocted by Geoffrey of Monmouth, whose 12th century *History of the Kings of Britain* is one of the principle sources of medieval Arthurian legend. Geoffrey's *History* includes the tale of how Merlin brings a stone circle called the Giants' Ring-Dance from Ireland and has it set up on Salisbury Plain, where it is now known as Stonehenge.

Geoffrey was particularly fascinated by Merlin, mystical adviser to Arthur's father, Uther Pendragon. Merlin uses his magic power to enable Uther to sleep with Arthur's mother, Ygrain, by making him appear to her in the shape of her husband. Geoffrey devotes two whole volumes to the legendary magician, *Prophetiae Merlini*, 'The Prophecies of Merlin,' written around 1130, and *Vita Merlini*, 'The Life of Merlin,' dating from about twenty years later. His Merlin is an amalgam of two men, both called Myrddin, who combine the skills of bard, ovate and Druid. Writing in Latin for a Norman French audience, Geoffrey may have thought it wise to change the name to Merlin because, when spoken, the Welsh Myrddin can sound uncomfortably like the French *merde*.

One of the two, Myrddin Emrys, 'Merlin Ambrosius,' is portrayed as a prophet, magician and advisor to the 5th century British King Vortigern. Legend tells how Vortigern tried to build a castle at Dinas Emrys in north Wales, but every night an earthquake caused it to collapse. Myrddin Emrys eventually divined that two dragons, one red, one white, were engaged in violent nightly combat in a lake beneath the site.

The second is Myrddin Wyllt, 'Merlin the Wild,' a household bard in 6th century Scotland. In around 575 he was present at a horrific battle and siege during which he saw his patron and all his companions killed. As a result, he suffered a mental breakdown, fled human society and lived for many years in a cave in a remote valley in the Forest of Celydon on the Scottish borders with a pig and a wolf for company, hence his epithet, 'the Wild.' He was clearly afflicted with what we now know as PTSD, post-traumatic stress disorder. Several poems in the mid-13th century *Black Book of Carmarthen* and the late 14th century *Red Book of Hergest* are attributed to him. As well as a bard, he developed a great reputation as an inspired prophet.

An important theme in Arthurian myth is the quest for the Holy Grail, supposed to be the chalice or bowl from which Jesus and his disciples drank at the last supper and/or the vessel in which Christ's blood was caught when he was pierced by a spear as he hung on the cross. Ostensibly a Christian symbol, the Grail can be seen as a version of the various magic cauldrons of pagan legend. Both Grail and cauldron have healing powers, strong feminine associations, and grant wisdom and inspiration, among other gifts.

The Matter of Britain ends with Arthur mortally wounded at the Battle of Camlann and sending Sir Bedivere to cast the sword Excalibur back into the lake from whence it came. Arthur is then borne away to the mystic Isle of Avalon, 'Apple-Land,' which some believe to be Glastonbury Tor in Somerset. Arthur, however, does not die but sleeps, awaiting the time when his country will have need of him once more. Hence he is called *Rex Quondam Futurum*, 'the Once and Future King.'

Arthurian legends have inspired generations of creative artists, from the 15th century poet Sir Thomas Malory, whose epic *Morte d'Arthur* is one of the great classics of English literature, through the artists of the 19th century Pre-Raphaelite Brotherhood to the film-maker, John Boorman, whose *Excalibur* (1981) is perhaps the most successful cinematic rendition of the Matter of Britain to date.

Sir Gawain & the Greene Knight

Of the many legends surrounding individual Knights of the Round Table, perhaps the most remarkable is the 14th century poem 'Sir Gawain and the Greene Knight.' It opens with Arthur and his knights celebrating Christmas and New Year at the court of Camelot. Their feasting is interrupted by the arrival of a huge, green-skinned man, dressed all in green and riding a green horse, holding a holly-branch in one hand and an axe in the other. The Greene Knight challenges the assembled knights to strike his neck with this great axe, with the proviso that he be allowed to strike a blow in return after a year and a day. Gawain accepts the challenge and strikes off the Knight's head with a single blow. The Greene Knight, however, picks up his severed head, which tells Gawain to seek out the Green Chapel after a year and a day to receive the return stroke. The Knight then mounts his green horse and gallops out of the hall.

Gawain journeys in search of the Green Chapel. Towards the end of the year he stays at a castle whose lord goes out hunting each day, telling Gawain that they must give each other whatever they receive during the day. While the lord hunts game, his lady hunts Gawain who reluctantly receives her kisses and later passes them on to her husband in return for his day's catch. On the third day, however, the lady gives Gawain her green silk belt and this he fails to pass on to the lord, knowing he will recognise it. When the time comes, Gawain keeps his appointment at the Green Chapel, a hollow mound beside a stream in a woodland glade. There he meets his opponent and stands to receive the axe-stroke, which cuts him only slightly. He then learns that, had he given the lady's belt to his host, he would have received no hurt at all, for the Greene Knight is none other than the lord, and he and his wife have been testing Gawain. Gawain returns to Camelot wearing the green belt as a symbol of his shame at having deceived his host, but Arthur's knights and their ladies think his adventure so worthy that they decide all Knights of the Round Table should henceforth wear a green belt.

Several legends recorded in the medieval literature of Wales are paralleled a few short miles across the sea in Ireland, and it is to that storied isle that we now turn our attention.

Ireland: The Mythological Cycle

Many of the foremost legends of Ireland are grouped into cycles dealing with the exploits of one or more central characters.

The Mythological Cycle is centred on a collection of tales known as

Lebor Gabála Érenn, 'The Book of the Taking of Ireland,' the earliest version of which is recorded in the 12th century *Book of Leinster*. This tells of five groups of invaders who come to Ireland before its current inhabitants, the Gaels. The first group consists primarily of women, led by Cessair. All her party die in a catastrophic flood except for her consort, Fintan mac Bochra, 'White Fire son of Ocean,' who lives on through all the subsequent arrivals. Fintan changes shape, becoming in turn a salmon, an eagle, and a hawk. The salmon is a giver of wisdom, the eagle symbolic of sovereignty. Irish bards looked to Fintan as the supreme authority in matters of tradition. With his store of ancient learning, Fintan is an archetype of the Druid bard, a role paralleling that of Taliesin in Wales. A number of later Druids share his name, as a number of later bards used the name of the 6th century 'historical' Taliesin, perhaps seeing themselves as reincarnations of their spirits. Fintan, or a later incarnation of him, appeared to Diarmaid mac Cearrbheoil [pron. Dermot mac Kurveal], the last pagan High King of Ireland, who reigned during the 6th century.

The second group of invaders is led by Partholon. He and all his followers save one perish in a plague. The sole survivor is Tuan mac Starn, whose story closely resembles that of Fintan. Tuan transforms into a stag, a wild boar and, like Fintan, an eagle and a salmon. In salmon form, he is caught and eaten by the wife of Cairell who later gives birth to him as Tuan mac Cairell. The 6th century Christian Saint Finnian is said to have interviewed this incarnation of Tuan and caused his story to be written down, preserving it for posterity.

The third invasion is led by Nemed. After many tribulations, his followers are forced to leave Ireland, but their descendants lead the next two invasions. The fourth group are the Fir Bolg, who seem to have been the earliest Celtic inhabitants of Ireland.

The fifth invasion brings the Tuatha Dé Danann, the 'Clan of the goddess Anu,' to Ireland. They are the gods of the Gaels, the second group of Celts to inhabit the land. The Gaelic gods include among their number the Dagda, or 'Good God,' the god of Druidcraft, presented in the literature as a sturdy, porridge-eating giant with a massive wooden club, a magical cauldron of plenty and a living harp carved from a single block of oak. Other members of the Tuatha Dé are the Morrigna, 'Great Queens,' a a trinity of fearsome battle-goddesses able to transform themselves into ravens, wolves, cows, horses or serpents; Nuada Airgetlam, 'Cloud of the Silver Hand,' sword-wielding ruler of the gods; and Brighid, 'Bright, or Powerful One,' daughter of the Dagda and goddess of childbirth, brewing, smithcraft and poetry.

The Tuatha Dé defeat the Fir Bolg in a great battle, and in a second conflict defeat the Fomoire, who may have been the gods of the Fir Bolg. This second battle, in which both sides invoke powerful magical forces, forms the climax of *Lebor Gabála Érenn*. After Nuada loses his arm in battle, Lugh, the young god of light, leads the immortal Tuatha Dé to victory, thereby clearing the way for the mortal Gaels to take possession of the country. After this the Fomoire and the Fir Bolg retire to the province of Connacht in the west of Ireland where they dwell still among the ancient stones and burial mounds that adorn its misty landscape. Some say that with the coming of Christianity, the Tuatha Dé themselves withdrew into the *sidhe*, the Faery mounds of Ireland, and live there still.

The Ulster Cycle

The Ulster Cycle centres on the great Irish hero, Cú Chulainn [pron. Koo-hullan]. As a child, the young warrior visits Cullan, an otherworld smith who lives on or in Slieve Gullion, a volcanic mountain in the south of County Armagh, Northern Ireland (pages 36-7). There he is attacked by Cullan's huge, fearsome guard dog. Despite his youth and small stature, he swiftly kills the great hound. In recompense, he takes the dog's place, thus earning his name, which means 'Hound of Cullan.'

Central to this cycle is the epic *Táin Bó Cúailnge*, the 'Cattle Raid of Cooley.' This tells of Cú Chulainn's single-handed defence of the province of Ulster against an army drawn from the other four provinces of Ireland and led by the warrior queen Maeve of Connacht, who wants to capture the magical Brown Bull of Cooley. Maeve's name in its original Irish form, *Medb*, means 'intoxication' and is the same as that of the honey-based alcoholic drink, mead, that was the foremost sacred intoxicant of our ancestors. Maeve times her attack for when the Ulster warriors are laid low by a periodic sickness that leaves them debilitated and unable to fight. Not having been born in Ulster, Cú Chulainn is immune. He is aided in the conflict by his father, the god Lugh, but hindered by the fierce goddess, the Morrigan, who is angered by his spurning of her sexual advances. In a particularly poignant scene, he is forced to face his own foster-brother in single combat at a ford. After battling alone for many days, Cú Chulainn is fatally wounded but uses his belt to tie himself to a standing stone so that even in death he will not fall before his enemies. In some versions, as he dies, the Morrigan perches on his shoulder in the form of a carrion crow.

If you find it hard to get into medieval literature, seek out Thomas Kinsella's English translation of *Táin Bó Cúailnge*. Called simply *The*

Tain and first published in 1969, it has been reprinted several times since and is the finest modern English rendering of any medieval tale I've found in nearly fifty years of reading them. Kinsella, who died in 2021 at the age of 93, was a talented poet and brings to his translation a poet's understanding of the sound of words, the layers of meaning they convey, and the emotions they evoke. The result is a medieval tale that moves me to tears every time I read it.

The Fenian Cycle

The Fenian Cycle is centred around the legendary warrior chief, Fionn mac Cumhaill [Finn mac Cool], 'White, son of Hazel,' and his war-band, the Fianna, elite bodyguard to the High Kings of Ireland. As a young man, Finn gains wisdom and clairvoyance by eating one of the salmon of wisdom that swim in the River Shannon. In some versions of the tale, this particular fish is called Fintan, perhaps the salmon incarnation of the aforementioned Fintan mac Bochra, who had been in Ireland since before the Flood. The salmon is given to Finn to cook by an elderly Druid, also called Finn (or Finegas), who has spent seven years fishing the river in the hopes of catching one of the sacred fish. While cooking it, Finn burns his thumb and puts it in his mouth, at which point the aged Druid realises that the salmon is not meant for him and gives it to the young warrior to eat with his blessings.

The tales of Finn and the Fianna involve much magic and mystery and constant traffic with otherworlds and their inhabitants. Finn's son, for example, is named Oisín, meaning 'Fawn,' having been born of an otherworld mother, Sadb, who had been transformed into a doe. Like King Arthur, Finn is said to be not dead but sleeping in a hidden cave surrounded by his warriors, awaiting the hour of his country's greatest need when he and they will rise again.

The Historical Cycle

The Historical Cycle consists of stories concerning the High Kings of Ireland who ruled from the ancient sacred hill of Tara, men such as Conn of the Hundred Battles and Niall of the Nine Hostages. These tales, while not quite in the same wildly magical mould as those of the other Cycles, still have their moments of enchantment. We are told, for example, how Niall obtains the High Kingship after embracing a hideous black hag who asks him for a kiss in return for a drink of water from her well. On receiving his embrace, she is instantly transformed into the most beautiful woman in the world, and when Niall asks, "Who art thou?," she replies "King of Tara, I am Sovereignty ... and your offspring shall rule over every clan." This theme of the hag transformed into a beautiful maiden by an embrace occurs several times in early Irish literature and in British and French ballads and romances.

A World of Legend

We have focused on tales close to my home, but every culture has its own myths and legends that perform similar functions and contain similar motifs. Bards in other lands will not have to look far to find traditional tales of their own cultures, whether it be the Norse legends of Odin, Thor and Freya; the Greek myths of Zeus, Hera and the Olympian gods; their Roman equivalents, Jupiter, Minerva *et al*; the Hindu gods of the *Vedas*, Brahma, Agni, Sarasvati, Shiva; Lakota tales of White Buffalo Calf Woman; the African Fang people and their legends of the sky father, Nzame, and the forest mother, Nyule; or the Buryats of Siberia with their tales of the great bull prince, Buxa Noyon, and the cow mother, Buxtan Xatun. The magic of stories and storytelling is universal.

As well as a store of ancient tales, most cultures have, or once had, their own specialists in the transmission of traditional songs and stories who are or were comparable to the bards of Britain and Ireland. Those great epics, the *Iliad* and the *Odyssey*, are attributed to Homer, a Greek bard who may have lived about 700 BCE. The Brahmans of Vedic India were priests who sang hymns in praise of the gods and were tasked with preserving and passing them on for future generations. The verses that tell of the exploits of Odin, Freya and their kin were the province of the *skald*, Norse equivalent to the Celtic bard. The medieval French *trouvere*, or *troubadour* performed a similar function, passing on songs telling of the exploits of Charlemagne and his knights among others.

Knowing the traditional tales of our own culture can lead to a deeper understanding of who we are, where we come from, and how we relate to our own and other cultures. This in turn helps us relate to our ancestors, both human and divine. Discovering the traditional tales of other cultures reveals how much people all over the world have in common. Wherever we look, fundamental themes are repeated: light and dark forces struggle against each other; mortal heroes stand against overwhelming odds, helped or hindered by the gods; gods and mortals live, love, and die; magicians, priests, Druids, shamans, wise women or medicine people strive to wrest knowledge and power from otherworlds. The fascination of such universal themes ensures that traditional tales continue to exert a timeless magic on the human mind. Hence modern bards not only pass on the old poems, songs and stories but create new ones based on them. Visual artists also find them potent sources of inspiration. The current resurgence of interest in the bardic tradition will hopefully ensure that they are well performed and passed on so that they can continue to inspire future generations.

But why leave it to others to carry the tradition? Why not become a bard yourself? First, find some poems to recite, songs to sing or stories to tell. Several books of British and Irish poetry, songs and myths are listed in the Resources section at the end of this book, as are websites where you can find many more. For those of other cultures, search online or try your local library. Or make your own. Listen to other bards. Recordings listed in the Resources section demonstrate the skills necessary to convey a poem, song or tale clearly and movingly. Of course, seeing a good bard in action remains, as it always was, the best way to learn. Movement and gesture, a look in the eye, direct interaction with an audience, are vital to the art. Again, the Resources section should help you track down a bard or two. Having found the sources and studied the techniques, practice. Share poems, songs and stories with your family and friends or join a story-telling group. This will help you find which material works best for you. You may find songs you absolutely love, but can't quite put across. You may find that stories you didn't think all that wonderful communicate brilliantly to an audience. The best way to find out is by trial and error.

Simple tricks can help keep an audience engaged. One of the most important is variation in tone. Remember, monotone gives us the word monotonous! Vary the volume, use different voices when different characters are speaking, raise and lower the pitch, speak faster when describing a chase or a battle, slower in more emotional passages. Make eye contact with your audience. If not seated in one place to accompany yourself on a harp or other instrument, keep moving, perhaps physically acting out actions in the tale. You could even get members of your audience to act out roles for you. This is not only great fun but makes the story much more memorable. Having a group running around being pigs in the *Mabinogion* story of Math, son of Mathonwy, while other audience members enact Gwydion and his brother trying to drive them around the room across mountains and valleys of the mind, can be simultaneously magical and utterly hilarious!

As suggested earlier, the magical nature of these ancient tales can be enhanced by telling them within a sacred circle. The act of casting the circle before beginning the telling can certainly help an audience find initial focus and retain it throughout the tale.

If you're concerned you might not be able to remember a lengthy tale, a useful trick is to break it down into its main events and characters using as few words as possible. It's usually possible to reduce three or four paragraphs to a single short sentence. Do this for the whole story and you'll have all the main 'beats' of the story and the characters involved in them in a much more readily memorable form. Commit this short-hand synopsis to memory, if necessary refreshing yourself on it just prior to performance. You'll then find you can fill in the gaps between 'beats,' often to an extent you would not have thought possible and even bearing a striking resemblance to the original text. Poems are much harder to reduce down in this way, but then you have rhyme to help you remember, and with songs you have both rhyme and melody.

So much for the nuts and bolts, but there is something else you need to be a bard: trust in the spirit of the material. Recognise that the poem wants to be heard, the song sung, the story to be told, that the characters within them want to come to life through your performance so that your audience will know and feel what those characters have known and felt. The material has a life of its own, you are just its means of transmission. Traditional songs and tales have often been passed down over many generations. Be aware of the line of bards who have sung the songs and told the tales before you. When the spirit of a story takes you, you may sense the presence of previous tellers standing behind you, urging you on. You may hear their voices adding extra phrases or incidents to the tale or reminding you of ones you had forgotten. Then you will know that you have been accepted by the tradition, and that this aspect of the way of the bard has truly opened to you.

In our electronic culture we have come close to losing the art of story-telling, except to our children at bedtime, forgetting that adults too respond to a well-told tale with a warmth, depth of emotion and intimacy that digital screens simply cannot match. There is an undeniable magic to sitting spell-bound around a late night camp-fire, or in a Gorsedd circle by the light of day, as a skilled exponent of the way of the bard paces the floor, unravelling some ancient tale of wonder, of dragons or witches, giants or Faery folk, brave heroes and beautiful maidens, brilliant women and foolish knights, or of the creation of the world. At such times we realise that the bardic arts will never die, for they carry with them a potency as old as the hills, a charm as fresh as spring-water. As my mother used to say, such things are "too good for the children!"

Part Three:
Healing & Awareness: the Path of the Ovate

Chapter 6:
Seership & Divination

We enter now upon the path of the ovate, a path that leads from communication towards understanding. Among the compasses used to navigate this path are seership and divination. Seership is the ability to see into other worlds, including those of nature spirits, the Faery folk and, at times, the future. Through exploring the bardic path, we open ourselves to the flow of *awen*, learning to recognize its presence and channelling it into creativity. The path of the ovate leads to a new understanding of *awen*, now seen as a conduit for information from other worlds. Divination is, literally, the art of communicating with the divine, discovering the will of the gods. If you have no belief in a god or gods, you may think of it as discovering the ways of fate. If you have no belief in fate, you may see it as a means of accessing your subconscious mind. Whatever your world view, divination provides a means to access otherwise hidden information in order to learn about ourselves and the world, to act wisely and live more effectively.

Many of our ancestors believed the patterns of our lives to be mirrored in the stars and other natural phenomena and that our destiny is controlled by fate (Welsh *tynged*), whether seen as an abstract power or the will of the gods. Even in antiquity some questioned this view, but it was the growth of scientific rationalism in the 18th and 19th centuries that produced the more mechanical, deterministic model of the universe that, in theory at least, prevails today. This sees life as an interplay of natural forces that science will one day both fully explain and give us complete control over. The development of chaos theory in the 20th century did much to restore the pagan idea that our lives are inextricably linked with the ebb and flow of seemingly random forces underpinned by subtle connecting threads. Through seership and divination we seek to understand the patterns of our lives in relation to the world around us, often through observing apparently random patterns such as the fall of a coin or card, the flight of birds, the flickering of firelight or shapes in the clouds.

The methods of divination used by Druids are many and varied, some ancient, some modern. Understood in its literal sense as communication with the divine, divination should be approached with the same reverence as prayer or ritual, otherwise it may lose its meaning and degenerate into mere fortune-telling. Before undertaking divination you might like to enhance your appreciation of its spiritual nature by lighting candles, burning incense, perhaps casting a circle. Certainly you should ask your ancestors, gods and guides for help and guidance.

Signs & Omens

Seeking signs and omens in natural phenomena such as clouds, water, fire, the movement of birds or animals, the shapes of trees or rocks or the patterns of the stars combines aspects of seership and divination and is probably as old as humankind itself. In the highlands and islands of Scotland, where seeking signs in nature was once common, it is called *frith* and those who practise it *fritheir*. Sometimes the talent for it is inherited, those who possess it being regarded as members of *Clann an Fhritheir*, 'the Clan of the Seer.' *Frith* is traditionally made before sunrise on the first Monday after each quarter-day (i.e. Candlemas, May Day, Lammas and Hallowe'en) and accompanied by fasting, prayer and meditation on the subject about which information is being sought. Some say the *fritheir* should be barefoot and bareheaded, some that she should begin by walking three times around her hearth fire, harking back to the days when most country folk lived in single-storey, turf-roofed houses heated by an open central fire. With closed or blindfolded eyes, she goes to the door of her house, opens it and places a hand on either door jamb. She then makes a final prayer to the all-seeing god for clarity of vision and understanding, opens her eyes and stares straight in front of her, taking careful note of whatever she may happen to see. If further information is needed the *fritheir* may circle her house once, sunwise, keeping her gaze fixed straight in front of her and again taking note of everything she sees. Tradition holds that it is more difficult to make the *frith* across water, particularly across the sea, the reason being that the spirits who inhabit water are more able and willing than those of the land to confuse the seer's vision.

Often handed down with the technique are instructions as to what sights are lucky (*rathadach*) or unlucky (*rosadach*). To see a brown-skinned man is a good omen. A man coming towards the seer or looking towards her is even better, a man moving or turning away is bad. The sight of a woman is likewise good, unless she is going away from the seer. A man or animal in the process of standing up shows that the one enquired about is casting off a problem or illness that has afflicted them. If they are lying down then the problem will continue. To see a dog, horse, foal, calf or lamb facing the seer is lucky, and to see a sheep is especially fortunate if the query is to do with a journey. To see a duck indicates good fortune for seafarers.

Bad luck is presaged by most members of the crow family, particularly if moving towards the seer. A pig with its back to the seer is a bad sign, as are cats, unless you are on good terms with witches or are a member of one of the Scottish cat clans such as the Mackintoshes or Macphersons. To see a goat is a bad omen for a journey.

A vision in a woodland glade a few years ago gave me a variation on the *frith* technique. When seeking an omen, hold your hands out in front of you at eye level, palms forward, fingers together and pointing upward, thumbs pointing downward, index fingers and thumbs touching. This produces a roughly triangular aperture that frames a small section of the world, helping to keep the attention fixed. For those who find vision-seeking difficult, it has the added advantage that the eyes will sometimes focus at the range of the hands, sometimes on the world beyond. This focusing and de-focusing can help the mind recognize objects, shapes and patterns that might otherwise be missed.

Through techniques such as those outlined, we attune ourselves to receive messages from this world and worlds beyond. With continued practice, we begin to shift our consciousness into a deeper understanding of those otherworlds of spirit, and how they interact with our lives.

Second Sight

This process of attunement can awaken us to direct visionary experience of other worlds. In his *Description of Wales*, the 12th century cleric, Giraldus Cambrensis, 'Gerald of Wales,' writes of a group of seers operating in his day called *awenyddion*, '*awen*-inspired ones,' who went into a trance during which they spoke prophecies in spontaneous verse. Some described the process as like having sweet milk or honey poured on their lips. On waking, they recalled nothing of what they had said. They worked with a companion whose task it was to interpret the poetry they created while in the trance state.

In Scotland, seership is commonly known as 'second sight.' It not only enables us to get glimpses of distant or future events, but also to see otherworld inhabitants such as tree spirits and the Faery folk. The reality or otherwise of such beings has been the subject of much debate. In Druidry, those who remain undecided are encouraged to accept their existence as a catma (see page 4), behaving as if they are objectively real and therefore treating them with due respect. Given the tricks some otherworld inhabitants are wont to play on unwary mortals, this is no more than sound common sense.

The other worlds that exist alongside our own are often said to be hidden from us by a veil of mist, as in the romance of Gereint son of Erbin (pages 112-3). For those gifted with second sight, the mist disperses and the spirits of nature, the Faery folk and their kin are more clearly seen. As we shall see in chapter 9, one of the defining abilities of the Druid is the ability to walk between worlds. To do so without stumbling, it is, of course, necessary to be able to see those worlds. The path of the ovate encourages the development of this ability.

Second sight requires a shift in consciousness. Some are born with an aptitude for it, others develop it as they grow, some work hard over many years to achieve it, some never do. The first requirement is to acknowledge that other worlds exist. The second is best described as a kind of de-focusing on the mundane world that allows visions of other worlds to come through. Here, the de-focusing technique described earlier may prove helpful. As with other talents, the way to develop it is either through good teaching or through lots of practice, preferably both. Those who are experienced in journeying between the worlds may act as guides, taking you on such a journey to awaken you to the sight of the spirit world, and to awaken the spirit world to you. Don't be in too much of a hurry though, for second sight may bring visions of ugliness as well as beauty, death as well as life. This is why many of those born with 'the sight' regard it as a curse rather than a blessing.

Learning to deal with both darkness and light is a vital part of the ovate path. Darkness and light continually strive for balance. While we may seek to become beacons of light, it is foolish not to acknowledge that darkness exists, both within us and without. It has often been said that the existence of darkness makes the light seem brighter still.

Edwardian children's books give a false impression of otherworlds and their inhabitants, in particular the Faery folk, who are often depicted as pretty little child-like beings with butterfly wings who devote their time to looking after flowers. In early Faery lore, they are nothing of the sort, most being human-sized and often averse to humans, particularly those who slight them in any way. Cutting down a solitary Faery hawthorn tree or building a house on a Faery path can lead to blighted crops, damaging accidents, illness, even death. Some Faery folk steal human babies, leaving weird changelings in their place. As with most spirit beings, however, if approached with kindness, care and respect, some Faery folk are not averse to giving gifts to us mortals. Records from the medieval era to the present day, for example, tell of harpers being given wonderful tunes by Faery musicians.

Which is not to say that flowering plants don't have indwelling spirits, just that they are of a different order to the Faery folk, although individual Faery folk may be protective of certain trees and plants.

The Language of Birds

Many forms of seership are variants of *frith* with more or less ceremony attached. One with a long history is divination by the behaviour of birds, known as augury or ornithomancy. In his 1st century CE *Geography* (book 4, chapter 4), the Greek writer, Strabo, refers to Gauls divining from the movements and speech of two crows whose right wings were white. A medieval Irish text called 'Prognostications of the Raven and the Wren' (translated by R. I. Best, in *Ériu*, Vol. 8, Royal Irish Academy, 1916, pages 120-126) sets out precise meanings to be drawn from the behaviour of those birds. For example, a raven calling from above an enclosed bed in a house is said to predict the arrival of a distinguished, grey-haired guest or of clergymen. If a lay cleric, the raven calls *bacach*, if he be in holy orders, the raven says *gradh gradh*. If the call is *grob grob* or *gracc gracc* then bardic satirists or warriors are coming. If a raven goes before you on a journey, this is a good sign. If it approaches from the left, this means an argument. If a wren calls from the north-east, a woman, either alone or with a companion, is coming to see you. If calling from the east, bards are coming, or news of them, if from the west, expect an unwanted visit from a relative. If singing from atop a standing stone, the death of a great man is signalled.

Such specifics as those set out in the 'Prognostications...' are interesting, though often not particularly useful in a modern context. Rather than holding to a rigid set of fixed meanings, it may be better just to be aware of traditional associations with birds, plants, trees and animals. Some of these are given elsewhere in this book, others will be found in works listed in the Resources section.

As well as ravens, jackdaws, hoodie crows, magpies, rooks and other members of the crow family have long been regarded as harbingers of fate. This must be in part due to our ancestors' awareness of how intelligent these bird people are. Intelligence tests consistently see ravens out-perform our closer genetic relatives, chimpanzees.

Divination by magpies survives in a popular childhood rhyme, of which this is one version:

One for sorrow,
two for joy,
three for a girl
and four for a boy,
five for silver,
six for gold,
seven for a secret
never to be told,
eight for a wish,
nine for a kiss,
ten for a marriage
never to be old.

As a small child growing up on the Sussex coast in the 1950s, my mother taught me to stave off the sorrow resulting from seeing a single magpie by saying, "Good morning, Mister Magpie, and how's your wife today?" This polite enquiry was deemed to earn the goodwill of the magpie. I still greet solitary magpies this way.

In ancient Ireland a group of specialist diviners called *Neladoir* divined answers to questions put to them by studying the shifting patterns and images in cloud formations. As a persistent daydreamer since childhood, so my parents and teachers constantly reminded me, this always seemed a particularly desirable job. Most of us will at some time or other have seen clouds that look like faces, animals or other things. Many of us will have stared into a fire and seen similar shapes in the flames. With focused intention, either can be a means of divination.

Ogham: the Secret Language

Another method of divination with a long history uses an alphabet called Ogham that was probably created in South-west Ireland during the 2nd century CE. It originally consisted of twenty letters to which a further five were added later. The original twenty letters each consist of from one to five straight lines or notches intersecting a stem line. The prevalence of the number five suggests that the alphabet developed from a system of counting on the fingers and then keeping tally by cutting notches into wooden staves. The earliest surviving Ogham inscriptions are carved on standing stones with the edge of the stone forming the stem line. Inscriptions are usually written from the base of the stone upwards, sometimes passing over the top and continuing down the other side. Although a bit clunky for writing much more than memorial inscriptions, Ogham nevertheless developed into a complex system in which each letter has many possible meanings, being used in magic, divination and possibly as an early form of musical notation.

Much of our knowledge of Oghams comes from *Auraicept na nEces*, '*The Scholars' Primer*,' a textbook used in the bardic schools of medieval Ireland, copies of which are found in manuscripts dating from the 12th century onward. The *Primer* was translated into English by George Calder in 1917. It tells us that Ogham is so called because it was invented by the god, Ogma Grianaineach ('Sunface'). The alphabet is also known as *Beth-Luis-Nion* after the Irish names of the original first three letters. Before the first stone inscriptions were carved, however, the letters N and F had been transposed so that the final order became:

B L F S N, H D T C Q, M G Ng St R, A O U E I

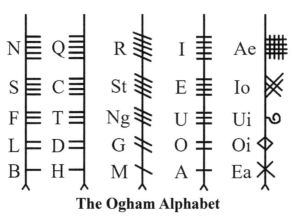

The Ogham Alphabet

Many Ogham letters derive their names from trees or shrubs, hence Ogham is often referred to as a tree alphabet. In fact, not all the letter names translate as tree species. *Luis*, for example, commonly translated as 'rowan,' actually means either 'flame' or 'herb,' the Old Irish word for 'rowan' being *cáerthann*. *Huath*, usually given as 'hawthorn,' actually means 'fear, or terror,' the Old Irish for hawthorn being *úath* without the initial 'h.' The erroneous translations of the names began with scholar and clan chief, Roderic O'Flaherty (1629-1718). His history of Ireland, which includes a section on the Ogham alphabet, was published in Latin in 1685 and later poorly translated into English under the title, *Ogygia, or a Chronological account of Irish Events* (1793). He seems to have felt that, since most Ogham letters

129

were named after trees and shrubs, they all should be. For those that weren't, he therefore invented his own tree names. His errors were continued by George Calder in his translation of *The Scholars' Primer*, and then by Robert Graves, whose 1948 book, *The White Goddess*, first alerted the general English reading public to the existence of Oghams. In the letter lists on subsequent pages, the actual translations will be given in round brackets (...).

As well as the alphabet itself, the name 'Ogham' also applies to secret languages and cyphers used among initiates of Irish bardic schools. The most common forms of Ogham speech used by them are not true languages but consist of ordinary Irish words disguised in various ways such as adding letters or syllables, changing initial letters or reversing words. The names in square brackets [...] in the following list are suggested equivalents for use in an English version of a spoken Ogham 'back-slang.' This was inspired by the work of Dylan ap Thuin, late Archdruid of the Insular Order of Druids. One method of creating a spoken Ogham is to select a single tree name and insert that name in place of its initial letter each time it appears. So, using the word 'sallow' in place of the letter 's,' the phrase "Listen, I must say something" becomes "Lisallowten, I musallowt salloway sallowomething."

The 'B' group:
⊢ B, *beith*, 'birch' [birch]

⊨ L, *luis*, 'rowan' ('flame, or herb') [larch]

⊨ F, *fearn*, 'alder' [fir, or fern]

⊨ S, *saille*, 'willow' [sallow]

⊨ N, *nion*, 'ash' [nut, or nettle]

The 'H' group:
⊣ H, *huath*, 'hawthorn' ('fear, or terror') [hawthorn]

⊣ D, *duir*, 'oak' [durmast]

⊣ T, *tinne*, 'holly' ('bar, rod,' or 'musical instrument') [trefoil]

⊣ C, *coll*, 'hazel' [cedar, or crabapple, depending on whether the 'c' is soft or hard]

⊣ Q, *quert*, 'apple' [quince]

The 'M' group:
✛ M, *muin*, 'vine' ('upper back, neck') [mistletoe]

✚ G, *gort*, 'ivy' ('a field') [gorse]

✚ Ng, *ngetal*, 'broom or reed'

✚ St, *straif*, 'blackthorn' ('red dye'?)

≋ R, *ruis*, 'elder' ('red') [rowan]

The 'A' group:
╀ A, *ailm*, silver fir ('pine tree') [apple, or ash]
╪ O, *onn*, furze ('ash tree') [oak]
≢ U, *ura*, heather ('earth, clay, soil') [ulmus]
≣ E, *ebad*, aspen [elder]
≣ I, *idho*, yew [ivy]

At some point a further five letters representing diphthongs were added to the original 20-letter alphabet, as follows:

✕ Ea, *eadha*, 'aspen' ('fitting, lawful')
◈ Oi, *oir*, 'spindle tree' ('gold'?)
⟙ Ui, *uillean*, 'ivy, woodbine or honeysuckle' ('elbow')
✖ Io, *pin*, 'gooseberry' (?)
▦ Ae, *emancoll*, 'witchhazel, or beech'

As some English letters and sounds aren't represented in the Ogham alphabet, the following could be added for the purposes of our back-slang:

J [juniper]
K [kelp]
P [pine]
Th [thorn]
V [vine]
W [willow, or witchhazel]
X [xylem]
Y [yew]
Z [zinnia]

Ogham Divination

An Irish legend, 'the Wooing of Étaín,' tells of the god Midir kidnapping Étaín, wife of King Eochu, who employs a Druid named Dalan to find where she has been taken. The Druid cuts four wands of yew wood on which he inscribes three Oghams and uses them to find the *eochra ecsi*, 'keys of divination.' They show him that she has been taken to the Faery mound of Breg Leith [pron. Bree Leeth].

Other Irish sources also refer to the divinatory use of four Ogham-inscribed yew wands called *fews*, 'woods.' The number four presumably relates to the division of the original twenty Ogham letters into four

131

groups of five. If the *fews* each have four sides and each of the twenty Ogham characters are cut across one angle, this results in three angles bearing one letter, the fourth having two. The Ogham or Oghams to be read would then appear on the uppermost face of the *few* when cast.

A method of Ogham divination employed by some modern Druids uses twenty (or twenty-five) *fews* made from the wood of each of the letter trees, each *few* having its letter cut on it. These *fews* are usually quite small, perhaps three or four inches long. They are placed in a bag, often of leather or some other natural material. The diviner then pulls out one or more *fews* at random, usually no more than three, and reads the answer to her question from them. Some cast the *fews* onto a cloth, reading information from the way they fall in relation to each other. The Roman historian Tacitus describes a similar method used in Germany in the 1st century CE. In this, a branch from a nut-bearing tree is sliced into strips which are marked with signs and thrown at random onto a white cloth. A priest, or the head of the family, then offers a prayer to the gods and, looking up at the sky, picks up three strips one at a time, reading their meaning from the signs marked on them.

A cloth decorated with a pattern of concentric circles with the Oghams marked around them is sometimes used for this purpose. This is one of several diagrammatic arrangements of Oghams found in *The Scholars' Primer.* Casting one or more *fews* onto a cloth marked with this pattern increases the range of possible readings by combining the letters on the *fews* with those on the diagram (opposite).

The words in the top left-hand corner of the diagram are *Fege Fin*, commonly translated as 'Fionn's Window.' *Fege*, however, is from Old Irish *fhéige*, meaning 'ridge-pole' or 'roof-tree.' In a modern house, this is the beam that lies horizontally along the ridge of the roof and to which the rafters are attached. Having built an Iron Age roundhouse, I believe an earlier use of the word refers to the central post that is the first to be erected, stands the full height of the roof, and is the hub around which the rest of the roundhouse is built. Roundhouses were the most common dwelling in the British Isles from the Neolithic through to around 800 CE in Ireland. When building is completed, the lower part of the roof-tree is removed, the post-hole filled in and a clay hearth laid over it for the central fire. The roof-tree echoes the concept of a central cosmic 'world tree' found in many cultures, often being a means by which shamans and spirit workers ascend to the Upperworld of the sky gods. The centre represents the point of unity, of perfect balance and, therefore, of illumination or enlightenment. The Fionn's Roof-Tree diagram certainly looks like a roundhouse roof viewed from above, while the introduction of the idea of the central ridge pole as world tree has poetic resonance alongside an alphabet in which most letters are named for trees.

On the diagram, the four rows of Ogham letters are marked with the word, *beiti*, 'birch,' at the top, the letter 'h' for *huath*, 'fear, or terror' to the right, the word *muin*, 'upper back, neck' at the bottom and the letter 'a' for *ailm*, 'pine tree' at the left.

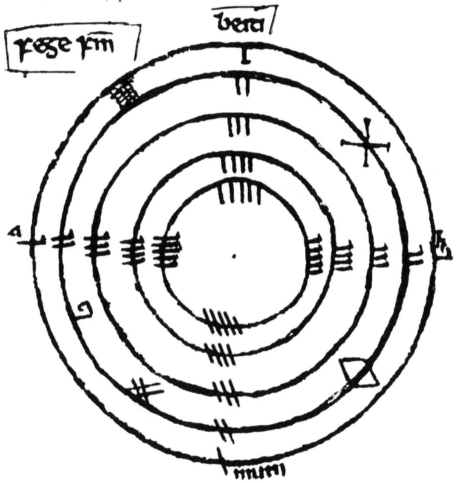

Fionn's Roof-Tree

Meanings attributed to the Ogham letters are set out in *The Scholar's Primer* in the form of lists of 'phrase Oghams,' the creation of which is attributed to various characters in Irish legend. These short, enigmatic phrases are reminiscent of the meanings of trigrams given in the *I Ching* in that their significance is often not immediately apparent. Below is my translation of the phrase list of Morann Mac Main. As

133

before, the actual meanings of the Ogham letter names are given in brackets (…). As you'll see, several of the phrase Oghams make more sense in relation to these meanings than to the 'standard' tree names.

The 'B' group:
⊢ B, *beith*, birch - faded trunk and fair hair
⊨ L, *luis*, rowan ('flame, or herb') - delight of eye
⊨ F, *fearn*, alder – forefront of Fiann warriors
⊨ S, *saille*, willow - complexion of the lifeless
⊨ N, *nion*, ash - checking of peace

The 'H' group:
⊣ H, *huath*, hawthorn ('fear, or terror') - pack of wolves
⊨ D, *duir*, oak - highest of trees
⊨ T, *tinne*, holly ('bar, rod,' or 'musical instrument') - a third part, or a good portion.
⊨ C, *coll*, hazel - fairest of trees
⊨ Q, *quert*, apple - shelter of a wild one

The 'M' group:
⤙ M, *muin*, vine ('upper back, neck') – strongest of effort
⤙ G, *gort*, ivy ('a field') – sweetest of grasses
⤙ Ng, *ngetal*, broom – power of a physician
⤙ St, *straif*, blackthorn ('red dye'?) - strongest of reds
⤙ R, *ruis*, elder ('red') - intensest of blushes

The 'A' group:
✛ A, *ailm*, silver fir ('pine tree') - loudest of outcries
✛ O, *onn*, furze ('ash tree') - helper of horses
✛ U, *ura*, heather ('earth, clay, soil') - in cold dwellings
✛ E, *eadha*, aspen - discerning wood
✛ I, *idho*, yew - oldest of trees

A second set of phrase-Oghams in the *Primer* is attributed to a pagan Irish god, Mac ind Oc, 'Son of the Young,' who may be another form of the god Ogma and may be equated with the British Mabon (page 110). Here is his list in my translation:

The 'B' group:
⊢ B, *beith*, birch - most silvery of skin
⊨ L, *luis*, rowan ('flame, or herb') - friend of animals
⊨ F, *fearn*, alder - guarding of milk

⊨ S, *saille*, willow - rejoicing of bees

⊨ N, *nion*, ash - contending of women

The 'H' group:

⊣ H, *huath*, hawthorn ('fear, or terror') - blanching of faces

⊨ D, *duir*, oak - carpenter's craft

⊨ T, *tinne*, holly ('bar, rod,' 'musical instrument') - fires of charcoal

⊨ C, *coll*, hazel - friend of nut-cracking

⊨ Q, *quert*, apple – power of solitude

The 'M' group:

✛ M, *muin*, vine ('upper back, neck') - proverb of slaughter

✛ G, *gort*, ivy ('a field') – area for a cow

✛ Ng, *ngetal*, broom or reed – clothing of a physician

✛ St, *straif*, blackthorn ('red dye'?) - increasing hidden wisdom

✛ R, *ruis*, elder ('red') - reddener of faces

The 'A' group:

✚ A, *ailm*, silver fir ('pine tree') - first answering

✚ O, *onn*, furze ('ash tree') – watching over liberty

✚ U, *ura*, heather ('earth, clay, soil') - propagation of plants

✚ E, *eadha*, aspen – synonym for a friend

✚ I, *idho*, yew – most withered of woods

Many other meanings besides trees and shrubs are attributed to the Ogham letters in the *Primer*, based on lists of words beginning with the same initial as the Ogham letter. Bird-Ogham, for example, begins with:

⊢ B, *besan*, 'pheasant'

⊨ L, *lachu*, 'duck'

⊨ F (V), *faelinn*, 'gull'

⊨ S, *seg*, 'hawk'

⊨ N, *naescu*, 'snipe,' &c

Using the same principle, English-speaking Druids might construct similar lists. An English bird-Ogham might begin with:

⊢ B, blackbird

⊨ L, lark

⊨ F (V), finch

⊨ S, swallow

⊨ N, nightingale, &c.

Various divinatory card decks based on the 25 letters of the full Ogham alphabet have been created, including my own *Druid Ogham Oracle* and Liz and Colin Murray's *Celtic Tree Oracle*. Other divinatory systems used by modern Druids include card sets such as my own *Druid Tarot*, Philip and Stephanie Carr-Gomm's *Druid Animal Oracle* and *Druid Plant Oracle*, the same authors' *Druidcraft Tarot*, and Will Worthington's *Wildwood Tarot*. See our Resources section. Others use more traditional tarot decks, runes, astrology or the *I Ching*. While personal inspiration is the best guide to which method will suit you best, there's plenty of information available online to help you decide.

We conclude this chapter with a simple exercise. Look again at the turning of the Wheel of the Year as set out in chapter 3. When you cast your circle, walk it sunwise (clockwise) from north to north, from the dark womb of Midwinter through the growth of springtime, the vigour of summer, harvest time and the fall of the year, finally returning to the womb of winter. This is the path of the ovate: the path of fate and of time. Studying the processes of birth, growth, death, decay and subsequent rebirth in the natural world, we come to understand the cycle of our lives. This is the root of natural philosophy, which is the core study of the ovate.

Chapter 7:
Healing

Healing in the Druid tradition is truly holistic, operating through all levels of being. As the practice of Druidry becomes more ingrained in day to day life, it becomes clear that every aspect of the path affects our spiritual, psychological and physical well-being. At the soul level, we seek to respond to the deepest needs of the individual, working through the pain of past lives to bring about healing in the present, reconnecting with our ancestors of blood and of spirit. We work through ritual and meditation. At the physical level we use herbs, massage and other techniques. Conventional medicine begins with the physical. In Druidry, we address the individual first and foremost as a spiritual being. The concept behind this is simple: the spiritual realm is seen as the origin of all other levels of being, so anything that has an effect in that realm naturally affects every other aspect of existence. The spiritual provides the blueprint from which emotion and intellect build the view of reality from which we construct our physical world, our environment and our relationships. So, by working with the spirit, we bring about changes in the emotional, intellectual and physical worlds, in heart, mind and body.

The common link in the healing modalities outlined below is, then, not so much the nature of the therapies themselves, which differ widely, but the attitude of mind that the ovate brings to them. It is not so much the illness that is treated as the person with the illness, each person being treated as an individual rather than a collection of symptoms. There is also a recognition that individuals should, as far as possible, be given full understanding of, and responsibility for, their own treatment.

Healing techniques employed by modern Druids include massage, aromatherapy, acupuncture and healing through spirit and sound. Some of these combine in a healing system derived from a short text inserted into a medieval Irish law code dealing with medicine. This text is called 'The Twelve Doorways of the Soul®,' and the BDO is doing pioneering work in restoring it as a viable therapeutic system. Working with health care professionals experienced in both conventional medicine and alternative therapies, it has produced impressive results. It has similarities with other ancient healing systems, including those of ancient Greece, India and China. At it's heart is the concept of good health depending on the free flow of *anma*, an Irish word meaning both 'breath' and 'spirit.' It's Welsh equivalent is *anadl*. Both derive from a proto-Indo-European word, *ane*, 'to breathe, blow,' which also gives us ancient Greek *ánemos*, 'wind,' Latin *anima*, 'a current of air, wind, air, breath, the vital principle, life, soul,' and Sanskrit *prana*, 'breath, life force, vital principle.' As a healing modality, the Twelve Doorways® operates by maintaining the flow of *anma* around the body or restoring it if it becomes blocked, thereby restoring the body, mind and spirit to health. The techniques involved are explored in depth in the BDO's ovate course (see our Resources section) and will be the subject of a forthcoming book by the present author.

Journeys of the Soul

A tenet held by many Druids is that we live not one but many lives. Most hold that we live again and again in this world, some that we pass through death to new life in other worlds. The 1st century BCE historian, Diodorus of Sicily, quotes his compatriot, Posidonius, as saying that,

> The teaching of Pythagoras prevails among the Gauls, that the souls of humans are immortal and that after a certain number of years they will live again, with the soul passing into another body. Because of this belief, some people at funerals will throw letters into the funeral pyre, so that those having passed on might read them.

Some believe we pass through many stages of being, experiencing the life of stone, grass, bee, tree, lizard, rabbit, raven, fish, deer, bear or other before or between our human lives. You may recall the various transformations of the bard, Taliesin, in the poem, 'The Battle of the Trees' (pages 99-100), or the animal transformations undergone by Fintan mac Bochra and Tuan mac Starn, as recounted in our section on the Irish 'Mythological Cycle' (pages 116-8).

Some believe this cycle of birth, life, death and rebirth leads ultimately to a point of understanding at which we identify ourselves fully with all the greater and lesser powers of the universe, from sub-atomic particles to black holes, galaxies and gods, merging our individual consciousness with the whole of creation. As noted earlier, indications in the poetry attributed to Taliesin and his Irish counterpart, Amergin, suggest that meditations aimed at bringing about such universal consciousness may have been practised in the bardic schools of medieval Wales and Ireland. They may lie behind the transformations in 'The Song of Amergin,' versions of which are preserved in the late 14th century *Book of Ballymote* and *Yellow Book of Lecan*. In my translation, this sees Amergin singing:

I am the wind that breathes on the sea,
I am a wave upon the ocean,
I am the murmur of the billows,
I am an ox of seven fights,
I am an eagle upon a rock,
I am a ray of the rising Sun,
I am the fairest among all plants,
I am a wild boar in valour,
I am a salmon in the water,
I am a lake upon a plain,
I am a word of cunning art,
I am the point of a spear in battle,
I am the god who puts fire in the head,
Who brings light to the hilltop gathering?
Who announces the ages of the Moon?
Who knows the place where the Sun has its rest?
Who finds springs of fresh, clear water?
Who calls fish from the ocean's deep?
Who causes them to come to shore?
Who changes the shape of headland and hill?
A bard whom seafarers call upon to prophesy.
Spears shall be wielded,
I prophesy victory,
And all other good things,
And so ends my song.

Most maintain that we grow in knowledge and experience through each of our lives, whether human or other. As the soul passes from life to life, we learn, at least in theory. Sometimes we learn well, other lessons may be forgotten in the space between lives or the trauma of being born, or lost among the overwhelming sensations of childhood. The pain of past lives can, however, remain with us even when the lives themselves have faded from memory and, if we don't acknowledge and free ourselves from it, we may be prevented from moving on in this life or those to come. We may then fall prey to the Spanish philosopher, George Santayana's well-known aphorism which holds that, "Those who cannot remember the past are condemned to repeat it." The exploration of past lives therefore offers a path to healing and freedom. Recalling severe traumas of past lives can be as traumatic as reliving those experiences in this life and may best be done with the help and guidance of a trained counsellor. However, guidance and healing may also be achieved through working with our ancestors of blood and spirit, our soul friends, gods and guides who may have been with us in those previous lives.

Earlier in this book we journeyed through the history of the Druid tradition, seeking our vision of the archetypal Druid. That journey may have awoken ancestors of spirit to our presence on the path. Below is a way to journey through our ancestral blood line, looking for blockages in the flow of spirit that may be caused by areas of trauma in our relationships with our DNA ancestors. The process of healing the past began earlier when we acknowledged and gave thanks for the gift of life bequeathed to us by our parents, grandparents and previous generations. The following exercise takes that initial healing further.

The Ancestor Tree

First, find a tree. Any tree might do, but try to find one with which you feel a kinship or resonance. You might, for example, feel drawn to the majesty and stability of the oak, the dark wisdom of the yew, the lively brightness of the rowan, the ethereal beauty of the silver birch. For more information on the meanings associated with trees, refer to the previous chapter and to our Resources section. As ever, you may also ask for guidance from your gods and guides.

When you have found your tree, pause when you reach the edge of the spread of its branches and ask the spirit of the tree, known to ancient Greeks as the *dryad*, to accept your presence and the work you are about to undertake. Be open to the response. If you sense that the tree is unwilling to help you, bid it a polite farewell and move on. Evidence of this might be, for example, a nut or twig from the tree falling on your head. If the tree is willing to accept you, perhaps indicated by something like a blackbird bursting into song nearby, move in under its branches and sit with your back resting against the trunk. Take a few deep, slow breaths to regulate your breathing. If it seems appropriate, you might like to chant the *awen* to awaken the flow of spirit.

Be aware of your physical body. Feel its solid presence beneath the tree. Make sure you are comfortable and well-supported. Feel the tree against your back. Think of it now as your family tree. The trunk against which you rest is where you are now, with all the support and strength that you have around you. Its roots are your ancestors, its branches your descendants. Today we are going to journey into the roots.

As in chapter 2 (page 32), the first step on the journey is to give thanks to your parents for the gift of life. Take this opportunity to heal any rifts between you and your parents, any blocks of anger or mistrust that still exist between you. As before, explore the negative aspects of your relationship, then find the positive results they may have had in your life. Has parental opposition strengthened your will, or parental absence increased your independence? Find what you have gained and give thanks.

Now sense how the tree is rooted deep into the earth. You too are rooted in the earth through the bloodline of those whose genetic inheritance you carry. Become aware of your grandparents and explore your relationship with them, looking again for what their lives and their inheritance has given you. When you are ready, move your consciousness back to your great-grandparents and so back through the generations. There is no need to visit every generation. You may find you skip some but are drawn to others. Some you may acknowledge briefly as you pass, others you may wish to spend time with, absorbing what they have to say. Bear in mind that the number of direct ancestors doubles with every generation, so that we have only to go back five generations to find 32 of them. It seems unlikely that you'll want to spend time with all of them. In practice, what normally happens is your journey will narrow to only those ancestors with whom you resonate most strongly, perhaps a single individual from each generation. Some generations may hold no one at all you feel drawn to, in which case, give thanks and move on. Go back through as many or as few generations as you feel comfortable with. You can always go back further another time.

As you journey, you may feel your consciousness sliding down the roots of your tree. If you do, go with the feeling as it is the way the spirit of the tree is responding to your journey. If not, don't worry, the tree is still there supporting you. As you move back in time, remain alert for any problems, tensions or blockages. When you find them, work through them as you did with your parents. Look for the roots of each problem and how it has affected subsequent generations. Then look beyond the problem to what positive results may have flowed from it. Offer this positive input to refresh and clarify your genetic stream.

If you have the time, patience, endurance and inclination, this mode of travelling into the past can carry you right back to the first uni-cellular life forms that existed in the primordial soup of planet Earth 3.8 billion years ago.

When you have journeyed as far as you wish to at this time, retrace your steps, giving thanks to each generation of your ancestors for the beneficial gifts they have passed down to you through your genetic line and that you may pass on to future generations. Where gifts are other than beneficial, work for healing, not just on your own behalf but for your ancestors, your children and generations as yet unborn. Make prayers or offerings for healing if this seems appropriate.

When you have moved back through the generations to the present day, bring yourself back to full awareness of the present by focusing on your breathing, becoming aware again of the physical reality of your body, feeling the earth beneath you and the firm presence of the tree at your back. Look around you. Take in the here and now.

When you are ready, give thanks to your ancestors, gods and guides and to the spirit of the tree. You might like to make some small offering before you leave, perhaps of flowers, bread, mead, water, a poem or song. All these things will feed the tree and the beings who live in and around it, both seen and unseen.

This exercise may be used to connect with your ancestors of spirit as well as those of blood. Incidentally, reaching the era of Iron Age Druids, before the Roman conquests of Gaul and Britain, requires going back through something like 75 generations.

The making of ritual, whether alone or in a group, is itself a healing process through the re-connection it offers with the spirits of the land, our ancestors, gods and guides, the cycles of our lives and of the world. Meditations like that described in chapter 4 (pages 89-91) offer similar opportunities for re-connection.

Herbs & Healer Gods

Among other traditional healing techniques used by modern Druids, herbalism is popular and widespread. The magical and medicinal use of plants fits well with our animistic vision of Druidry that sees all things as sacred, imbued with spirit. The use of medicinal herbs in Druidry goes back a long way. The quotation from Pliny the Elder given in chapter 2 (page 52) refers to Druids in 1st century CE Gaul calling mistletoe by a name meaning 'all-heal.' Despite being toxic in all but very small doses, mistletoe was long used to stop internal bleeding and to treat epilepsy and other convulsive disorders. More recently, it has been explored as a treatment for some types of cancer.

Most plants have some medicinal properties. In the Taliesin poem, 'The Battle of the Trees,' Gwydion, the archetypal enchanter of the *Mabinogion*, invokes the powers of thirty-five different species of tree, shrub and herb, from "alders at the head of the file," to "shy chestnut, fierce adversary among mighty trees." Of the thirty-five, twenty have diuretic properties, nineteen astringent, sixteen tonic, fourteen are used to treat fevers, thirteen are anti-inflammatory, eleven used for skin conditions, ten to treat rheumatism, nine are expectorant, seven antiseptic, and another seven are used to treat kidney problems. The alder alone has medicinal properties that include being used internally as an emetic, purgative, alterative, astringent, cathartic, febrifuge and tonic, and externally for skin conditions and rheumatism, while a decoction of its leaves has been used in folk remedies for treating cancer of the breast, duodenum, oesophagus, face, pylorus, pancreas, rectum, throat, tongue, and uterus. The second tree invoked by Gwydion is the willow, whose bark contains the compound Salicilin, the basis of aspirin, the most widely used medicine in the world. The use of willow bark as an analgesic and fever-reducer is first recorded in Egyptian papyri 3,500 years ago. Our ancestors certainly knew a thing or two about healing plants.

'The Battle of the Trees' demonstrates a Druidic approach to healing that combines magic with medicine in which plants are invoked to defeat

> … a great beast, horny-scaled,
> on whom were a hundred heads
> and a fierce war-band
> beneath the root of his tongue.
> Another war-band is found
> in each of his necks' napes.
> A black-forked toad
> with a hundred talons.
> A serpent, speckled, crested,
> a hundred souls for their sins
> are tormented in his flesh.
> (Translated by Frank Olding)

As elsewhere in our medieval literature, disease is represented as a destructive, poisonous monster. 'The Battle of the Trees' supports other sources in suggesting that it can best be defeated by combining magical incantations and spiritual invocations with the application of healing herbs, steam baths and other physical therapies. I have some experience of this, having developed pleurisy after a vision in which a large black serpent flew into my room and attacked my chest. This led me to create a healing chant based on an early Irish poem in which the healer god, Dian Cécht, burns a disease-bringing serpent to ashes. This and other healing chants and prayers can be found on the BDO YouTube channel at https://www.youtube.com/channel/UCsI19GdnuCqvoUbKxyo39bA

An ancient legend of the Tuatha Dé Danann, the old gods of Ireland, tells how when their leader, Nuada, lost his hand in battle, Dian Cécht, their chief physician, made him a replacement of silver every bit as supple and strong as the original. Dian Cécht had a son, Miacha, who inherited his father's healing skills. Indeed, some said he was a better healer than Dian Cécht. On hearing this, Nuada sent for the lad. Miacha asked where Nuada's severed hand was and, on learning it had been buried, he dug it up, removed Nuada's silver hand and held the withered hand of flesh to the stump. As he did so, he uttered the incantation, "Sinew to sinew and nerve to nerve be joined." After three days and nights, the hand had grown back to the arm and was as good as ever.

On learning of his son's achievement, rather than swelling with paternal pride, Dian Cécht flew into a rage at having been outdone by a mere youth. Attacking Miacha with his sword, he cut through his skin. Miacha healed the wound instantly. With his next blow, Dian Cécht hacked his son to the bone but again Miacha healed himself. The third blow clove through Miacha's skull and deep into his brain. Again the lad healed himself. His father then struck a fourth blow, cleaving his skull completely in two so that he finally died. Appalled at what he had done, Dian Cécht buried his son. On his grave grew three-hundred and sixty-five healing herbs, each one a cure for a different ailment. Miacha's sister, Airmid, took each of these plants and laid them out on her cloak according to what ailments they would cure. Dian Cécht was furious at what she was doing in her brother's memory, angered that, if the healing properties of these plants became known, no one would honour him any more for his healing gifts. So he snatched up the cloak and shook it vigorously, scattering the plants in confusion. Had it not been for this act, we would now have a cure for every illness and be practically immortal. Thanks to Dian Cécht's rage, subsequent generations have had to do what we can to rediscover the lore of herbs. Fortunately, there are now numerous books and study courses available for would-be herbalists, some of which are listed in our Resources section.

The story of Dian Cécht illustrates how our ancestors saw the gods as able to give or promote healing, or to deny it. As said, in 'The Battle of the Trees,' the healing powers of the plants are invoked by the enchanter, Gwydion. The poem also refers to Math who, with Gwydion, conjures the maiden, Blodeuwedd, from flowers of oak, broom and meadowsweet, to Modron, mother of the Mabon, to Dylan eil Ton, the twin brother of Lleu Llaw Gyffes, and to Lleu himself.

Some deities are seen as having influence over particular areas of health. The Irish Brighid (Welsh Ffraid), for example, is especially invoked in pregnancy for protection of the unborn child, in labour for a safe and speedy delivery, and for the protection of young children. The Romano-British god Nodens, equivalent to the Irish Nuada, Welsh Nudd, seems to specialise in the healing of wounds, particularly those received in conflict. Others, such as the goddess Sulis, patroness of the healing waters at Bath in Somerset, offer more general healing.

Healing & the Faery Folk

A Welsh folktale tells how a poor farmer met a beautiful maiden who lived in a lake in the Black Mountains. She agreed to marry him and make him wealthy, on condition that he would not strike her three blows. When he did strike her three times, albeit by accident, she returned to the lake. While they were together, she had borne him three sons. When these three went down to the lake shore their mother appeared, gave them a bag of medicines and told them they would be great physicians and so would their children after them. Her prediction proved correct. Their fame spread and they and their descendants were long known to Welsh tradition as the Physicians of Myddfai. Many of their remedies were recorded and have since been published. Again, see our Resources section.

The Physicians of Myddfai offer just one of many examples of the Faery folk helping humans to heal. Some have given healing stones which, when placed in water, give it curative properties. A few such stones have been preserved, passed down for centuries through the families to whose ancestors they were given.

Whenever we receive a gift from the spirit world, whether it be of teaching, wisdom, inspiration or, as in these tales, something more tangible, we should always give something in return. This may be an offering of bread, mead or flowers, a song or poem, an act of generosity towards someone, a donation to a charity or a simple acknowledgement of the gift and honouring of the giver.

The Place of Healing

Each person has their own place of healing, either in this world or another. It is a calm spiritual centre, a place of perfect peace and security from whence healing can begin. Visiting your place of healing can bring specific guidance on how treatment should proceed. You may be shown what you need to restore spirit, mind and body to health and well-being.

The place of healing can be found through meditation, divination, or with the help of a spirit guide or someone experienced in guiding spirit journeys. It can emerge from a dream or may be found during waking life. For some it may be the white sands of a tropical beach, for others the secure darkness of a deep cave, a sunlit forest glade, a rock shelf behind a waterfall, a softly-turfed hollow on a mountainside, a mossy tree beside a woodland stream, the heat of the desert or an Arctic ice-flow. It may be a particular place you knew in childhood, an ancient sacred site, or some enchanted place that you may never have seen in this world.

Ask your guides to help you find your place of healing. I cannot take you there through the pages of this book. It is too intimate, too personal to you. It is your place. Those who walk with you in spirit, whether in this world or the worlds beyond, may help you to find it. Then, when you are troubled in spirit, mind or body, you may go there. In the peace that you find there, you may be given what you need to restore you to health and well-being.

A Time to Live, a Time to Die

Of course, there comes a time in every life when no amount of prayer or healing can any longer delay the moment of death. In Ursula leGuin's magical *Earthsea* sequence of novels, the supreme teacher of healing is the Master Herbal, who says that the beginning and end of the healer's art can be summed up as, "Treat the illness, heal the wound, but let the dying spirit go." Perhaps the hardest of all the healer's tasks is to recognize when healing can, or should, no longer be attempted, when the spirit must simply be allowed to pass on.

A friend discovered a potent talent for healing in a particularly dramatic way; his arm began to glow like several 100-watt light bulbs, visible both to himself and his terrified girlfriend. After some notable early successes, he quickly gained a local reputation as a spirit healer. Then he was asked to intervene for a man with advanced stomach cancer. My friend immediately felt resistance to treating this man, but was reluctantly persuaded to do so by the concerned relative who had approached him. He then attempted healing in spite of his own deep misgivings. Not only did the healing not work, but the man's condition worsened and my friend lost his ability to heal. This tale should serve as a warning that, as a spirit healer, it is vitally necessary to listen to the promptings of one's own spirit while attempting to heal others. My friend eventually recovered his healing ability, but had learned his lesson. There are folk whose time has simply come, and attempting healing in such circumstances can do more harm than good.

Our pagan ancestors in Europe used to celebrate death with

feasting and rejoicing, happy that the soul of the dead person was passing on to a blissful new life in an otherworld of ecstatic beauty, serenity, peace and plenty, surrounded by friends and relatives, like that described in the song, 'The Islands of the Blest' (pages 98-9). This belief was so strong that people were known to throw themselves onto the funeral pyre of a friend or loved one in order to join them in the Blessed Realm. In more recent years, we have come to fear and shun death. Any real sense of the afterlife as a place of wonder and beauty seems to have been lost under Anglican Christianity. The best most people seem to hope for now is that, in the words of David Byrne, "heaven is a place where nothing ever happens" ('Heaven,' from the 1979 album, *Fear of Music*, by Talking Heads).

In the Irish tradition of the wake, the body in its coffin took pride of place in the parlour while friends and relatives came to the house to drink toasts to the deceased and eat and drink while sharing stories about their lives. Now, when our loved ones die, they rarely stay in our homes with us. Instead, they are swiftly taken away to funeral parlours or held in hospital morgues, appearing again briefly in a closed coffin in a chapel before being removed for burial or cremation away from their friends and relatives. Many of the processes of death are thus hidden from our sight, as if this will somehow make our own part in the process easier. I believe it does the exact opposite, divorcing us from the reality of death, making it more difficult to deal with it appropriately or well.

As Druids, we may seek to regain control over the processes of dying, working with the dead person in body and in spirit, through ritual and physical preparation of flowers, perfumed oils, incense and offerings, as well as food and drink for those joining the celebration. And we do very much celebrate the life of the individual and their newfound spiritual freedom, as well as mourning their physical passing.

Hindus in the UK will often be present during the cremation of deceased relatives. There is no reason why Druids should not do the same. It was, after all, a Welsh Druid who made cremation legal in the UK. This was Dr. William Price (1800-1893), a brilliant and generous physician who, long before the NHS, often treated poor patients for free. When his infant son died, Dr. Price built a large funeral pyre for him on a hillside near the family home. The hillside overlooked the local chapel and, it being a Sunday, half the town came out of the chapel as the fire took hold. Horrified chapel goers snatched the child's body from the pyre and Dr. Price was arrested, still wearing his ceremonial regalia which included a hat made from the complete hide of a fox, since he believed the fox to be the foremost animal spirit honoured by Druid healers. A subsequent post mortem showed that, as Dr. Price said, his child had died of natural causes. At his trial, the court realised that there was actually no law forbidding cremation, so found Dr. Price (right) not guilty of any offence. When Price himself died a few years later, his open air cremation was witnessed by a crowd estimated at 20,000.

The vital thing to remember about death is that it is only the physical body which dies; the spirit lives on and journeys to another realm where, assuming that the deceased has lived anything like a decent life, a joyous reception awaits from those who have gone before. For the person who dies, it is not an end but a change. They are on the path to freedom and joy, and then perhaps to rebirth in this world or another. This is particularly true of those who have suffered long and debilitating illnesses or some types of serious injury. For them, the body may have become a cruel prison, perhaps even a torture chamber. When someone in this position dies, they are released from the cage of the flesh, exchanging it for the ecstatic flight of the spirit between worlds. If we grieve then, we are grieving not for them, but for ourselves who are left behind to miss their physical presence in our lives.

Just as life is a process of continual change, so death is a vital part of that process. Both are essential phases in the great interlocking cycles of being. To fear one is to fear the other. May you be free from fear.

So may it be.

Part Four:
Ritual & Change: the Path of the Druid

Chapter 8:
Ritual

Ritual is the grammar that shapes and gives pattern and meaning to the language of our lives. Through it, we express recognition and reverence for those things we hold sacred and sanctify those things we hold dear. Ritual provides a focus for prayer and meditation, an avenue for healing, a vehicle for shifting between worlds. In Druidry, many ceremonies have a specific focus, perhaps working for the healing of an individual, a shift in the focus of a group or the protection of a particular vulnerable ecosystem. Others are more general in their intention, though they may still incorporate working towards specific goals. We gave some examples of how different types of ceremony impact the lives of modern Druids on pages 34-8.

We mark with ceremony the passage of the Sun through the seasons and the changes that flow through spring, summer, autumn and winter. For an understanding of seasonal rites, see our section on the Wheel of the Year in chapter 3 (pages 74-80). Many Druids also honour the monthly course of the Moon with ceremonies, often at the full or new Moon. The rites of Sun and Moon are primarily celebratory, honouring the natural world and the spirits of land, sea and sky. They honour the gifts of creativity and inspiration, those present sharing poetry, music, songs and stories. They include offerings of mead, wine, water or other drink in honour of the sky father whose rain fertilizes the Earth, and of bread or other food to the Earth herself as the nurturing mother who feeds us and to whose embrace we return when our time is done. Through these rites we attune ourselves with the natural processes of the world.

In industrial and post-industrial nations many of us live lives largely divorced from the world of nature, our hermetically sealed homes protected from seasonal variations in temperature by double-glazing, central heating and air conditioning. Most of us are urban dwellers, detached from the processes of agricultural production, getting our food pre-packaged from supermarkets rather than directly from field and hedgerow as our ancestors did. Electric lighting lessens the impact of nightfall. Street lighting obscures the stars. This is the life many of us have chosen. Don't get me wrong, industrialisation brings many benefits. I'm writing this on a desktop computer and love my android phone, flat-screen TV, digital recording equipment and electronic music. However, when we lose touch with the natural world, we lose an intimacy of contact with the cycles of birth, life, death and decay that shaped the world of our ancestors and inspired their spirits. We also lose contact with the spirits of nature that are a vital part of Druid tradition. In losing these things, we are cut off from potent sources of teaching, healing and inspiration. On healing alone, recent scientific studies have shown what many of us instinctively knew, that even being able to see trees through a window has measurable benefits on mental, emotional and physical health and well-being. Through ritual we can re-establish vital connections with our ancestors and the natural world.

Just as we make ceremonies that mark the flow of the changing seasons of Sun and Moon, so we mark the flow of our lives with rites of passage that acknowledge and celebrate the changes that come with birth, puberty, commitment to a partner, menopause, death. Through ritual, we explore the meaning of these changes and the ways in which they affect our lives and our relationships with the world around us, preparing us for each new stage in life's journey. The construction and performance of such rituals is an important part of the work of the Druid.

Many ceremonies have no set text, deriving from an immediate, spontaneous response to time, place, people and spirit. Others are more formal, especially where many of those taking part may be unused to the shape and nature of ritual. As Druid priests, we increasingly find ourselves called upon to make rites of passage with and for non-Druids. In such circumstances, we often begin with a written script that will then be adapted to fit specific needs. For example, when performing a Druid wedding or handfasting we will speak with the couple beforehand to discuss what we and they will say and do during the rite, ensuring that its meaning is as deep and powerful as possible for them. Within the basic framework of Druid ritual we will work with their needs and expectations to ensure that their own gods and ancestors are appropriately honoured, their friends and relatives included, the site properly prepared, music provided, &c.

This brings us to the portmanteau rite that follows. Among other things, it contains within it rites of blessing for children, handfastings, a form of bardic initiation and an honouring of the dead, any of which might be extracted or expanded for use on their own.

The Gorsedd Rite

A *gorsedd* is a gathering of bards. The Welsh term *gorsedd* [pron. GORSE-eth], literally 'high seat,' may have originally referred to prehistoric sacred mounds, sometimes with single trees growing on them, that were places of tribal assembly, festival celebration, law-giving and the inauguration of kings during which, in times past, kings were ritually wedded to a queen who was a female representative of the spirit of the land. At some point, the gatherings themselves came to be called *gorseddau* [GorseETHeye] after the mounds on which they were held.

The ceremony that follows forms the basis of open *gorsedd* celebrations that have taken place at each of the eight festivals of the year at sacred sites in Britain and overseas, first under the aegis of the British Druid Order, then independently. The rite as given here does not include specific seasonal elements as these will obviously change from festival to festival. Such seasonal elements often include the acting out of mythical dramas appropriate to the festival, primarily drawn from the medieval literature of Wales and Ireland we looked at in chapter 5. See chapter 3 on the Wheel of the Year for additional guidance.

The original ceremony on which the rite given here is based was created by the present author for a multi-faith gathering held among the great stone circles of Avebury in Wiltshire at the autumn equinox of 1993. That ceremony resulted in the formation of the Gorsedd of Bards of Caer Abiri, which continued to celebrate the turning of the seasons at Avebury for many years. Following Iolo Morganwg, places where Gorseddau are regularly held are often given names beginning with *Caer*, which means 'fortification' but may originally have indicated a circular bank-and-ditch earthwork. Abiri is an old name for Avebury. Again following Iolo, I created a motto for the Avebury Gorsedd; "In the Spirit of Freedom and for Freedom of the Spirit." That first Gorsedd led to many others, including the Gorsedd of Bards of Cor Gawr at Stonehenge, which was instrumental in getting the henge re-opened for public celebration of the summer solstice in 2000 and which still celebrates Midsummer and Midwinter there.

The version given here is the original Avebury rite as revised by Emma Restall Orr and myself for a ceremony held in Volunteer Park, Seattle, in 1997. It draws on historical sources, our own inspiration, and contributions from members of the Avebury and Stonehenge Gorseddau. It includes elements common to Druid ritual as performed in the BDO and other groups, including the Ancient Druid Order and the Order of Bards, Ovates and Druids. As my old friend Philip Carr-Gomm reminded me, it is thus a bricolage, a text that incorporates elements from various sources. It is not to be taken as holy writ, but as a source of guidance and inspiration. The words spoken should come from the heart, reflecting the spirit of the rite rather than slavishly following the written text.

BDO Gorseddau began as open, multi-faith celebrations at which folk of many spiritual traditions gathered together to honour their gods, the earth and each other. In this, they reflect central tenets of our Druidry such as inclusivity, acceptance of many gods, and tolerance for the beliefs and practices of others. Within the Gorsedd circle we celebrate the turning of the year through the cycle of eight festivals recognised by many modern pagan traditions. We also celebrate rites of passage, offering Druid weddings or handfastings, blessings for children, croning, and remembrance of the dead. Most celebrations include initiations into the Gorsedd for those wishing to make a personal dedication to the spirit of the place and the way of the bard, which is to learn to express *awen*, the spirit of inspiration, through the creative arts. Bread and mead are blessed and shared during rites, which include eisteddfod sessions where bards are encouraged to offer stories, poetry, music, song or dance.

The lead celebrants are two Druids. In 1997, since Bobcat and I usually worked group celebrations together, we designated these roles 'priest' and 'priestess,' though neither of us were very happy with those terms. In this edition, they are replaced with the non-gender-specific 'Druid' and differentiated by being designated 'Druid 1' and 'Druid 2.'

Before the ceremony begins, the lead Druids invite others to participate in it as follows: a person (often, though not necessarily, a woman) to represent the guardian spirit of the place; three bards or musicians to assist in weaving the circle; four people, perhaps from different spiritual traditions, to make the calls to the four directions; two further celebrants to help with the sharing of bread and mead.

Once everyone has assembled, the gathering forms two groups. One, sometimes called the goddess party, led by the representative of the guardian spirit of the place, goes to the place at which the ceremony will begin. Often, they will drum to awaken the spirits of the place. Meanwhile, the other group, sometimes called the god party, led by one of the lead Druids, takes another route, processing sunwise to bring them to the point where the two groups meet again and the rite begins.

Words that are to be spoken are given in standard text. Those not to be spoken, such as ceremonial instructions, are given in *italics*.

Druid 1: "Once again the solar wheel returns to [*insert the name of the festival here*], and we come to this most sacred place and ask the guardian spirit of [*insert the name of the place here*] to accept the gifts we bring and bless us as we enter in to celebrate the sanctity and beauty of our Mother Earth."

He/she presents a gift to the Guardian.

Druid 1: "That which comes from the Earth, returns to the Earth."

Guardian: "In the name of the mother of all living, the guardian spirit of [*insert name of place*], and the ancestors of our people, I accept the gifts you offer. All who come here are welcome, but thrice blessed are those who come with reverence and love.
The blessings of the goddess be with you,
The blessings of the guardian be with you,
The blessings of the ancestors be with you, and with our children,
With you and with our children.
Enter now and welcome."

Others may also present gifts to the Guardian and receive a blessing from the Guardian in return. The lead Druids then guide both groups to the place where the Gorsedd circle is to be formed.

Opening the Circle

The place where the ceremony is to be held is often prepared in advance, a circle marked out and cleared, perhaps decorated with seasonal vegetation, an altar may be set up, candles, water bowl and incense provided. The presiding Druids may begin with a short purification ritual in the circle before the main ceremony begins, if this is deemed appropriate.

The ceremony proper then begins with greeting the spirits of the land and of our ancestors, welcoming all who have come.

Druid 2: "Hale, O spirits of this place, you who are the embodiment of this sacred land on which we are gathered. As we honour you, so I ask that you accept our presence here. Hale, O ancestors, you who have walked these ways before us, you whose songs echo in the air around us, whose tears and laughter echo in our hearts. Hale to you, both seen and unseen, who gather here this day. Let all who come in peace be welcomed to our circle. Hale and welcome!"

All: "Hale and welcome!"

Druid 1: "We begin this celebration by calling for peace, that in peace the voice of spirit may be heard.

May there be peace in the east.

May there be peace in the south.

May there be peace in the west.

May there be peace in the north.

May there be peace throughout all the world.

So may it be!"

All: "So may it be!"

Druid 2: "We gather here in peace to celebrate this Gorsedd of Bards of [*name of place*], and the festival of [*insert name of festival here*], and the sanctity of our Mother Earth. Let us now weave our circle, that the spirits of those who are gathered here may be blended in one purpose, one voice and one sacred space."

The circle is woven (see chapter 1) by Druid 1 and bards, or by both lead Druids. The circle may also be consecrated with incense and water. An incense burner or saining herbs are carried around the circle, the smoke wafted over each person present. A bowl of water is then taken around the circle, each person being sprinkled with a few drops.

Druid 2: "Let us call now to the quarters, that our ancestors may know the old ways are not forgotten."

Calling the Quarters

Calling the quarters is a part of many traditions, invoking different energies from each of the cardinal points. Representatives of different faiths are invited to call the quarters, each in their own way. The following are merely suggestions, firstly in the Druid tradition:

East: "I call to the spirits of air, the breath of life; to the spirit of the Eagle who brings the gift of vision far and clear, the spirits of the wild east wind, of sunrise and of spring, of new life and new growth. May all within this circle know the power of your blessings. So I bid you hale and welcome!"

All: "Hale and welcome!"

South: "I call to the spirits of fire, of energy, of passion; the spirit of the Wild Cat, who kindles within us the strength and beauty of the untamed places; spirit of the noonday Sun, the heat of summer, vitality

154

and abundance. May all within this circle know the power of your blessings. So I bid you hale and welcome!"

All: "Hale and welcome!"

West: "I call to the spirits of water, of the ebb and flow of emotion; to the spirit of the Salmon, who fills us with the wisdom welling up from deep within the earth, of open seas and running streams, of cleansing rain; spirit of the evening Sun, of twilight and of autumn. May all within this circle know the power of your blessings. So I bid you hale and welcome!"

All: "Hale and welcome!"

North: "I call to the spirits of earth, of the womb of creation; to the spirit of the great Bear, who draws us into the nourishing darkness of the cave; spirits of the night and the snows of winter, deep roots and ancient stones. May all within this circle know the power of your blessings. So I bid you hale and welcome!"

All: "Hale and welcome!"

And here are some suggestions from other traditions:

East [Christian]: "The eye of the great God,
The eye of the God of glory,
The eye of the King of hosts,
The eye of the King of the living,
Pouring upon us
At each time and season,
Pouring upon us gently and generously.
Glory to thee
Thou glorious Sun,
Glory to thee, thou Sun,
Face of the God of life."

South [Shamanic]: "You, O Fire,
Our mother with thirty teeth.
You ride a red mare of three springs,
Your red cloak flying in the wind.
Through your garments run chains of mountains.
In your veins the rivers flow.
Provide for us by day
And protect us by night.

155

Light the way for those who depart
And lead the others homeward.
O Fire, Great Mother, be with us."

West [Wiccan]: "Ye Lords of the Watchtowers of the West, ye Lords of Water, ye Lords of Death and of Initiation; I do summon, stir and call you up, to witness our rites and to guard the Circle."

North [Heathen]: "Hale to Woden, wisest of wights,
Howls of Wolves and Ravens' cries,
Be sig-runes writ on this bright day.
Hale to Freya, fiery love-queen,
Witch-wife, healer, warrior of trance.
Hale to the gods and goddesses all,
Hale to the ancient ones,
Spirits most wise."

Druid 1: "The circle is unbroken,
The ancestors awoken.
May the songs of the Earth
and of her people ring true.
Hale to the spirits of this place;
of root and branch, tooth and claw,
fur and feather, of earth and sea and sky.
Hale and welcome!"

All: "Hale and welcome!"

Handfasting

Handfasting is a traditional form of marriage once common in parts of Britain and treated as binding by the couple themselves, their families and communities. As I prepare this edition, the UK parliament is in the process of updating the law regarding marriage. This may allow Druid handfastings to be legally recognised. Until then, couples often follow a handfasting with a legal marriage in a registry office.

Druid 2: "At sacred times and places such as this our ancestors clasped hands when they would wed, and such handfastings were lawful, true and binding, for as long as love should last. Would any couple who would wish to make such vows, or to reaffirm existing vows, witnessed by this gathering, now come forward."

The couple requiring handfasting join hands. Their hands may be loosely bound with a silk scarf or other light material.

Druid 2: "As the Sun and Moon bring light to the Earth, do you [*insert first name here*] and [*insert second name here*] vow to bring the light of love and joy to your union?"

Both: "I do."

Druid 2: "And do you vow to honour each other as you honour that which you hold most sacred?"

Both: "I do."

Druid 2: "And do you vow to maintain these vows in freedom, for as long as love shall last?"

Both: "I do."

Druid 1: "Then let the Earth bear witness that [*insert name*] and [*insert name*] are joined in love and joy and freedom. So may it be!"

All: "So may it be!"

The couple are then encouraged to exchange any personal vows of their own, either privately or so that all may hear, after which the assembly may again say: "So let it be!" *to signify that they have witnessed these vows. They may also exchange rings and/or blessings, love tokens, &c, sealing their bond with a kiss.*

Druid 1: "Let all bear witness that [*name*] and [*name*] are joined in love. May their love partake of the beauty, majesty and power of the sacred land, and may they grow together in wisdom, joy and harmony. My own blessing, and the blessings of all those assembled here be with you,"

Druid 2: "The blessings of the gods be with you,"

Druid 1: "The blessing of the ancestors be with you"

Druid 2: "And with all that flows from your union,"

Druid 1: "So may it be!"

All: "So may it be!"

Blessing for Children

Druid 2: "Our circle is a symbol of the eternal, and yet it is made anew each time we meet. And so it is with ourselves; we each hold

157

within us a spirit that is eternal, and yet we are reborn many times as we journey towards the centre. And at each moment of rebirth we are touched by the eternal spirit that guides us on our journey.

Let the children who would be blessed come forward, creating a circle within the circle of our community."

Babies and young children may come forward, with or without their parents. Each child is given a blessing by Druid 2 (below) that introduces them to the elements of Earth, Air, Fire and Water. During the blessing, these may be represented by soil or stone; a wafting fan, feather or wing; a candle, incense or a saining stick; a bowl of water.

If there are many children to be blessed, it may be good to open a first eisteddfod session while this is being done. This is coordinated by Druid 1 who invites members of the assembly to come forward with appropriate stories, poems and songs.

Druid 2: "I baptise thee with Mother Earth,
from whose loins we come
and to whose arms we fly
when our journey here is over.
I baptise thee with the winds
that come from the four corners
of the Earth, the winds that
scatter the seeds of the harvest
and blow away the snows of winter.
I baptise thee with fire
so that thy spirit may be
purified and thy days
be long and fruitful.
I baptise thee with the waters
of life, the waters that
no living thing can do without.
Give thanks to our Lady
for thy bounteous harvest,
and may she bless you and keep you
all the days of your life."

Druid 2: "Within the Gorsedd circle is the circle of our children, blessed by the gods, blessed by our Mother Earth and by the elements of earth, water, fire and air. Let us welcome them into our community of spirit and of song. Children of our Mother Earth, I bid you hale and welcome!"

All: "Hale and welcome!"

Bardic Initiation

This simple form of initiation offers an opportunity to make a commitment to the bardic path and to the spirit of the place.

Druid 2: "As we are born into the life of the body, so we may be born into the life of the spirit. Initiation into the Gorsedd offers an opportunity to dedicate to the spirit of place, the community of bards and kindred of the spirit. It is free and open to all who wish to receive it, welcoming followers of all spiritual traditions within one circle. In offering this initiation, we ask that you make a personal commitment to walk the path of the bard in beauty and in peace, using what inspiration you may gain to find your own spirit's true path of creative expression, and using your creativity for the benefit of your community and of the Earth."

Druid 1: "Let those who wish to be initiated into the Gorsedd of Bards of [*name of place*] and to receive the spirit of inspiration that we call *awen*, the flowing spirit, step forward now to the centre of the circle."

The candidates for initiation gather at the centre of the circle, linking hands to form an outward facing circle of their own. All then repeat the following, one line at a time, after Druid 2:

Druid 2, followed by **All**: "We assemble here at [*name of festival*] of the year [....].
We assemble in the face of the Sun; the Eye of Enlightenment.
We assemble on the Gorsedd mound of Mother Earth.
We assemble here to constitute ourselves a Gorsedd of Bards of the Isles of Britain."

Druid 1: "In the name of the ancient Order of Bards, and by the authority of those here present, I hereby proclaim this Gorsedd of [*name of place*]; may it be a meeting place of love, and truth, and light. So may it be!"

All: "So may it be!"

Druid 2: "Let us now invoke the *awen*, the holy flowing spirit of the bardic tradition, and direct its shining stream of inspiration towards those gathered in the midst of our circle, that they may receive its glowing gifts of clear sight, wisdom and strength of spirit. And let those in the centre join the chant, visualising the stream of inspiration flowing

159

into you, and through you, to energise and inspire not only yourselves, but the land of [*name of place*] and all the worlds beyond."

Those in the outer circle link hands. Those who have already received the awen *visualise its stream of inspiration flowing into the circle, directed through them to those gathered in the centre.*

All: "Awen, awen, awen."

*All in the outer circle then give the following blessing, repeating each group of three lines after **Druid 1***:

Druid 1 (*followed by* **All**): "Wisdom of Serpent be thine,
Wisdom of Raven be thine,
Wisdom of the valiant Eagle.

Voice of Swan be thine,
Voice of honey be thine,
Voice of the son of stars.

Bounty of sea be thine,
Bounty of land be thine,
Bounty of the boundless heavens."

Druid 2: "Step forward now, Bards of the Gorsedd of [*name of place*], and take your place within the circle of initiates."

All now return to their places in the circle.

Druid 1: "Let us now proclaim the Gorsedd Prayer."

All: "Grant, O gods, thy protection,
and in protection, strength,
and in strength, understanding,
and in understanding, knowledge,
and in knowledge, the knowledge of justice,
and in the knowledge of justice, the love of it,
and in that love, the love of all existences,
and in the love of all existences, the love of the
gods and all goodness."

Druid 2: "Everything the power of the world does is done in a circle. The sky is round, and I have heard that the Earth is round like a ball, and so are all the stars. The wind in its greatest power whirls, and birds make their nests in circles, for theirs is the same religion as ours. The junction of heaven and earth, the horizon, is its circle of enclosing

160

stones, for it is beyond the air that heaven and earth meet, and that junction is the circle of enclosing stones. Let us then complete our circle by joining hands to swear the Oath of Peace."

All join hands and repeat the following three times:

All: "We swear by peace and love to stand, heart to heart and hand to hand, mark, O spirit, and hear us now, confirming this our sacred vow."

Honouring the Departed

Druid 1: "The Otherworld is known by many names. Some call it the Islands of the Earthly Paradise, or the Isles of the Blest. These islands lie beyond the western ocean, where the souls of the departed are carried on the rays of the setting Sun to the place of peace and healing."

Druid 2: "Those among us who have friends or loved ones who have taken or are about to take that journey are invited to speak their names, either aloud or in your hearts, that we may honour them."

Those who wish to may say the name or names aloud. Others may make their dedications in silence. A bard may sing a song or play a melody in honour of the departed and for the strengthening of those they leave behind. A suitable song would be 'The Islands of the Blest,' the lyrics of which are given in chapter 4.

Druid 2: "We give thanks, in the name of our gods, for all those who have shared with us their lives, their wisdom and their love. Hale, O ancestors, those newly departed and those of old."

All: "Hale, O ancestors!"

Sharing Bread & Mead

Druid 1 and Druid 2 or two other designated celebrants then bless the bread and mead. No one is, of course, obliged to drink the mead. For those who wish it, a non-alcoholic substitute may be provided.

Druid 1: "We gather here today to celebrate [*name of festival*], the festival of [*say what the festival is about*]."

Druid 2: "Let us now give thanks to our Mother Earth, from whom we all were born, and to whom we shall return at the end of our days."

The bread and mead are then brought into the centre of the circle to be blessed by Druid 1 and Druid 2 or another couple.

Druid 2: "Mother Earth, in the name of our gods and the gods of our ancestors, we give you thanks. You nourish us body and soul with your gifts of life, beauty and abundance. As you honour us with such precious gifts, so we honour you. I bless this bread in the name of our great Mother Earth [*and/or whatever other spirit or deity may be deemed appropriate*]."

Druid 2: "This bread is blessed. To our Mother we give the first. With this gift, I leave corn and milk in your land, and mast in your woods, and increase in your soil."

Druid 2 breaks the bread and scatters some over the earth.

Druid 1: "Father Sky, in the name of our gods and the gods of our ancestors, we give you thanks. Light of the Sun and blessings of rain fall upon the body of our Mother, bringing forth her gifts. To you, O Father, we give thanks. I bless this mead in the name of the great Sky Father [*and/or whatever other spirit or deity may be deemed appropriate*]."

Druid 1: "This mead is blessed. To you, our Mother, we give the first. With this gift, I leave corn and milk in your land, and mast in your woods, and increase in your soil."

Druid 1 pours some on the earth.

Druid 2: "Let us eat, that none may know hunger."

Druid 1: "Let us drink, that none may know thirst."

Druid 1 and Druid 2 give to each other. With the help of their assisting celebrants, the bread and mead is shared with the gathering, passing sunwise around the circle. Mead was traditionally passed in a shared mead-horn. In these infection-conscious times, individual vessels may be used. While the feast is shared, the eisteddfod begins.

Druid 1: "As we give thanks for the gifts of food and drink that sustain our bodies, so let us now give thanks in music, poetry and song for the gift of inspiration that uplifts our spirits."

Bards of the Gorsedd are now invited to make offerings of music, poetry, song or story in honour of the season, of the Earth and of the community. Such offerings should not be too long and should preferably have some connection to the particular festival when the rite takes place

(see, for example, pages 102-5).
When the eisteddfod ends, the circle is closed.

Closing the Circle

Druid 2: "I call upon the guardians of the quarters to close this Gorsedd circle."

North: "Spirits of the North; spirits of Earth, we give thanks for the gifts of strength and endurance that you have brought to our circle. May these gifts remain with us as we prepare to depart this place, and as we bid you hale and farewell!"

All: "Hale and farewell!"

West: "Spirits of the West; spirits of water, we give thanks for the gifts of deep wisdom and free flowing that you have brought to our circle. May these gifts remain with us as we prepare to depart this place, and as we bid you hale and farewell!"

All: "Hale and farewell!"

South: "Spirits of the South; spirits of fire, we give thanks for the gifts of passion and energy that you have brought to our circle. May these gifts remain with us as we prepare to depart this place, and as we bid you hale and farewell!"

All: "Hale and farewell!"

East: "Spirits of the East; spirits of air, we give thanks for the gifts of clarity and far sight that you have brought to our circle. May these gifts remain with us as we prepare to depart this place, and as we bid you hale and farewell!"

All: "Hale and farewell!"

Guardian: "I give thanks to all those, both seen and unseen, who have gathered here today. May all be blessed."

Druid 2: "Spirit of this place, we give you thanks for your blessings. Hale, O ancestors and you, O great gods both old and ever-young. We give thanks for your presence, your guidance and inspiration. May these gifts remain with us as we bid you hale and farewell!"

All: "Hale and farewell!"

Druid 2: "Let the circle be opened that these blessings be shared

163

throughout the world."

Druid 1 and three bards then unweave the circle.

Druid 1: "This rite ends in peace as in peace it began. May the spirit of [*name of place*], the light of Sun and Moon, the blessings of our ancestors and the power of the old gods go with us all to nourish, strengthen and sustain us as we depart this place. Peace without and peace within, until we meet again. So may it be!"

All: "So may it be!"

Here ends this Gorsedd rite.

This portmanteau rite incorporates many elements of our tradition. It was designed as an open, public representation of Druid practice, offering an opportunity for rites of passage to be witnessed and acknowledged by a broad community. Many find their spiritual needs well met by such open rites, so much so that for a while in the 1990s our Gorsedd ceremonies at Avebury were attended by up to a thousand people. Others wish for individual rites of passage to be more private and more tailored to their own needs. A Druid priest will respond to these needs by working closely with those requiring the rite to ensure that their requirements are well and fully met.

The ceremony given here is fairly complex. Within Druidry, most rites are much simpler, consisting of a few words we might say when we light a candle of blessing for a friend, greet our ancestors before our altar, pray for guidance for a loved one in need or honour the spirit of a tree in a forest glade. These things generally have no written text. Like all the best ceremonies, they are spoken from the heart.

Notes on the Gorsedd Ceremony

The Call for Peace beginning "May there be peace in the east" (page 154) is adapted from that used by the Order of Bards, Ovates and Druids (OBOD), who may have inherited it from the Ancient Druid Order (ADO).

The Calls to the Quarters on pages 154-5, composed by Bobcat and myself, were adapted for use in the closing ceremony of the London 2012 Paralympics. The call to the East quotes from my song, 'Lord of the Wildwood.' The speech beginning "The circle is unbroken..." on page 156 was also used in the Paralympics ceremony. Its first line is the title of one of my favourite Robin Williamson songs, written by him for

The Incredible String Band and featured on their 1968 double LP, *Wee Tam & The Big Huge*. I sang it and played it on penny whistle during the first Gorsedd rite at Avebury in 1993.

Of the alternative calls on pages 155-6, the Christian call to the East is from Alexander Carmichael, *Carmina Gadelica*, vol. 3, 1940, page 307; the Shamanic call to the South is from a 'Prayer to Fire' from Alfonso M. Dinola, *The Prayers of Man*, William Heinemann Ltd., 1962, pages 62-3; the Wiccan call to the West is found in many sources, including Janet & Stewart Farrar, *Eight Sabbats for Witches*, Robert Hale, 1981, pages 39-40; the Heathen call to the North was, I believe, gifted by a Heathen who attended an early Avebury Gorsedd rite.

Handfasting (pages 156-7) is a form of marriage that was formerly legally binding in the UK but, at the time of writing (January 2023), is so only in Scotland. The UK government has, however, published a proposal to alter marriage laws across the UK in ways that will enable Druid, Pagan and Heathen celebrants to conduct legally recognised weddings. The Druid Network, the Pagan and Heathen Symposium and the Pagan Federation are among many groups who provided information in support of this welcome proposal.

The Blessing for Children on page 158 was given to us by a Druid named Septimus Bron, a regular attendee at our Avebury ceremonies, now departed for the Islands of the Earthly Paradise.

The bardic blessing on page 160 is adapted from a 'Good Wish' found in Alexander Carmichael, *Carmina Gadelica*, vol. 3, page 241. For various versions of the Gorsedd Prayer, see J. Williams ab Ithel (ed.), *The Barddas of Iolo Morganwg*, Weiser Books, 2004, volume 1, pages 361-5. The speech beginning "Everything the Power of the World does..." is from John G. Neihardt, *Black Elk Speaks*, Abacus, 1974, page 139. Neihardt compiled it from various interviews conducted with Black Elk in 1931 and 1944. I included it in the original Gorsedd rite because it is a splendidly animistic statement of why the circle is sacred and its reference to the "circle of enclosing stones" seemed to sit well in a rite conducted among the old stones of Avebury.

"Let us eat, that none may know hunger" and "Let us drink, that none may know thirst" on page 162 are, I believe, from OBOD.

Greeting the Day

As said, most Druid ceremonies are far less complex and much shorter than the Gorsedd rite. For example, a short ceremony consisting of a single spoken prayer is a good way to start each day, renewing our connection with beings and concepts that are central to our spirituality and, therefore, our lives. Hence I get up each morning, open the curtains, look out at the new day and say:

> Hale to Gwydion, antlered lord of forests.
> Hale to Arianrhod of the starry skies.
> Hale to Cunomaglos, lord of Wolves.
> Hale to Nudd of the healing shrines.
> Hale to Lleu Llaw Gyffes, lord of light.
> Hale to Sulis of the flowing waters.
> Hale to Ceridwen of the cauldron bright.
> Hale to the gods and goddesses all!
> Hale to the ancient ones, spirits most wise!
> May your blessings of light and life,
> strength and healing,
> guidance and protection,
> wisdom and inspiration
> be with us this day,
> this day and all days.
> So may it be!

The deities named have a particular resonance for me at this time in my life. Several feature in the *Mabinogion*. Two are local to my home. Cunomaglos is a god of healing, hunting and protection revered at a ceremonial complex at Nettleton Shrub in Wiltshire, about 20 miles from where I live. Sulis is a native goddess primarily associated with the healing springs at Bath in Somerset, but also linked with waters in neighbouring Wiltshire. Some names are different from those included a few years ago. No doubt the list will continue to change and evolve. Your own morning prayer should include those deities who mean most to you now. The principle remains that making such a prayer is a good way to begin each day, reminding us of our spiritual connections at the same time as invoking the guidance and protection of beings of great power, both for ourselves and for all those who live with us. The prayer begins by wishing health (hale) to the gods, which seems only right when one is asking assistance from them.

May they, and you, be blessed.

Chapter 9:
Change

This final chapter is where you might find yourself most in need of the concept of catmas introduced in our Preface (page 4). If you skipped it, or have forgotten what it is, go back and look now.

For me, the Druid is a walker between worlds. We have taken some initial steps along that path in previous chapters of this book, journeying in imagination and in spirit. To fully become a Druid in the sense in which I understand and practice the craft, it is necessary go to the threshold between life and death, between this world and the worlds beyond, and step over it into new realms of being.

A legend common to many traditional cultures tells of a Golden Age when those who walk between the worlds did so in body, not in spirit. This Golden Age is looked upon as a remote mythical past when humans talked freely with all other creatures and when the gods lived permanently in this world. Such tales often tell how humankind became divorced from the gods and the rest of the natural world, usually through some monumental act of human arrogance or stupidity. The gods then withdrew into other worlds, humans and other animal people lost the ability to speak with each other and spirit worlds were hidden from human sight. The role of the Siberian *Shaman*, Icelandic *Seiðkona*, Lakota *Wichasa Wakan*, Yaqui *Brujo* and European *Druid* is both to re-establish communication between the worlds and to move between them, bringing back messages from ancestors, gods and spirits for the benefit of our communities.

In most traditional cultures, illness or injury are believed to result from harm done to the sick person's spirit. Sometimes a part of the spirit becomes lost, detached or stolen. Sometimes the whole spirit is lost or taken. The job of those who walk between the worlds is then to journey to the right area of the other worlds, search out the missing soul-stuff and bring it back, restore it to the person and, in so doing, bring about their cure. Healing has been an important part of native European religion for millennia and there are Druids today who work healing in many ways, including those described in chapter 7. As we saw there, traditional cures often combine herbs, rituals, prayers, chants and other elements but, whether openly acknowledged or not, the recovery of the patient's soul-stuff often lies at the heart of the process.

Boundaries Between the Worlds

The role of walker between worlds encourages a regard for boundaries and doorways that has long been part of Druid tradition. Any boundary or doorway, whether in time or space, in this world or those beyond, is seen as a potential passage by which we may pass between worlds. Hence our recent ancestors made prayers or ritual gestures each time they entered or left a house while our more remote ancestors buried humans or other animal people at the entrances to shrines or stone circles, their spirits becoming guardians of the threshold. We recognise seasonal festivals as doorways between the worlds just as they are doorways from one part of the year to another, from spring to summer, autumn to winter. Hallowe'en and May Eve in particular, but other festivals too, are seen as times when the dead mingle with the living, when the inhabitants of the Faery realm show themselves in wild dances beneath the Moon. The twilight boundaries between day and night are also seen as peculiarly potent times to make ritual or seek inspiration and visions. We recall such traditions when approaching a sacred grove or circle, when we pause at the gateway to honour, greet and be greeted by the spirit guardian of the place before we enter.

To be a walker between the worlds takes other forms besides spirit journeying. So Druids may act as bridge-builders, promoting understanding and reconciliation between different interest groups or cultures. Many Druids promote and take part in interfaith dialogues or work for peace between opposing factions through ritual, prayer or pilgrimage or through more direct forms of mediation.

Since first discovering Druidry in the 1970s, I have felt it to be equivalent to shamanism in other cultures, Druids interacting directly with supra-physical realities beyond those which our physical senses normally perceive. Hence such things as second sight, shape-shifting and otherworld journeying. These skills of the Druid can, however, be a double-edged sword. Working in a world of spirit that most people don't see, or deny the existence of, can cut off those who take this path from family and friends. My own family can vouch for the fact that it takes considerable tolerance and understanding to live with a Druid. Also, things encountered in the spirit world are not always pleasant. Dealing with folk who are sick in mind, body or spirit is difficult and demanding, yet once one has developed the skill it becomes very hard to turn away from it. To compensate for these difficulties, we may receive assistance from ancestors, gods, guides, and animal helpers. The latter are so prominent in traditional cultures all over the world that the American mythographer, Joseph Campbell, called shamanism, which he loosely defined as "a collection of ways of interacting with spiritual realities that are beyond normal awareness," "the way of the animal powers."

Power Animals & Animal Powers

The concept of power animals is common to many traditional cultures. They are individual beings who are strongly connected to us, spirit to spirit, while also representing a conduit through whom we connect with the great archetypal spirit of their species and, through them, with other animal, plant and mineral species who comprise our and their environment. They often act as guardians, guides and teachers as well as potent sources of energy and inspiration, *awen*. Sometimes a power animal will remain with us for life or we may have a succession of them. Most people have one. The few who don't are often extremely unwell. To begin to work with your power animal you first need to know who he or she is. There are many ways to find out. One is to go on a spirit journey with an experienced guide who will help you discover and meet your power animal. If this is not an option, you might look for an animal who crops up repeatedly in dreams or waking visions or who intrudes on your life in other ways. Or you might try meditation or divination within the sacred circle, preceded by an *awen* chant.

Having discovered the identity of your power animal, you can begin to work with her or him by finding information about the species, its habitat, food and behaviour. This will help you form a relationship. You may find a piece of fur, feather, skin or scale, tooth or claw that will help bring you closer to your power animal. You may be given, find, create, or hear in your head a song or chant that will also help. Play-acting your power animal can also be rewarding, as can making a mask or costume that represents it. Dancing your power animal is another potent way to connect. Once the initial connection is made your own intuition, with guidance from your power animal itself, should help you to build and maintain a good relationship with her or him. Such relationships can be invaluable in pursuing the Druid path. *Sacred Animals* by Gordon MacLellan, published in 1997, is an excellent and very practical guide to finding and working with power animals.

Aware that baldly describing things like power animals is not really enough to convey the reality of their being, one way to bring that reality to life may be to recall two powerful interactions between myself as a modern Druid and animals who have played a significant role in shaping my own developing spirituality.

In the Paw-prints of the Wolf

In Druidry, a single ceremony can sometimes change not only your spiritual outlook but the whole direction of your life. Many years ago, I was blessed to find such a rite on a Druid summer camp. At a morning meeting it was announced that Georgien Wybenga, a shamanic teacher from the Netherlands, would be conducting a sweat lodge the next day. I had heard of sweat lodges, even seen one in the Somerset cottage garden of fellow Druid, Tim Sebastion, but had never experienced a ceremony in one. For some reason, I felt that this was the right time to do so.

About a dozen of us devoted the whole day to preparing for the ceremony, cutting hazel rods to make the frame of the low, domed bender in which the rite would be held, digging two pits, a large one for the fire that would heat the hot rocks over which water would be poured to create the steam to heat the lodge, a smaller one in the centre of the floor into which the hot rocks would be placed, making the bender frame, covering it with canvas, gathering wood for the fire, building the fire with the carefully-selected stones in the middle of it. This physical work was all done with an awareness of its spiritual purpose. Before cutting the rods, we spoke with the hazels to make sure they were OK with what we were doing. Offerings of herbs were put into the earth where the pits were dug, and into the holes into which the hazel rods were pushed. All of this added to the power of the build-up to the ceremony itself, preparing us for what was to come.

In the late afternoon, we lit the great fire with the rocks inside it. As orange flames and curls of smoke first gently lapped and then roared into the cooling air, we drummed, danced and sang. It was beautiful and powerful. When the time came, we stripped off our clothes, got down on hands and knees and crawled into the little bender.

Inside the lodge, our naked bodies were huddled close to each other in the total darkness that enveloped us once the door flap was lowered. After giving safety instructions, Georgien raised the flap again and asked Walter, our fire-keeper, to bring in the first rocks. A shovel duly appeared at the door with three large stones on it, glowing red. They were welcomed as honoured ancestors and carefully tipped into the central pit, after which the shovel withdrew and the flap was pulled down again. A ruddy glow from the stones now marked the position of the central pit. Georgien scooped water from a vessel at her side and laved it onto the stones. A great, hissing cloud of steam burst from them, filling the interior of the little dome. The temperature rose rapidly. By the time a few more scoops of water had gone on, more rocks had been welcomed in, and more water poured over them, it was so hot in the lodge that the only way I could remain conscious was to get my head low down to the ground where the air was slightly cooler. After a while, I was able to sit upright again.

We had four 'rounds' within the lodge, between which we were allowed to go out. Despite the heat, I chose to stay inside. Georgien had been guided to make sweat ceremonies by two American First Nations' teachers, Sun Bear and Archie Fire Lame Deer. Hence, in the round during which we were introduced to the guardians of the four quarters, she mentioned coyote in the south. For the first time that day, this struck me as being out of place. We were, after all, in a field in southern England where no wild coyote had ever walked. I wondered who our native equivalent might be. The answer should have been 'fox,' since fox fulfils a trickster role in British folk tales similar to that of coyote in America. Instead, the word that instantly came to mind was 'wolf.'

No sooner had the word entered my head than a full-grown adult wolf appeared, curled up in the pit in the centre of the lodge, the hot rocks glowing inside his body. Although startled by his sudden appearance, I was deeply intrigued. After a few moments, the wolf stood up, still with the stones in his belly, and looked straight at me. He jerked his head to one side in a gesture that clearly meant, "follow me." He walked out through the closed door of the bender. My spirit left my body, stood up and followed him. Outside, instead of the fire-pit and English summer field, were the snow-covered slopes of a great mountain. Some way up the slope, maybe half a mile away, was the dark line of a dense pine forest. The wolf padded away across the snow, heading towards the treeline. I followed, trying to place my footfalls into his paw prints so as to disturb the pristine snow as little as possible. This was purely instinctive. It wasn't until much later that I thought about the symbolic significance of my following in the paw-prints of the wolf.

I followed him to the treeline where rows of great pines towered high above us, their massive trunks forming cathedral-like spaces that merged in the deeper darkness further into the forest. A path ran between the trees, thick with fallen pine-needles and cones, visible for some way in until it too faded into shadow. The wolf turned and looked at me. Speaking straight into my head, he told me his name, that he had to go

171

on alone now, but that next time we met he would guide me deeper into the forest. Thanking him and bidding him farewell, I turned and made my way back across the snow towards the little canvas dome lower down the slope. Reaching it, I re-entered it and my body. The intense heat inside was much more bearable following my stroll in the snow.

Finally crawling out of the bender a little before sunrise, I was delighted to find the grass soaked with deliciously icy dew. I rolled on my back and laughed. When eventually able to stand, I made my way to the big water-butt by the side of the bender and drank as much as I could of the cool, clear liquid.

At lunchtime that day I was supposed to conduct a Gorsedd ceremony for a couple of hundred people among the great stone circles of Avebury. By mid-morning, however, my spirit was still soaring to such an extent that I wondered if I would be in a fit state to conduct the rite. Seeing fire-keeper Walter crossing the field, I intercepted his path and asked him how long the effects of the previous night's ceremony were supposed to last. He looked at me as though I were either a bit simple or slightly insane and said, "Well, forever." Finally, I understood. I asked about my wolf vision and Walter suggested I should find something physical to connect me with wolf spirit. Never having seen hide nor hair of a wolf in my entire life, this seemed highly unlikely, but I thanked him for the advice and reassurance. The ceremony at Avebury went well. I may have been unusually in tune.

The weekend after the camp, a friend, Andy, invited me to his parents' house for a garage sale. Ellie and I duly packed the kids into her car and drove over. On arrival, the first thing I saw was a large fur draped across an old water tank. As soon as I saw it, I thought, "that's wolf," immediately followed by, "no, it can't be … can it?" Getting out of the car, I took a closer look. It was a wolf-skin rug that had been in the house when Andy's parents bought it in 1947. They didn't like it, bundled it into a bag and put it in the loft. Nearly 50 years later, on the very day I entered the sweat lodge, Andy found it there and brought it down to add to the garage sale. I told Andy and his mother about my wolf vision and came away with the rug, which was made from the hides of six wolves. Removing the heavy woollen backing, I added some ties and made it into a cloak to wear in ceremonies, the best way I could think of to honour this extraordinary gift, received just eight days after the wolf came to me in that sweat ceremony vision.

The wolf who had come to me during the rite subsequently became my guide, companion and teacher in many further adventures. Following

172

on from the cloak, further wolf gifts came thick and fast; a tooth from an American friend, a chant given among the old stones of Avebury, my spiritual heartland, and many more. The six wolves who comprise my cloak turned out to have distinct personalities and became the pack 'my' wolf and I lead. Wolf spirit guided me to the Quileute Reservation on the Olympic Peninsula in the Pacific Northwest region of the United States. There I sang the wolf chant I had been given at Avebury and was honoured to be welcomed into their drum circle. I then learned that the Quileute people are descended from shape-shifted wolves and that, five days before my arrival, the weekly meeting of the tribal elders had been told that Greywolf was "either here, or he's coming." Years later, I found a second wolf-skin cloak, just a few miles from where the first one came to me, but that's another story...

While working with a spirit animal can bring huge benefits, it also entails responsibilities and should therefore not be undertaken lightly. Making the initial connection is one thing, maintaining it quite another. It requires continual work and attention. As with any relationship, if you fail to work at it, you risk losing it. In the case of a power animal, losing it can result in debilitating loss of vitality, quite possibly resulting in physical or mental illness. On the other hand, maintaining it regularly and well can benefit every aspect of your life. This is why something like my wolf chant is important, representing a way in which you can simply sit down with a drum and remake your spiritual connection with your power animal through chanting its spirit song. As said, other ways to maintain the relationship include dancing as your power animal, finding out information about the species along with associated folklore, and surrounding yourself with images of your animal helper.

Some folk may be upset by my encountering Wolf spirit during a sweat ceremony conducted in Lakota style by a European woman on an English Druid camp. It smacks of the sort of cultural appropriation that rightly angers many First Nations people. Anger against Europeans is entirely justifiable, given that Europeans slew the ancestors of present day Native Americans, drove others from their ancestral homes, stole their sacred land and rendered them second-class citizens in their own country, forcing them onto reservations where poverty and sickness remain rife and infant mortality, teenage suicide and addiction are common. Who wouldn't be angry? Many then see the appropriation of sacred ceremonies as a final insult piled on top of centuries of appalling injury and injustice. Sun Bear and Lame Deer, the two elders who encouraged Georgien to begin conducting sweat ceremonies, have been criticized from within their own communities for sharing sacred rites with non-Indians. Both have defended their right to do so and spoken and written of their reasons for doing so.

At the time of my wolf vision, I had never visited America and was unaware of the seething tensions surrounding cultural appropriation. I have since been to the US several times and met many First Nations people. Almost without exception, they are strongly supportive of our attempts to recover our own native traditions, not least because our vision of Druidry as an indigenous British and European spirituality offers a genuine alternative to seekers who might otherwise be tempted to join the widely despised tribe of Wannabee Indians.

The overwhelming power of that first sweat ceremony led me to wonder if my ancestors had ever conducted similar rites. I soon found that Britain and Ireland are rich in what archaeologists call 'burnt mounds,' piles of stones that show clear signs of prolonged exposure to fire. Most date from the Bronze Age and many are found near stone or timber water troughs into which hot rocks were placed to heat the water. Some troughs were within structures very like the type of lightly-framed bender used in Lakota sweat lodges, others inside small, circular, domed, drystone walled huts. In south-west Ireland, the remains of two such huts, and their adjacent burnt mound, are within 40 paces of the Drombeg stone circle. Another early example on the Orkney island of Westray is part of a complex of buildings the earliest of which date from the Neolithic era, circa 4000 BCE. Similar stone sweat houses were still used for healing purposes in parts of rural Ireland in the 19th century.

Medieval Irish literature refers to *fulachta na Morrigna*, 'hidden places of the Morrigans,' some of which are associated with sacred hills and Faery mounds. The Morrigans, 'Great Queens,' are a powerful trio of goddesses able to transform into a variety of animals, including ravens, crows, wolves, snakes, horses and cattle. *Fulacht* sites are commonly crescents of drystone walling surrounding a water-trough with accompanying fire-pit and pile of burnt stones. Those associated with the Morrigans seem to have been used for ritual purposes. An Irish triad states that, "Three things give sacred status to a smith: the stake of Neithin, the *fulacht* of the Morrigans and the anvil of the Dagda."

Sharing my findings with Georgien and others in the Druid community, we devised a sweat ceremony rooted firmly in our own tradition. We remain hugely grateful to those First Nations' teachers who helped us rediscover this lost aspect of our spiritual heritage.

Shape-Shifting

For me, shape-shifting is one of the archetypal skills of the Druid. In the mythical Golden Age the power to shape-shift is said to have physically transformed spirit-workers' bodies from human to animal, bird or fish. Nowadays most shape-shifting occurs in spirit and bodily transformations are rare, though not entirely unknown. Shape-shifting may serve many purposes. For some, such transformations are part of the process by which they move between worlds, using the senses, strength or speed of a particular animal to facilitate their journeying. This can certainly be an extremely powerful way of cementing your relationship with your power animal.

So what does it feel like to shape-shift? Well, strange. Some level of human consciousness generally remains, sometimes as a passive observer in the background while the main part, that which senses the world and governs our interaction with it, makes decisions and acts upon them, shifts entirely into the animal state. At other times, human and animal consciousness may be evenly balanced, or the human may be dominant. The following example from my own life illustrates one form the process can take.

Eagle Dancing

Bobcat and I had been asked to put together a ceremony for about a hundred people on a Druid summer camp. The weather had been

175

blisteringly hot and dry for weeks, the ground on the camp site was parched and cracking, tempers fraying, arguments flaring. Some rain-making was clearly needed to benefit both the land and the people on it, but how to do it? Sympathetic magic seemed an obvious starting point with a firm basis in European magical tradition. We would take containers of water into the circle and sprinkle some on the ground to emulate rain and encourage the real thing to come. A Native American, John Two-Birds, was on the camp to give a talk. Being open to interfaith cooperation, I asked John if he knew any techniques we might try. He said his grandfather had taught him a rain-making spell, adding that "the trouble is, he never taught me how to turn it off." I said we'd try our way first, keeping his grandfather's spell in reserve.

Immediately before the ceremony began, I saw a shallow silver bowl suspended above the entrance to the sacred circle, from which silver liquid was spilling onto the parched ground. I recognised this as a sign that I should abandon our planned ceremony and let *awen* guide me. A little way into the rite, I looked up into the cloudless sky and realised that to effect a change in the weather meant getting up there. Having previously encountered a spirit eagle, I began a spontaneous eagle dance, letting my body decide how to move, whirling around, holding my wolf-skin cloak out as wings and flapping them. It may have looked weird but had the desired effect. The eagle I had met before flew into the circle at speed, diving out of the clear sky, slamming into and through my body, exchanging spirits in a split second so that he took over my body and I his. Rising swiftly on powerful wings, I looked down at the circle below and saw my body still dancing, the eagle now inhabiting it still flapping wolf-skin wings, paralleling my dance in the sky. Soon I was too high to make out what was happening in the circle. I was joined by three more eagles who soared in swiftly from the west. The four of us flew in circles, wide at first but spiralling in towards a common centre. As we did so, a few little fluffy white clouds appeared on the horizon and we began to draw them in towards us. Larger grey clouds followed, brought ever closer by our beating wings, becoming thicker and darker until my eagle kin and I were flying in a vertical, tunnel-like space at the heart of a raging storm with thunder crashing and brilliant bolts of blue-white lightning coruscating all around us, thrilling our every cell with electrical energy. It was glorious!

When a lightning bolt zapped along the oaken staff I held in my talons, I knew we had done enough and it was time to return to my human body. Bidding farewell to my winged companions, I swooped down towards the camp while they flew back westward. Diving into the sacred circle, I did as the eagle had done, slamming into my human form so that we exchanged bodies again. Coming so suddenly back into my human body, which had been whirling all the time, I found myself dizzy, disoriented and unable to stay upright. Falling to the ground, I rolled on one shoulder, came back up and continued dancing. This happened several times before I regained balance and was able bring the dance to a halt. To many in the circle, it must have looked as though I had completely taken leave of my senses. In effect, I had.

At midday the following day the sky darkened, thunder rolled, lightning flashed and warm summer rain fell in torrents from the sky. A spectacular thunderstorm swept across the country in a narrow arc on either side of which twenty-three buildings were struck by lightning, though no one was injured. At the centre of it all was our camp, where Druids emerged from their tents to whoop and dance naked, rejoicing in the wonderful, refreshing downpour. The land got the drenching it so desperately needed, the atmosphere of tension on the camp broke and peace was restored. Despite which, some folk on the camp complained that, because of our Native American visitor, we should have made what they termed a 'proper' Druid ceremony. And yes, several of them did think I'd entirely lost my mind. Two-Birds, on the other hand, was quite impressed. For me, a 'proper' Druid ceremony is one that works.

After telling a Scottish Pagan with an interest in shamanism about this ceremony, his response was to stroke his chin thoughtfully for a moment and then say in a questioning tone, "and you did this *without* drugs?" Absolutely. Except in some South American cultures, most traditional spirit workers don't use drugs to shape-shift or make spirit journeys. In Siberia, where the word 'shaman' comes from, one who needs drugs to help him is considered a pretty poor shaman.

Some months after my eagle flight I read a novel called *The Way of Wyrd* by Brian Bates in the first chapter of which the central character, a Saxon sorcerer, wears a wolf-skin cloak and performs a whirling dance flapping his cloak while summoning the spirit of an eagle. I also learned after the event of a Welsh folk tradition that storms are created by eagles who dwell in the clouds around the summit of Mount Snowdon (*Yr Wyddfa*, 'the High Place') in north Wales. The eagles who joined me above the circle that day came from the direction of Snowdonia and headed back that way when they left. Years later, taking time out from creating group ceremonies in north Wales, I stood alone on a steep hillside looking towards Mount Snowdon, stretched out my arms and became eagle again. Flying to the summit, I located my storm-brewing colleagues and thanked them for the help they had given me that day and subsequently. As said elsewhere, giving thanks for gifts given is a strong part of Druidry. It was good to see them again and to experience once more the wonderful freedom of flight.

I have also shape-shifted as wolf. Sometimes this has followed the same pattern as with the eagle, the wolf leaping through my body to initiate an instant consciousness exchange, leaving him in control of my body while I inhabit his. At other times, I have initiated the shift by drumming, chanting my wolf chant, getting my body into a wolf-like posture and howling, even by playing guitar. There are few hard and fast rules. One of the greatest lessons I've learned in nearly fifty years as a Druid is that if something feels right, it probably is, alongside the similar advice to 'follow your nose.'

Shape-shifting is a fair exchange. We both get to feel what it's like to be each other. In general, as wolf, eagle or other being, my human consciousness exercises a fair amount of control over the actions of my shape-shifted self. That said, I am also aware of the altered priorities of the being whose form I am inhabiting. For example, I once shape-shifted into wolf whilst in a blind rage at three men who had gate-crashed a camp I was running and were going round campfires demanding money with menaces and threatening children. On becoming wolf, blind rage changed to focused action. I sniffed out the three, briefly snarled their spirit animals into submission, we had no more problems from them that night and in the morning they sheepishly apologised. This taught me that, unlike humans, wolves do not waste time and energy on futile anger. We have much to learn from wolves and other animal people.

On the Edge, Between the Worlds

How, then, do we develop the ability to shape-shift, to walk between the worlds? Usually not through choice. Such talents often arise as a result of serious illness, either mental or physical, events that lead us to the edge of death, the gateway between this world and the worlds of the ancestors, the Faery folk and the gods. I had twenty years of such experiences before finally meeting my wolf companion during the ceremony described earlier. Which leads to our next question: given the dangers, difficulties and responsibilities involved, why should we want to shape-shift or walk between the worlds? Many of us don't, so the observations that follow are primarily aimed at those for whom it is not a choice but a desperate need, felt with every fibre of their being.

On or beyond the borderline between worlds, ancestral teachers or spirit guides, either human or animal, may bring gifts of healing and explain how healing may be achieved. Often, the recipient of such gifts will have been observed from early childhood to be an otherworldly loner, a daydreamer. Often, they will have been plagued by persistent dreams or wild imaginings, turning to the spirit world in desperation to find out how to cope with them. The gifts received once they break through into other worlds will thus often be used first to heal themselves before they are able to help others. An old piece of Welsh folklore tells how spending the night within certain ancient sacred shrines at pivotal times of the year such as May Eve, Midsummer's Eve or Hallowe'en will render one either an inspired poet, insane, or dead by morning. Becoming a 'shamanistic' Druid entails much the same risks. The reason those of us who pursue this path undertake it in the first place and continue to walk it is that we are driven to do so. We have no choice. Should we succeed, the rewards can be substantial. As said earlier, encountering wolf spirit changed my life, taking me to extraordinary places where I have met equally extraordinary people, both human and otherwise, and have had many of the most remarkable experiences of my by now quite long life.

Some who possess such talents are willing to teach them to others. Teaching is another traditional role of the Druid and there are those in the tradition today who run teaching groves or take on apprentices who want to learn skills that can't adequately be passed on through a book, even this one...

By no means all Druids develop the skills of shape-shifting, otherworld journeying or soul healing, nor is it necessary that they should. There are other, equally valuable areas in which to work. Teaching is a traditional Druidic role that can be intensely rewarding. The construction and performance of group ceremonies is another, as are counselling and peace-making. Just as some artists work in paint, others with clay or steel, dance or music, film or digital technology, so those who walk the Druid path find their own individual ways to express their *awen*, their connections with the sacred land, its human and non-human inhabitants, our gods and ancestors.

In walking the Druid path it is not even necessary to become a Druid as defined here. As we have seen, Druidry also encompasses the various roles of the bard and ovate. If you have a particular gift for the written word, poetry, music, song, dance, film-making, story-telling or some other art or craft, the complete fulfilment of your physical, mental and spiritual journey in this life may lie in bringing that art to the highest peak of perfection you can attain. Is a great bard any less valuable than an ovate healer or seer, a Druid counsellor, teacher or ceremonialist? Of course not. Likewise, if your nature is that of a healer or seer, then the ovate path can offer everything you need to reach your greatest potential and lead a rich, fulfilling life of great value to your community.

We each achieve our best life by following our own *awen*. This is similar to what mythographer, Joseph Campbell, meant when he said, "follow your bliss." It's also what my spirit guides mean when they advise me to follow my nose. We are all individuals, with individual needs, capacities, understandings and abilities. Part of the magic of Druidry is that it encourages all of us to become our best possible selves.

We have spoken of following our *awen*. Sometimes it seems as though *awen* is guiding us. At other times, it may feel more as though it is sweeping us along in a raging torrent. At others, we may feel it has deserted us completely. This may be especially so if we suffer from depression, as so many creative, imaginative, sensitive people do. At such times, it may be helpful to keep in mind that *awen* exists at all times and in all places, everywhere around us, wherever we are. *Awen* never deserts us. All that we may temporarily mislay is our ability to sense its presence clearly. This is why, earlier in this book, we suggested building up what amounts to a store of *awen* by taking note of those things that most inspire us, whether individual works of art, particular musicians, awesome sunsets, thunderstorms, autumn trees or what-have-you. Having this store of *awen*, we may then turn to those things whenever we feel lost and disconnected. Knowing they have had power to enthuse and enliven us in the past, we may expect them to lift our spirits again. Likewise chanting *awen*, or exercising our own *awen* through acts of creativity can reconnect us to its enchanting flow. Having suffered from depression since childhood, I speak of that which I know.

That said, the most frequent advice I've received from the spirits who guide me, and certainly among the most wise, is encapsulated in the simple phrase, 'it will be what it will be.'

Hale & Farewell

This book is intended to give a taste of contemporary Druidry as it is lived and to explore some of its roots. To capture any spiritual tradition on a page of text is never easy. As I write, I am conscious of my words flowing across the page like quicksilver, their meaning becoming elusive, sliding from the mind like rainwater from a puddle slips through the fingers of a child. It is the way of *awen*, the flowing, feminine spirit of the Druid tradition, that it seldom remains still for long, but continually changes, flowing ever onward, linking us spirit to spirit with our ancestors, with the changing tides of Sun, Moon and seasons, with the old gods and spirits of the land, the teachers of our tradition and more as its silvery, gleaming rivulets run out across the world from our personal cauldron, sometimes meeting larger streams or roaring rivers, ultimately feeding into the great ocean of creation. Our task is to allow ourselves to flow and change with the *awen*, riding its currents like the salmon of wisdom in the legends of our ancestors, gaining fresh inspiration from each breath we take as we follow the rushing stream to the ocean, periodically tracing it back to its source, as salmon return upstream to their spawning grounds, to that ultimate well-spring of the creative spirit, the cauldron of Ceridwen from which all *awen* flows. The great bard, Taliesin, found within the cauldron the gifts of poetry, prophecy and shape-shifting, and the ultimate treasure of oneness with the gods and with the universe, an existence that transcends time and space. May your journey be similarly blessed so that you too may one day sing, as Taliesin sings in Frank Olding's translation of 'The Battle of the Trees':

> The wisdom of sages conjured me
> before the creation of the world,
> when I had my being,
> when the world was still small.
> A lovely poet of prophetic gifts,
> I possess in song
> all the utterance of tongues.

Until that blessed day, may there be peace without and peace within, until we meet again, as for this time and from this place I bid you ...

Hale and farewell!

Resources

Druid Groups

Initial interest in Druidry is often followed by a desire to connect with others in the tradition. This is usually achieved by joining one or more of the many Druid groups that exist in Britain and around the world. Many offer training, companionship, celebration, ritual or networking. Some offer all these things. Among the biggest and best are:

The British Druid Order (BDO) The BDO has an international membership and is known for its animistic, 'shamanistic,' Pagan style of Druidry and the depth and quality of its distance learning courses, of which noted historian of paganism, Ronald Hutton, has said, "there is certainly no other course of which I know for would-be modern Druids that has the erudition, sophistication and density of material as yours." Courses are available via the website, along with free downloadable sample booklets, a forum and lots more about the Druid, bard and ovate paths. - https://www.druidry.co.uk - or write to: BDO, PO Box 1217, Devizes, Wiltshire, SN10 4XA, England.
BDO Blog - https://britishdruidorder.wordpress.com
Greywolf's Lair – Your humble scribe and BDO founder, Philip Shallcrass' blog, is located at: https://greywolf.druidry.co.uk
BDO Ritual Online – the British Druid Order's YouTube channel has videos of chants, songs, poems, stories and other elements of ritual: https://www.youtube.com/channel/UCsI19GdnuCqvoUbKxyo39bA

The Order of Bards, Ovates and Druids (OBOD) Currently the largest Druid group worldwide, with seed groups and groves in many countries. Founded by Ross Nichols in 1964, it lapsed following his death in 1975 until revived by Philip and Stephanie Carr-Gomm in 1988. Its correspondence courses offer a well-balanced, structured introduction to its version of contemporary Druidry. – www.druidry.org – or write to: PO Box 1333, Lewes, East Sussex, BN7 1DY.

Reformed Druids of North America (RDNA) - Their large and informative website can be found at http://rdna.info/

Ár nDraíocht Féin, **a.k.a. A Druid Fellowship (ADF)** - Another excellent website: https://www.adf.org/

The Ancient Order of Druids in America (AODA) - https://aoda.org/

The Gorsedd of Bards of Cor Gawr - for ticketed ceremonial access to Stonehenge at Midsummer and Midwinter, visit https://bards.org.uk

There are far too many other groups to list here. A useful umbrella group is **The Druid Network (TDN)**. TDN is currently (2023) the only UK-based Druid group registered as a religious charity. Founded by former BDO joint chief and OBOD tutor, Emma Restall Orr, its website has excellent content. www.druidnetwork.org

Pagan, Ecological & Conservation Groups

The Pagan Federation (PF) is a useful umbrella group for Pagan Druids. Founded in the UK in 1971, the PF now has branches in many countries and does sterling work supporting Pagans, actively campaigning for rights and recognition and promoting accurate information about all Pagan paths. It publishes the excellent magazine, *Pagan Dawn*. https://www.paganfed.org

The Pagan & Heathen Symposium is an umbrella group that brings together leading figures within various traditions, including Druidry, to discuss and take collective action on issues of mutual interest. https://pagansymposium.org – Among other things, the Symposium has contributed information to an online resource for Religious Education teachers. See - https://www.reonline.org.uk/knowledge/pagan/

PaganAid is a UK-based charity that supports indigenous peoples engaged in sustainable development projects. https://www.paganaid.org

Universal Declaration of the Rights of Mother Earth leads calls for the United Nations to adopt the Declaration which would change the way humanity interacts with the living world. The website has a copy of the Declaration, a petition page and lots of information about positive action. https://www.rightsofmotherearth.com

Extinction Rebellion (XR) is controversial because it uses direct action to draw attention to the global crisis represented by human-created climate change. The fact that it does is, of course, what makes it such an effective campaigning group. While not specifically Pagan, XR does have a lot of support among Pagans. Check social media platforms for XR Druid and Pagan groups. https://extinctionrebellion.uk - https://rebellion.global/

Honouring the Ancient Dead (HAD) promotes cooperation between archaeological interests and the wider community, exploring issues around the storage and display of ancient human remains and the possibilities for respectful reburial. https://www.honour.org.uk

Bibliography & Discography

There are more books in print about Druidry now than at any time in history. I have therefore been very selective in those listed here.

Contemporary Druidry

Kevan Manwaring, *The Bardic Handbook*, Gothic Image Publications, 2006. A complete guide to how to be a bard in the 21st century. Kevan really knows what he's talking about, being an excellent bard in his own right. As well as authoring several books, Kevan gives talks and workshops. He can be contacted via his website.
The Way of Awen, O Books, 2010. An excellent companion to *The Bardic Handbook*, this goes into the nature of *awen* and how we relate to it in much greater depth.

Emma Restall Orr (Bobcat), *Principles of Druidry*, Thorsons, 1998. An excellent introduction to the broad spectrum of Druidic belief and practice. As joint chief of the BDO from 1995-2002, Emma's books naturally reflect a very 'BDO' approach to Druidry.
Spirits of the Sacred Grove, Thorsons, 1998 (reprinted as *Druid Priestess*, 2002). A deeply moving personal account of the life and work of a Druid through the eight festivals of the sacred year.
Ritual: A Guide to Life, Love and Inspiration, Thorsons, 2000. A unique guide to the function, construction and performance of both personal and group ceremonies.
Living Druidry: Magical Spirituality for the Wild Soul, Piatkus, 2004.
Kissing the Hag: The Dark Goddess and the Unacceptable Nature of Woman, O Books, 2008.

Danu Forest, *The Druid Shaman: Exploring the Celtic Otherworld*, Moon Books, 2014. Integrating folk traditions, literary sources and archaeology with contemporary practice, Danu combines strong and spiritually apposite ideas with wise and sensitive advice.

Philip Carr-Gomm, *The Druid Way*, Element Books, 1993. A sacred journey through the landscape of the South Downs, weaving the author's experience of Druidry with philosophy, history, ritual and folklore.

184

Philip was Chosen Chief of OBOD from 1988-2020.

Carr-Gomm (ed.), *The Druid Renaissance* (revised and reprinted as *The Rebirth of Druidry*, 2003), Thorsons, 1996. A wide-ranging collection of articles by many leading figures in modern Druidry (including the present author).

What Do Druids Believe?, Granta Books, 2006. An excellent short introduction to Druidic belief and practice, also covering the history and development of the tradition.

Maya Sutton & Nicholas Mann, *Druid Magic: The Practice of Celtic Wisdom*, Llewellyn Publications, 2000. A truly excellent and remarkably comprehensive guide to the paths of bard, ovate and Druid, based firmly on original sources and the practical experience of its authors.

Kristoffer Hughes, *Natural Druidry*, Thoth Publications, 2007. Kris is chief of the Anglesey Druid Order and this is his story of how he came to understand Druidry as the natural religion of his native Wales.

The Journey Into Spirit: A Pagan's Perspective on Death, Dying and Bereavement, Llewellyn Books, 2014. Having worked for the UK Coroner's office for 25 years, and being a Pagan Druid funeral celebrant, Kris could scarcely be better placed to write on this subject.

Brendan Myers, *The Other Side of Virtue*, O Books, 2008. See pages 27-8.

The Earth, The Gods and The Soul: A History of Pagan Philosophy from the Iron Age to the 21st Century, Moon Books, 2013. Philosophy was invented by pagans and this fascinating book follows its development from 'Barbarian' Europe through to Emma Restall Orr, John Michael Greer, Vivianne Crowley and Michael York.

Sharon Paice MacLeod, *Celtic Myth and Religion: A Study of Traditional Belief*, MacFarland & Co., 2012. The old gods and ways.

Celtic Cosmology and the Otherworld: Mythic Origins, Sovereignty and Liminality, MacFarland & Co., 2018. A brilliant survey of all the surviving sources that tell us how our ancestors viewed this world and the worlds beyond.

Historical Druidry

Ronald Hutton, *The Druids*, Hambledon Continuum, 2007. The various ways in which Druidry has been perceived and presented, from the Classical era to the present day. Ronald is widely recognised as a world authority on paganisms ancient and modern.

Blood & Mistletoe, The History of the Druids in Britain, Yale University Press, 2009. A chronological history of Druidry in Britain, from the Iron Age to the 20th century.
Pagan Britain, Yale University Press, 2013. Comprehensive survey of what archaeology can tell us about the spiritual life of Britain from the first inhabitants onward.

Miranda Green, *Exploring the World of the Druids*, Thames & Hudson, 1997. Very good on early history and medieval references, excellent illustrations, a little shaky on contemporary Druidry.

Peter Berresford Ellis, *The Druids*, Constable, 1994. Good survey of Druid history, rather dismissive of some contemporary Druidry.

Bardic Tales

Sioned Davies, *The Mabinogion*, Oxford University Press, 2007. Absolutely the best English translation of this classic compendium of medieval Welsh folklore and legends. Sioned excels partly because she never forgets that these tales were originally designed to be told aloud rather than read on the page.

Rachel Bromwich, *Trioedd Ynys Prydein: The Triads of the Island of Britain*, 3rd edition, University of Wales Press, 2006. Superb translation of the 97 surviving medieval Welsh bardic Triads, detailing their origins, significance and relationship to other texts and, where possible, identifying the characters and places referred to in them.

John T. Koch & John Carey, *The Celtic Heroic Age: Literary Sources for Ancient Celtic Europe & Early Ireland & Wales*, 4th edition, Celtic Studies Publications, 2003. Comprehensive 440-page collection of translations from Gaulish prayer tablets, classical Greek and Roman texts, plus numerous medieval Irish, Welsh and Breton poems and legends.

Thomas Kinsella, *The Táin*, Oxford University Press, 1970. A poetic, powerful rendering of the story of Ulster's great champion, Cú Chulainn, and my personal favourite English translation of a medieval text.

Lady Augusta Gregory, *Gods and Fighting Men*, Colin Smythe, 1970. Poetic English rendering of the Irish *Book of Invasions* and the legends of Finn mac Cool.

Huge numbers of classic collections of 'Celtic' legends and Faery tales, including Lady Gregory's, are available free online at:

Bardic Poetry

Marged Haycock, *Legendary Poems from the Book of Taliesin*, CMCS, 2015. Brilliant scholarly translations and analyses of 26 Taliesin poems, including 'The Battle of the Trees' and 'The Spoils of Annwn.'
Prophecies from the Book of Taliesin, CMCS, 2013. Companion volume to the above, featuring 10 more poems, including 'The Awen Fortells.'

Gwyneth Lewis & Rowan Williams, *The Book of Taliesin: Poems of Warfare and Praise in an Enchanted Britain*, Penguin Classics, 2019. Good modern translations of all the poems in the 14th century *Book of Taliesin* by an award-winning poet and a former Archbishop of Canterbury who is a considerable poet in his own right.

Frank Olding, *The Taliesin Sourcebook* (provisional title, not yet published, February 2023). Beautiful English translations of all the Taliesin poems and both early versions of the Story of Taliesin.

Bardic Music

Sally Harper, *Music in Welsh Culture Before 1650*, Routledge, 2017. A magisterial survey of just about everything there is to know about bardic music in medieval Wales.

Keith Sanger & Alison Kinnaird, *Tree of Strings: Crann nan teud: a history of the harp in Scotland*, Kinmor Music, 1992. Classic work on the history of the harp from its earliest appearances on Pictish symbol stones.

Bardic Performance

Robin Williamson CDs: A founder member of The Incredible String Band, Robin is the finest living exponent of the traditional bardic arts, a magical storyteller, singer-songwriter and award-winning harper. Among the more traditionally bardic of his more than 50 albums are:
The Celtic Bard, Gason (Sweden), 2008. Wonderful selection of Robin's work, including three tracks from his *Mabinogi* album and a great retelling of the Irish 'Voyage Of Mael Duinn.'
Gems of Celtic Story, volumes 1, 2 & 3, Pig's Whisker Music. 1) features the *Mabinogi* tale of Culhwch and Olwen. 2) features four Irish tales, including the Birth of Lugh. 3) recounts tales from the Irish *Book*

of the Taking of Ireland, central to the Mythological Cycle.

Music for the Mabinogi, Flying Fish, 1983. 21 tracks Robin created for an open-air theatrical production of the Four Branches of the *Mabinogi* in which he appropriately played the part of the bard. An online search for 'Robin Williamson Mabinogi 1984' should locate the original four-part television series which is well worth checking out.

Among Robin's other albums, a couple of personal favourites are:

The Island of the Strong Door, 1999, Pig's Whisker Music, which is just breathtakingly beautiful from start to finish, and...

A Glint at the Kindling, 1979, which includes 'By Weary Well,' my favourite track by anyone ever, and 'Five Denials on Merlin's Grave,' a 14-minute epic poem devoted to the mythical history of the British Isles. Later CD reissues include bonus traditional material from Wales and Ireland including 'The Spoils of Annwn,' 'The Battle of the Trees,' and 'The Voyage of Bran.'

For more about Robin's music, paintings, books, tours and workshops, go to: www.pigswhiskermusic.co.uk – or write to: Pig's Whisker Music, PO Box 114, Chesterfield, Derbyshire S40 3YU, England.

Ronald Hutton, *The Mabinogion*, Talking Myth, 1997. Readings of the Four Branches with musical accompaniment. As far as I can discover, these are now only available via iTunes. Ronald is a captivating speaker. If you get an opportunity to hear him live, take it.

The Ritual Year (Ovate)

Ronald Hutton, *Stations of the Sun*, Oxford University Press, 1996. A history of the ritual year in Britain, including the origins of the eight seasonal festivals that make up the Wheel of the Year.

F. Marian McNeill, *The Silver Bough*, 4 volumes, 1957–1968, reprinted by Stuart Titles, Glasgow, 2012. Classic collection of Scottish folklore and folk customs. Wonderful stuff.

Otherwise, search online for each of the festivals by name.

Divination (Ovate)

Philip Shallcrass (Greywolf), *The Druid Tarot*, British Druid Order, various editions from 1998 to present. 29-card set based on original woodcuts from 3000 years of European pagan iconography. Available from the BDO website – www.druidry.co.uk

A Druid Ogham Oracle, British Druid Order, fully revised edition, 2022.

25-card set featuring full-colour illustrations of each of the trees, shrubs and herbs associated with the 25 letters of the Irish Ogham alphabet plus a booklet setting out its origins, meaning and use in divination and magic. Available from the BDO website – www.druidry.co.uk

Philip & Stephanie Carr-Gomm & Will Worthington, *The Druid Animal Oracle*, Simon & Schuster, 1995 (reprinted several times since). Superb illustrations by Will make this one of the most beautiful divinatory card sets available. The accompanying book contains fascinating folklore about our animal kin as well as the divinatory use of the cards.
The Druid Plant Oracle, Simon & Schuster, 1998 (reprinted several times since). The same size as the *Animal Oracle* cards so that the two decks can be used together. Will's wonderful illustrations again make this a truly beautiful deck.
The Druidcraft Tarot, Connections, 2004. Again featuring Will Worthington's superb art, this 78-card deck draws inspiration from both the Druid and Wiccan traditions as well as other threads of European magic and spirituality.

Mark Ryan, John Matthews & Will Worthington, *The Wildwood Tarot*, Eddison-Sadd Editions, 2011. This gorgeous deck draws inspiration from the history and prehistory of British and European paganism, folklore, legend and the natural environment in which they originated and continue to flourish.

Nigel Pennick, *The Secret Lore of Runes and Other Magical Alphabets*, Rider, 1991. Norse Runes, Irish Oghams, Welsh Coelbren and more.

Trees (Ovate)

Danu Forest, *Celtic Tree Magic: Ogham Lore and Druid Mysteries*, Llewellyn Publications, 2014. Does exactly what it says in the title…

Fred Hageneder, *The Living Wisdom of Trees: Natural History, Folklore, Symbolism, Healing*, Duncan Baird Publishers, 2008. Beautifully illustrated guide covering 55 tree species. Fred sometimes performs musical pieces inspired by trees. If you ever get the chance to see him do so, take it. You'll be in for a magical experience.

Jaqueline Memory Paterson, *Tree Wisdom*, Thorsons, 1997. An excellent compendium of Druidic tree lore.

Marcel de Cleene & Marie Claire Lejeune, *Compendium of Symbolic and Ritual Plants in Europe*, 2 volumes, Man & Culture, 2002. Brilliant, comprehensive guide to the folklore and magical uses of trees and herbs.

Herbs (Ovate)

Jo Dunbar, *The Spirit of the Hedgerow*, Local Legend, 2016. Jo, a Druid and medical herbalist, gives us a practical, illustrated guide to 66 medicinal and magical plants, from aconite to yew, associated with every month of the year.

Jocelyne Lawton, *Flowers & Fables: A Welsh Herbal*, Seren, 2006. A beautifully illustrated guide to the habitat, history, folklore and medicinal properties of numerous herbs.

John Pughe (translator), *The Herbal Remedies of the Physicians of Myddfai*, originally published in 1861, reprinted by Llanerch Press. Complete English translations from two manuscript sources. Of great historical interest but, as with other early herbals, extreme caution must be employed in using any of the recipes.

Animals (Druid)

Gordon MacLellan, *Sacred Animals*, Capall Bann, 1997. This inspiring book is by far the best source of practical advice for working with spirit animals. The author, also known as Gordon the Toad, is a gifted otherworld worker, walker and educator.

See also the *Druid Animal Oracle* under 'Divination.'

Wyrd

Brian Bates, *The Wisdom of the Wyrd*, Rider, 1996. The world-view of Anglo-Saxon sorcery made accessible for today. Meeting Brian at a conference years ago, after an evening in a pub swapping wolf tales we found so much in common that we created the concept of Wyrd Druidry.

Robert Wallis & Nathan Johnson, *Galdrbok: Practical Heathen Runecraft, Shamanism and Magic*, The Wykeham Press, 2005. Superb guide to practical working with Heathen traditions. Quite simply one of the best books on any Pagan tradition ever published.

Kveldulf Gundarsson & Others, *Our Troth*, 2 volumes, first published 1993, revised and expanded since. Massive, comprehensive, practical guide to Heathen gods, traditions and practices.

Index

Main entries are highlighted in **bold**.

Alban Arthan, 'Birth of the Bear Quarter' ... **74-6**, 103

Alban Eilir, 'Birth of the Spring Quarter ... **76-7**, 103

Alban Elfed, 'Birth of the Ripe Quarter' ... **79**, 104

Alban Hefin, 'Birth of the Summer Quarter' ... **78**, 103

Amergin ... 138-9

Ancestors ... 10-12, **20-22**, 25, **31-4**, 60-1, 88, 97-8, 104, **140-2**, 153, 156-7, 161, 163, 170, 178-9

Ancient Druid Order (ADO), a.k.a. the Druid Brotherhood of the Universal Bond ... 39, **44-5**, 49, 152, 164

Ancient Order of Druids (AOD) ... v, **47-9**, 183

Anglesey ... 18, **56-7**, 63, 91-2, 100, 109, 185

Anglesey Druid Order ... 18, 185

Animism ... 20, **24-7**, 66

Arianrhod, 'Silver Wheel' ... 7, **102-3**, 109, 165

Arthur, King ... 51, 71, 74, 105-6, 110-2, **114-6**, 119

Avebury Gorsedd ... v, 151, **164-5**, 172

Avebury stone circles ... v, 19, 34, 46, 48, 151, 165, 172-3

awen chant ... 18, 34, **89-90**, 140, 159-60, 169, 180

awen (meaning) ... 23, 29, **85-6**

awen (nature of) ... 11-2, 18, 23, 29, 34, 37-8, 48, 51, 71, **85-92**, 94, 97, 99-100, 113, 125, 140, 152, 159-60, 169, 175, 179-81

awenyddion ... 125

bardic initiation ... 150, **159-61**

bardic schools ... 17, **50**, 86, 91, 129-30, 138-9

bards ... 14, 17, 19, 23-4, 45, 48-51, **53-5**, 85-6, 88, 91-2, 95, 97, 100, 102-3, 107, 110, 113, 116, 119-20, 122, 127, 151-2, 154, 159-62

Bates, Brian ... 177, 190

'Battle of the Trees, the' (poem) ... **99-100**, 138, **142-4**, 181, 187-8

bear ... 35, **72-4**, 76, 83, 88, 103, 138, 155

Beltaine ... **77-8**, 102-3

Blake, William ... 47, 49

Blodeuwedd, 'Flower-face' ... **103-4**, 109, 144-5

Bobcat (Emma Restall Orr) ... 1, 8, 20, 41, 89, 151, 175, **183-5**

Book of Taliesin ... 99-100, 114, 187

Brân the Blessed ... 107-8

Branwen, daughter of Llyr ... 107-8

Brigid/Brighid/Brigit ... 76, 86, 102, 117, 145

British Druid Order (BDO) ... 1, 3, 18, 20-1, 24-6, 30, **40-1**, 66, 77, 85, 89, 94, 106, 137, 143, 151-2, **182**, 183-4, 189

Bronze Age – circa 2300-800 BCE ... 17, 35, **59-62**, 107, 174

bull ... 52, 72-3, 83, 110, 118, 120

Caer Abiri ... v, 151

Cailleach ... 80

Calan Mai ... **77-8**, 102-3, 105

Candlemas ... 17, **76**, 102-3, 124

Carr-Gomm, Philip & Stephanie ... 7, 18, **39-40**, 89, 136, 152, 182, **184-5**, 189

'Cattle Raid of Cooley, the' ... 55, **118**

cauldron ... vi, 16, 23, **28-30**, 32, 37, 51, 71-2, 85-6, 89, 108, **112-3**, 115, 117, 166, 181

'Cauldron of Poesy' ... vi, **28-9**

'cell of song' ... **91-3**, 96

191

Ceridwen ... 7, 23, 29, 40, 72, **85-6**, 102, **113**, 166, 181

chants, chanting ... 16, 18, 32, 34, 37, 62, **88-90**, 97, 100, 140, 143, 159, 167, 169, **172-3**, 178, 180, **182**

circle, sacred ... 35, 43-4, **65-83**, 88-91, 121-2, 124, 136, **152-6**, **158-65**, 168-9, 173, 175-6

circles, stone ... 12, 36, 43, 45-6, 48, **59-61**, 114, 151, 168, 172, 174

Cor Gawr ... v, 7, 61, **151**, 183

crows ... 57, 72, 118, 125, **127-8**, 175

Cú Chulainn, 'the Hound of Cullan' ... **118**, 186

Dagda, 'the Good God' ... 71, 117, 175

dana ... 11, **86**

Dian Cécht ... 71, **144**

Diodorus of Sicily ... **53**, 56, 138

divination ... 23-4, 28, 51, 54, 86, 110, **123-4**, 127-9, 131-6, 145, 169, 188-9

Dôn ... **14**, 103

Dragon Hill ... v, 35

dragons ... 36, 71, 109, 114-5, 122

drums, drumming ... 7, 22, 32, 35, 37, 62, 152, 170, 173, 178

Dylan eil Ton ... **102**, 144

eagle ... 14, 70, 87, 99, 104, 110, 116-7, 139, 154, 160, **175-8**

Epona ... 107

Excalibur ... 71, 114-5

Extinction Rebellion ... 10, 19, 183

Faery folk ... 76, 97-8, 112, 122-3, **125-7**, 145, 178

Faery mounds ... **36-7**, 101, 110-2, 116-7, 131, 151, 174

fate ... **69**, 109, 123, 127, 136

Fege Fin, 'Fionn's Roof-tree' ... v, **132-3**

Ffraid, Saint ... 76, 102, 145

Fianna ... 17, 63, 114, **119**

Fionn mac Cumhail, 'Finn mac Cool' ... 114, **119**, 132, 187

fire ... 1, 13, 17, 21-2, 29, 35-6, 51, 60, 70-3, **77-8**, 80, 86, 100, 123-4, 128, 132 135, 139, **154-6**, 158, 163, 165, 170, 174

frith, fritheir ... **124-5**, 127

Gardner, Gerald ... 39

Gawain & the Greene Knight ... 116

'Gereint, son of Erbin' ... 112-3

Giraldus Cambrensis, 'Gerald of Wales' ... 125

Golden Dawn, Hermetic Order of ... 18, **44-5**

Gorsedd of Bards of the Isle of Britain ... 18, 45-6

Gorsedd Prayer, the ... 13, **45-6**, 160, 165

Gowdie, Isobel ... 63

Graves, Robert ... 7, 41, 87, 95, 130

Gundestrup cauldron ... v, **29**

Gwydion ap Dôn, 7, **103-4**, 108, 113, 121, 142-4, 166

Gwyl Awst, 'August Feast' ... **78-9**, 103

Gwyl Forwyn, 'Feast of the Maiden' ... **76**, 102-3, 105

Hallowe'en ... 17, **79-80**, 102, 104, 124, 168, 179

harp, harpers ... **50**, 96-7, 100, 106, 117, 121, 127, 188

Harner, Michael ... 64

hawthorn ... 77, 109, 126, 129-30, 134-5

Honouring the Ancient Dead (HAD) ... 20, 183

horse ... 14-6, 28, 35, 57, 62, 72, **107**, 111-2, 115-7, 124, 134, 174

Hughes, Kristoffer ... 18, 185

Hutton, Prof. Ronald ... 7, 182, **185-6**, 188

'Islands of the Blest, the' (song) ... 2,

98-9, 147, 161

imbas, imbas forosnai ... 11, **86**

Incredible String Band ... 6, 96, 164, 187

initiation ... 6, 113, 150, 152, 156, **159-61**

Iolo Morganwg (Edward Williams) ... v, 13, **45-9**, 77, 85, 151, 165

Iron Age – circa 800-0 BCE ... 9, 14-5, 37, 41, 49, **53-4**, **57-60**, 91, 97, 105, 108, 132, 142, 185

Julius Caesar ... **13-4**, 48, 50, 56, 59

Kat Godeu, 'The Battle of the Trees' ... **99-100**, 138, **142-4**, 181, 187-8

Kundalini ... 29

Lebor Gabála Érenn, 'The Book of the Taking of Ireland' ... **116-7**, 188

Lludd Llaw Ereint ... 105, **109**

Lleu Llaw Gyffes, 'Light of the Steady Hand' ... 70-2, **102-5**, 109, 144, 166

Lugh Lamhfada, 'Light of the Long Arm' ... **70-2**, 75, 79, **105-6**, 117-8, 188

lyre ... 50, 53, **55**, 97

Mabinogion, The (*Mabinogi*) ... 40, 75-6, 85, 102-4, **106-15**, 121, 143, 166, 186, 188

Mabon ... 75-6, **110**, 134, 145

magpie ... v, **127-8**

Math, son of Mathonwy ... 76, 102-3 **107-9**, 113, 121, 144

May Day ... 2, 17, **77-8**, 80, 102-3, 124

mead ... 43, 53, 95, 100, **118**, 142, 145, 149, 152, **161-2**

meditation ... 12, 29, 34, 65, **90-1**, 124, 137-8, 142, 145, 149, 169

Merlin ... 31, 51, **114-5**, 188

Midsummer ... v, 17, 29, 47, 61, 71, **78**, 102-3, 151, 179, 183

Midwinter ... 17, 62-63, **74-6**, 78, 102-4, 136, 151, 183

mistletoe ... **52**, 130, 142

Morrigan ... 57, 72, 117-8, 175

Myrddin Emrys ... 114-5

Myrddin Wyllt ... 114-5

nemeton ... **54**, 56

Neolithic – circa 4000-2300 BCE ... 15-6, 43, 54, **59-62**, 91, 101, 132, 174

Nichols, Philip Ross ... **39**, 182

Nodens/Nodons ... 109, 145

Nos Galan Gaeaf ... **79-80**, 102, 104

Nuada Airgetlam ... 71-2, 109, 117-8, **144-5**

Nudd ... 71-2, 80, 105, **109**, 145, 166

oak ... **52**, 88, **103-4**, 117, 130-1, 134-5, 140, 145, 176

Ogham alphabet ... v, 51, **128-31**, 133, 135, 188

Ogham divination ... **131-6**, 188-9

Ogham speech ... 130-31

Order of Bards, Ovates and Druids (OBOD) ... 18, **39-40**, 89, 152, 164, 182

ovates ... 14, 19, **22-4**, 35, 45, 47, 53-4, 86, 113-4, **123-48**, 179-80

Pliny the Elder ... **52-4**, 142

poetry ... 11-2, **28**, 34, 46, **50**, 53, 62, 72, 76, 85-7, **91-6**, 97, 100, 113-4, 117, 125, 138, 152, 162, 179, 181, 187

Pretani ... 58

Price, Dr. William ... **147-8**

Quileute ... 7, 173

ravens ... 36, 57, 72-73, 83, 101 **108**, 110, 117, **127-8**, 138, 156, 160, 175

Red Book of Hergest ... 107, 115

Restall Orr, Emma (Bobcat) ... 1, 7, 20, 41, 89, 151-2, 175, **184-6**

Rhiannon ... 57, **107-8**

193

rites of passage ... 6, 10, 12, **34-5**, 150, 152, **156-8**, 160, 164

Roman Britain ... 15, **56-7**, 62, 91-2, 107-10, 142, 144

salmon (of wisdom) ... **71**, 110, **117**, 119, 139, 155, 181

Scholars' Primer, The ... **129-30**, 132-3

serpent ... **29**, 76, 111-2, 143-4, 160

'Seven Fires Prophecy, The' ... 21-2

shamanism ... 6, 10, 25, 31, 41-2, 51, **62-4**, 120, 132, 147, 155, **167-79**, 182, 184

shape-shifting ... 23, 57, 72, 86, 113-4, 168, **175-9**, 181

sidhe ... **36-7**, 113, 118

Spear of Lleu ... 104-5

Spear of Lugh ... 71-2

staff, Druidic ... 31, 47, 103-4, 108-9, 176

Stonehenge ... v, 19, 44-9, **59-61**, 114, 151, 183

Strabo ... 52, **127**

Sulis-Minerva ... 15, 57, 145, 166

summer solstice ... 44-5, **78**, 151

sweat ceremony ... **170-2**, 174-5, 179

sword ... 14, 37, 45, 53, 69, **71-2**, 99-100, 114-5, 117, 144

Sword of Nuada/Nudd ... 71-2

Tacitus ... 52, **56**, 92, 132

Táin Bó Cúailnge, 'The Cattle Raid of Cooley' ... 55, **118**, 186

Taliesin (Primary Chief Bard of Britain) ... 40, 51, 85-6, 88, 96, 99, 102, 108, **113-4**, 117, 138, 143, 181, 187

Taliesin, the Story of ... 40, 85, **113**

'Three Cauldrons' ... **28-30**, 32

triads ... **50-1**, 157, 186

Tuatha Dé Danann, 'Clan of the Goddess Anu' ... 71, 86, 105, 109, **117-8**, 144

Twelve Doorways of the Soul® ... 137-8

Uffington White Horse ... 35, 107

'Voyage of Bran, the' ... 2, **98-9**, 188

Wheel of the Year ... v, 39-40, **74-80**, 136, 149, 151, 188

White Book of Rhydderch ... 107

White Goddess, The ... 41, 130

Wicca ... 7, 11, 18, 25, **39-40**, 42, 45, 156, 165, 189

Williamson, Robin ... 6, 96, 101, 164 **187-8**

winter solstice ... **74-5**, 103

Witchcraft ... 7, 39, 63

wolf, wolves ... 7, 17-8, 62-3, 71, 88, 101, 109, 115, 117, 134, 156, **170-4**, 176-9

Wybenga, Georgien ... 7, **170-1**, 174-5

Yoga ... 29

194

Milton Keynes UK
Ingram Content Group UK Ltd.
UKHW041506040823
426337UK00001B/90

9 781915 604019